THE COMPLETE GUIDE TO

Flower

ARRANGING

THE COMPLETE GUIDE TO
Flower
ARRANGING

Introduction by Shirley Monckton · Edited by Diana Brinton

WH SMITH

EXCLUSIVE
· BOOKS ·

This edition published 1990 by
W. H. Smith Limited
by arrangement with Merehurst Limited, Ferry House, 51–57 Lacy Road, Putney,
London SW15 1PR

Edited by Diana Brinton
Designed by Clive Dorman
Jacket design by Bridgewater Design
Typeset by Avocet Robinson, Buckingham
Colour separation by Fotographics Ltd., London – Hong Kong
Printed in Italy by New Interlitho S.p.A., Milan

Jacket photography by Guy Ryecart
Photography on pages 10, 11, 12, 13, 15, 18, 19, 20, 21, 22,
23, 24, 27, 28, 29, 33, 34, 35, 44, 45, 47, 48, 49, 50, 51, 54,
55, 56, 57, 58, 59, 64, 65, 66, 67, 68, 69, 75, 76, 85, 86, 87,
88, 89, 90, 96, 97, 98, 99, 101, 106, 107, 126, 127, 128, 131,
132, 133, 134, 135, 138, 139, 140, 141, 143, 145, 146, 147, 152,
153, 156, 157, 158, 159, 160, 161, 162, 163, 164, 165, 176, 177,
185, 187, 188, 189, 190, 191, 207, 219–252 by Steve Lee, assisted
by Cliff Morgan; pages 16–17, 52, 53, 60, 61, 105, 109, 110,
111, 112, 120–121, 125, 137, 141, 151, 154, 155, 166, 167, 168,
169, 170, 171, 172, 173, 174, 175, 179, 184, 186, 192, 193, 194,
195, 203 (bottom) by Jon Stewart, assisted by Alister Thorpe, styling
by Barbara Stewart; page 211 by Graham Tann

All other photography by Helen Pask

ISBN 1 85391 138 0

The publishers would like to thank the following for their
contributions to the book:

Susan Conder, Hannah Stanley and Dee Hine pages 18, 85, 86, 87,
188, 189, 207, 211
Anne Hamilton, Kathleen White and Sandra Munro pages 88, 89,
90, 176 (top), 190, 191, 219, 220, 221, 222, 223, 224, 225, 226, 227,
228, 229, 230, 231, 232, 233, 234, 235, 236, 237, 238, 239, 240, 241,
242, 243, 244, 245, 246, 247, 248, 249, 250, 251, 252
Barbara Mallard pages 47, 56, 57, 64, 65, 66, 67, 68, 69, 70–71, 78,
83, 94–95, 123, 124, 143, 145, 146, 147, 148–149, 152, 153, 159,
165, 178, 181, 187, 203 (top), 204, 205
Ming Veevers-Carter pages 52, 53, 60, 61, 105, 109, 110, 111, 112,
120–121, 125, 137, 141, 151, 154, 155, 166, 167, 168, 169, 170, 171,
172, 173, 174, 175, 179, 184, 186, 192, 193, 194, 195, 203 (bottom)

All other arrangements by Shirley Monckton

Our thanks also to:

June Cutmore of Cutmore Florists, Maidstone, Kent
The Final Touch, Units E & F, Canada House, Blackburn Road, London NW6
for supplying the christening cake on page 178

CONTENTS

INTRODUCTION

More people than ever before are enjoying the pleasure of arranging flowers, and with it an awareness of the ever-growing range of beautiful materials that are available. The reason for this growing enthusiasm is not difficult to find – flower arranging is a life-enhancing form of creativity that it is possible for anyone, professional or amateur, to enjoy.

In this book there is something for everyone with an interest in flowers. There are chapters devoted to the choice and conditioning of materials, mechanics and suitable containers, the basic design techniques that are used by professionals, drying and preserving, silk flower making, and arrangements for situations ranging from the simplest of supper parties to the most grand wedding reception, with a wealth of ideas to inspire both the novice and the expert alike.

Arranging flowers is an ephemeral art, for even the most successful of your arrangements will have a strictly limited life, but the pleasure and delight in remembering such beauty will be a joy forever.

SHIRLEY MONCKTON

A selection of flowers has been conditioned and prepared for arranging.

BASIC TOOLS AND TECHNIQUES

If you are new to flower arranging, you may be relieved to discover that there are very few tools that are absolutely necessary or that you will not already possess for other household purposes. At the same time, it is useful to have a stock of the basic mechanics, such as floral foam, that are used in one way or another in most of the arrangements in this book.

Just as you do not need many tools, you will find that it is not necessary to acquire a range of expensive vases. Almost any container that will hold water, or can be made to hold water, can be used, and you may discover that a converted biscuit tin, painted to look like marble, is of more practical value than a genuine antique stand.

It is important, however, to know how to select top quality flowers, and to condition them so that you get the best possible value from them. The tip given here about placing rose stems in hot water, for example, may sound bizarre if you have not tried it before, but you will find that it works. So even if you already have some experience of flower arranging, you may find that some of the ideas here can help you to improve your skills.

Most arrangements are best made in situ, *using whatever mechanics may be needed, but if the flowers are intended as a gift, the recipient may appreciate your thought all the more if you arrange the flowers first, and present a finished design. Here, an arrangement is being assembled on a work-table, ready to be presented as a bouquet.*

9

TOOLS AND EQUIPMENT

Many of the tools of the flower arrangers' art are part of basic household/garden equipment, but there are a few specialist supplies that it is useful to have in stock.

WIRE NETTING

Also known as chicken wire, wire netting is essential for successful flower arrangements, as it holds the flowers in position. Choose holes of either 3.75cm (1½in) or 5cm (2in). The cheapest is the best for this purpose, because it is also the finest mesh, and is available by the metre (yard) from any good ironmonger's.

Not so easy to find, and more costly, is a good-quality wire covered in soft plastic, but if you can track it down it is well worth the extra expense. For example, it doesn't scratch precious surfaces and, because the plastic is dark green in colour, it is less difficult to camouflage in an arrangement than the silver grey of galvanized wire.

To use the wire, first cut off the edging, then take the container you plan to use and measure one-and-a-half times the diameter of the top by the width of the container plus approximately 7.5cm (3in). You will now realise how useful a pair of flower scissors can be! Roll the wire very loosely lengthways into a Swiss roll shape, then place in the container. The prongs at the sides should fit over the edge to keep the wire netting in place. Finally lift the centre of the netting a little. This roll of netting will give you several layers of wire and a variety of spaces into which you can place your flowers. If your design is to be quite large, with heavy stems, then it is a good

idea to secure the netting with wire or string to the container, tying it as you would a parcel. The ties can be cut away afterwards if not required.

Before arranging your flowers, you should check that the netting is secure. To do this, try to lift the container by the netting, but keep one hand under the container just in case! It should stay firm; if it doesn't then you must start again. No flowers will stay in place if the mechanics are not stable. When working with glass containers, a little netting cap that is placed over the top of the rim will hold the stems in place but will be invisible once the plant material is in position. Floral foam can be used in the top, but I always think a glass container looks a little strange without the stalks showing!

1   Always try to use plastic-covered wire netting when working with china vases, as it protects their surface. Roll the netting into a Swiss roll shape and then place it in the vase, lifting the centre a little and making sure the wire is well spaced.

2   Hold the netting in place with string, tying it as you would a parcel and catching the string in the netting occasionally. If the netting is not secure, the flowers will move about in the container and render the mechanics useless. Once the netting is firm, fill the vase with fresh water.

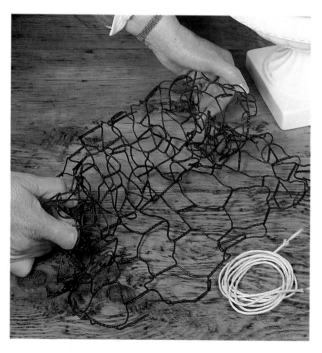

PINHOLDERS

These are very useful devices for holding flowers in place, and are known as *kenzans* in the Japanese school of flower arranging. They are available in a wide variety of shapes and sizes.

A pinholder has a heavy lead base, to give weight, in which sharp, pointed metal pins are embedded. When you buy a pinholder, ensure that it has the required long, sharp, pointed pins, and don't be tempted to buy a cheaper version – it will soon become misshapen and useless. To prolong its life, keep it dry and clean when not in use. Even greater support can be given to a pinholder by pressing a

A little cap of netting is all that is needed when preparing the mechanics for a small vase. Stretch the netting over the mouth of the vase, hooking the prongs over the rim to hold it in place. Once again, plastic-covered netting is best.

little crumpled wire netting into the pins.

Unfortunately, pinholders are unsuitable for dried flowers, as they cause the stems to split.

MASTIC

Often – if you plan to use heavy branches, for example – a pinholder will need to be held in place very firmly. To do this, press a thin circle of plasticine or mastic on the bottom of the pinholder, then press it firmly into the container.

There are several mastic products on the market. One is sold on a reel, and is the type normally used by professional florists; it is available from many florists' shops.

General purpose blue mastic is equally suitable. The surface of the container must be dry, to ensure firm adhesion. Mastic can be re-used, though it tends to harden with age.

FLORAL FOAM

Floral foam is a plastic foam that you will either love or hate. It holds flower stems exactly where they are inserted, with the result that arrangements can sometimes look explosive and angular. Lovely, curving arrangements can also be produced with this foam, however, so its dubious reputation may perhaps be a case of the poor workman blaming his (or her) tools.

There are two basic types of floral foam: grey or brown foam is used for dried or silk flowers; while green foam is water-retentive and designed for use with fresh flowers.

Rather like a sponge, green foam absorbs water, but remains firm enough to allow stems and branches to be pushed into it, and then holds them in place while supplying them with water. Not all plants like floral foam, but many do, taking up as much water as they need and revelling in the moist humid atmosphere that the foam creates.

Although not all flower arrangers like floral foam, one of its benefits is that it allows you to create flower designs that would not be possible with wire netting and pinholders alone, and it is very useful for creating a downward flow of plant material. It also prevents the plant stems from rotting.

Ideally, once an arrangement is finished you should store the damp foam in a plastic bag to keep it moist, but even if the foam has dried out completely you can revitalize it by adding a small amount of washing-up liquid to the water that you will use for re-soaking. If the foam has been used several times and now seems to have served its purpose, it can be placed in a plastic bag with a little water and a drop of washing-up liquid, and crushed. You can then press it into awkward corners of unusually-shaped containers that would be difficult to fill with solid foam. Surprisingly, washing-up liquid does not affect the flowers at all, but it will have to be thrown away if left in stale flower water. Turning the block upside down can also give it a new lease of life.

There are several types of floral foam on the market, intended for differing uses such as soft spring stems, so do check that you are buying the right kind for the flowers you will be using. Floral foam is cheapest when bought in large bricks, which you can then cut up according to your needs and soak well in cold water for the amount of time specified by the manufacturers before using. Buckets or a zinc bath are ideal for soaking the bricks, and if your sink has a wire basket, you will find that it is not only marvellous for the dishes, but is also very useful for lifting the wet blocks of foam out of the water to allow them to drain!

1 *When using floral foam in the vase, fix a holder firmly in the bottom of the vase with adhesive clay or Plasticine.*

FLORISTS' TAPE

Florists' tape, available in either green or white, is used to secure raised blocks of floral foam to containers.

FROGS AND HOLDERS

Several good accessories are available to hold the foam firmly in the container. One is a heavy lead base with widely-spaced pins; it looks rather like a near-bald pinholder and it is secured to the base of the container with mastic.

A similar, but smaller, device is known as a frog. It is often sold with an adhesive base and is ideal for smaller arrangements.

An economical alternative, suitable for medium-sized or small arrangements, is to use a 2.5cm (1in) base of mastic, then insert two 90-gauge wires bent into hairpin shapes, curved-side down. Impale the floral foam on the wires.

SELF-DRYING CLAY

A thin layer is spread over the surface of dry (brown) floral foam before dried flowers are inserted. The coating hardens, securing the arrangement permanently and adding weight.

GLUE

Clear, quick-drying adhesive is generally useful for attaching errant dried flower heads to stems, fixing ribbons down, and so on. A refinement, but very expensive, is a hot glue gun. This looks like a fat pen, and works rather like a piping tube, releasing a small stream of special glue heated to 160°C (360°F). The glue dries very quickly, and can be highly controlled. It is especially useful for attaching heavy floral decorations to lightweight containers.

STRING

Ordinary brown or white string is useful for binding moss to containers and re-tying bunches of dried flowers.

CELLOPHANE TAPE

Both double-sided and single-sided tapes are useful for taping liners to the inside of baskets.

SCISSORS

No arranger can work without scissors – not such an obvious statement as it may first appear! I know many arrangers who manage with old kitchen scissors or even a pair of dressmaking shears, not realizing how much easier life would be with the proper kind. These are blunt-ended, with serrated blades and a small sharp inset curve that is specially

2   Put the wet foam on top of the holder then tape it in place, pressing it firmly on to the sides of the vase. White tape is more easily hidden on a white vase than green tape.

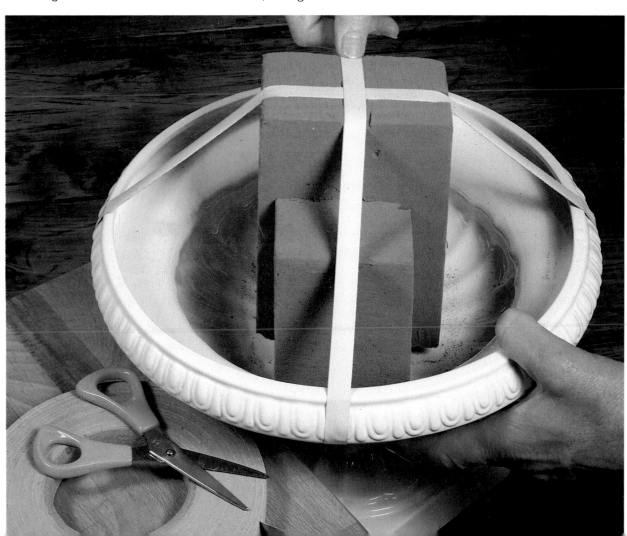

designed to cut wires and stout sharp branches. Light secateurs or a sharp knife can also be used.

KNIFE

A knife is needed to cut and shape floral foam, but any sharp kitchen or pocket knife will do.

SECATEURS

These are useful for general work, including cutting flowers for drying, if you have no florists' scissors.

FLORISTS' TUBES AND CONES

Made of metal or plastic, tubes and cones are a great asset and are invaluable when you need to give added height to the flowers or foliage in an arrangement. They are either pushed into the wire or foam or securely attached to a cane or green garden stick to give even greater height. The cones or tubes themselves should be filled with wire or foam in which the material can be arranged.

CANDLECUPS

Very useful yet inexpensive, candlecups are made from metal or plastic and are used to make arrangements with candlesticks. The candlecup is placed into the space left for the candle, but foam usually has to be placed in the surround. This mechanic is very effective and allows one to create a good downward design using very little plant material. Once the arrangement is completed, the candle is replaced in its recess.

RUBBISH BAGS

Baskets, in particular, need to be lined with dark plastic, such as cut-up rubbish bags. If you are making large arrangements, the amount of rubbish created will also be large, and plastic bags will also be useful for instant disposal.

DUST SHEETS

If you are working on several arrangements, or a very large one, spread a dust sheet out first, around the area in question, to collect all the trimmings and odd bits and pieces.

APRONS

If you do a lot of flower arranging, an apron with pockets is extremely useful, especially if it slips on over your head and ties at the back. An apron pocket is the ideal place in which to tuck your scissors, reel wire and other small mechanics when you are in the middle of creating an arrangement, because scissors, especially, can disappear among foliage, even if they have red or orange handles. Much valuable time can be saved if you keep them handy in your apron pocket!

The simple waist apron can become uncomfortable after a while, as it has to be fastened fairly tightly to stay in place – and if you've put a heavy pair

of scissors and a reel of wire in one of the pockets, slipping can certainly be a problem! A plastic apron with pockets is a good idea, but can become rather warm in hot weather. A simple linen or cotton apron may well be the best choice, because not only will it be more comfortable to wear but it will also be easy to wash.

WORK BOXES

Another helpful idea, particularly if you are working away from home, is a box or container in which to keep all your mechanics and equipment. The divided work boxes that are made from plastic and are used by carpenters and the like are marvellous, and very cheap to buy. The divisions are very handy and will take all your equipment, including florists' tape, wire, string, knives, scissors, adhesives, pins, glue and so on. Extras such as wedges and additional bases will fit happily in the bottom of the box.

BRUSHES AND BROOMS

When creating an arrangement away from home, you will not normally be required to clean before you start work, but you will have to clear and clean up after you have finished working. This is part of the job, whether you like it or not, and no one will be very pleased if you leave a mess behind you, so do be prepared to clear away afterwards.

If you clear your arrangements away when they are no longer needed, you will be able to remove any mechanics that you wish to keep, as well as any treasured containers that you may have used. Otherwise, some well-intentioned helper may not realize how expensive pinholders are to replace, nor how much you value that chipped soup tureen, and throw them away with the rest of the rubbish! If you won't be able to clear away the faded arrangement, then you may prefer to use simple plastic trays and the cheapest mechanics. This won't mean that you skimp on the arrangement – simply that you won't be so out of pocket if the worst happens and they are accidentally discarded.

A dustpan and brush is a great help, as is a soft broom if you are working in a church or hall. A mopping-up cloth is an absolute essential, since even the best arrangers have accidents, and you must always be prepared for one. A plastic bag into which you can place the wet cloth is also useful, and a duster is necessary if you need to polish a shiny surface or clear away any small pieces of foliage.

BUCKETS AND WATERING CANS

Ideally, you should have three buckets for conditioning, and although you can get by with the ordinary household type, the best bucket for the flower arranger is specially made of plastic, with solid handles on either side, making it much easier to pick up when loaded with flowers and water. The normal handle invariably decapitates the bucket's contents!

Florists' flower buckets are available in two sizes, although very small flowers can be conditioned in any container that will hold enough water and provide adequate support. A child's beach bucket or even aspirin bottles are very good.

A watering can with a long spout is invaluable, and a fine mister spray is very useful for freshening up plant material. A dust sheet or plastic cover is essential, because not only can it be used to carry your plant material but it also protects floors and furniture, and can be used when removing the rubbish afterwards. Try to find one that has integral handles, which will make it easier to carry. You can also buy an excellent large plastic bag which is fitted into a simple lightweight frame on wheels, making an instant wheelbarrow – a wonderful way to lighten the load you sometimes have to carry.

FIRST AID KITS

Sharp knives and scissors can cause accidents, so always carry a mini first aid kit around with you. Pack it with plasters and an antiseptic cream and also include an ointment that will ease insect bites – often a hazard when working with flowers.

Another important part of your equipment, if you will be working away from home, is a flask of hot coffee or tea, or perhaps some cold drinks in the summer. It is always a good idea to have a short rest in the midst of arranging flowers, as not only will it give you a breather but you will also have the chance to contemplate your designs from a distance, and correct any glaring faults that become apparent.

As you may have appreciated by now, good mechanics are an essential element of successful flower arranging, but the golden rule to remember is that they must not be visible in the finished design. So, whenever you create an arrangement, be it tiny or enormous, make sure that you practise the art of invisible mechanics!

WIRE AND STEM TAPE

For certain types of work, such as bridal bouquets and coronets, it is necessary to use wires and stem tapes. These are covered in the section on Wiring Flowers, on pages 62–69.

You will not always need a complete range of equipment when arranging flowers away from home, but it is essential to have a florists' bucket, practical containers for your mechanics, and a mister.

FLOWER ARRANGING EQUIPMENT

When creating your own arrangements, you may find some of the following equipment useful:

1 Green and brown floral foam
2 Watering can
3 Florists' bucket
4 Green garden sticks
5 Tubes
6 1.25 and 0.72mm (18- and 22-gauge) stub wires
7 1.25mm (18-gauge) short stub wires
8 Thick and thin silver wires
9 Silver reel wire
10 Black reel wire
11 Gutta percha
12 Green and white florists' tape
13 Satin ribbon
14 Pins
15 Florists' scissors
16 Floral foam tray
17 Spray mister
18 Dust sheet
19 Black plastic bag

Accessories that are particularly useful for dried flower arrangements include moss, pine cones, gourds, nuts, raffia, ribbon, spray paints and stones. All can be used to add variety of colour, texture and interest.

CONTAINERS

These are, of course, of vital importance, since not only will they contain the arrangement, but in many cases they can also increase its effectiveness and attractiveness.

UNUSUAL CONTAINERS

It was Constance Spry who was the main inspiration behind the use of unusual containers, and these can be as varied as there are ideas. You need never worry that you don't have a suitable vase in which to arrange your flowers, because a little lateral thinking should reveal the perfect container of one sort or another. For instance, any relatively well-stocked kitchen will yield a vast number of suitable containers: jugs, gravy and sauce boats, baking tins, vegetable dishes, and even the food and water bowls of animals can all be used with a little imagination.

Hunting in junk or thrift shops for unusual containers can be great fun, so don't imagine that all the best bargains have already been snapped up by enthusiastic flower arrangers, because they haven't. Old soup tureens or teapots, now without lids, are often inexpensive yet attractive, and you are unlikely to need the lid anyway. Don't be put off if an item, otherwise ideal, is cracked or damaged, because it may be easily repaired. Even if the piece you have chosen will not hold water it can be given a waterproof lining. Once you start looking, you will see that the opportunities are endless for finding interesting containers. Happy hunting!

VASES

If you would prefer to buy a vase from a shop, you may well be overwhelmed by the array on offer. If so, try to avoid succumbing to a sense of panic or

Once you start looking around junk shops for interesting containers you will find an enormous variety from which to choose. The ideas are limitless and with a little ingenuity you should be able to convert all sorts of objects into containers for flowers.

confusion that makes you buy the first thing you see in the hope that it will do. Firstly, the colour is important, and a neutral or earthy shade is a very wise choice – it may be difficult to find flowers that blend with very strongly-coloured vases. As for the shapes, simple pottery urns and shallow oval or round bowls are suitable for a variety of floral designs. These shapes can also be purchased in plastic. I like to have pairs of identical containers or pedestals whenever possible, as they have so many more uses, to create balanced arrangements on either side of a mantelpiece, altar or doorway, for example.

Terracotta pottery containers are ideal for all types of plant material, whether they are in the shape of formal tubs for planted trees or generously rounded jugs for flowers.

CHINA CONTAINERS

China, pottery and porcelain containers are all easily obtainable but are fragile and may therefore be the cause of much heartbreak if you have a habit of dropping things! Even so, you have a wide choice of shapes and designs, including pretty china baskets, shells supported by cherubs and sweetmeat dishes, and should be able to find the perfect containers to match your taste, style of arrangements, budget and home, whether they are found in antique or junk shops, or are good modern designs.

METAL CONTAINERS

These are probably more practical than china and porcelain, and well-shaped bowls, jugs and mugs are readily available in copper, bronze, tin and brass. Some of these materials may also be given an antique

China and silver containers are among my favourite choices for flowers. They often lend themselves to rather fragile and delicate-looking arrangements.

The warm colours of copper and brass make them particularly suitable as flower containers, especially if you are able to make a feature of their wonderful reflections, smooth textures and lovely sheens.

appearance which means that they don't require cleaning! Silver is a lovely foil for flowers and an oval or rectangular silver plated entrée dish looks wonderful on a dining table.

MARBLE CONTAINERS

Marble, alabaster and onyx are expensive stones, but they make marvellous containers. Alabaster must be given an inner lining as water will roughen its surface. If the container is not a family heirloom, then a little clear varnish painted on the inside will prevent any water damage. The shapes and forms of these containers are beautiful and well worth the money spent, as their textures blend so well with the plant material.

The cool, smooth contours of marble and alabaster are very beautiful, especially when enhanced by the particular beauty of fresh flowers and foliage.

Glass containers come in all shapes and sizes, and as well as the ones designed specially for the purpose, you can also put such objects as wine glasses, mustard pots and dessert bowls to good use in your arrangements.

GLASS CONTAINERS

Glass has recently been out of fashion, but there are some very good shapes to be found at the moment. The simple designs of the Munstead vases that were commissioned by Gertrude Jekyll, for example, are lovely, and when placing one within another, as she suggested, the possibilities are endless and exciting. What is more, her ideas can easily be adapted for modern glass containers. The only drawbacks with glass are that to look its best, it must be kept spotlessly clean, the flower water must always be clear and fresh, and the visible plant stems must look attractive.

WOODEN CONTAINERS

These are an interesting choice, and such containers as garden trugs, boxes, platters and bowls are ideal partners with plant material. Some of the most beautiful pedestals are wooden, making it a pleasure to use them, and very often they can take the place of a table for an arrangement.

When using a wooden container, try to let the beauty of the wood enhance your arrangement. In most cases you will have to protect the wood from water by using a waterproof lining or placing a smaller container of water inside the wooden one.

Baskets and wickerwork look especially attractive when combined with plant material, and there is a wide range of styles, shapes and textures from which to choose. The container will have to be given a waterproof lining before it is used.

USING BASKETS

Most arrangers own a basket, but it isn't always the most suitable shape. Invariably its handle is too short, and so is covered by the arrangement (unless it is very squat), thereby giving a most unsatisfactory design and effect. One of the best basket shapes to use is an old-fashioned picking basket, although you will have to line it first, with either tin foil or a sheet of black plastic.

WALL-MOUNTED VASES

Wall vases are not as popular as they once were, but nevertheless they are useful for a narrow hallway. Simple containers arranged on little shelves also look charming, and very elegant designs can be achieved with ivies and other downward-flowing plants.

ADAPTING UNSIGHTLY CONTAINERS

Many containers are made of plastic, but although some of them are available in very good shapes, their colours may leave much to be desired. Luckily, this can be easily remedied by repainting or spraying with aerosol paints. The real problem with plastic containers is their lightness, because although that makes them easy to transport from place to place, once they are filled with flowers they can become perilously top-heavy. Even if the plastic container feels heavy when first filled with wet floral foam and water, once these dry out the container can easily topple over. To overcome this hazard you will have to weight the base, either with sand for a non-permanent weight or ready-mixed concrete for a permanent solution to the problem.

Plastic and fibreglass pillars are also extremely useful, although it is even more important that these should be adequately weighted to prevent accidents. They are generally white, and although this is agreeable, they are much more attractive when made to resemble such materials as stone, marble or terracotta. It is great fun to transform pedestal shapes, and you will gain enormous use from them in the process.

USING BASES

Very often an arrangement is given extra impact or height with the use of a base. These come in many guises, from beautifully designed metal, carved wood and Chinese-style designs, to simple wooden stands or even a cake board covered with the fabric of your choice. In many cases they give the design just the special touch that is required. On a practical note, the base can also protect the surface of furniture from water damage. Protecting furniture is essential and an invaluable tip is to cover the underside of the base with a piece of plastic that has been cut and trimmed to shape.

CONTAINERS FOR DRIED FLOWERS

The general requirements for a container for dried flowers are the same as those for fresh flowers, but as dried flowers do not need water, a variety of non-watertight containers can be used. Hairline cracked china is useless for fresh flowers, but fine for dried; quite lovely antique pieces can often be bought at affordable prices. Terracotta flower pots, complete with drainage holes, can hold informal dried flower displays as well as the more usual, formal lollipop trees. Woven baskets are the epitome of non-waterproof containers, and probably the ones most frequently used in commercial dried flower arrangements. Natural pieces of wood and bark offer more opportunities.

Because there is no water to provide weight and stability, dried flower arrangements, especially large ones in lightweight containers, can topple over. Dried sand, pebbles, flower pot shards or marbles placed in the bottom of a lightweight container help to prevent mishaps later.

Dried flowers are on the whole rigid-stemmed, so there is no natural arching or drooping in an arrangement to break the line of the container, and informality can be difficult to achieve. Open weave containers, whether natural or wickerwork or woven porcelain, are particularly suitable, because the dried flowers and foliage can be inserted between gaps in the weave as well as in the top.

Another particular problem is the too-small neck syndrome. Some containers have a small neck in relation to their width, which can give an uncomfortable pinched look to an arrangement of erect-stemmed dried flowers. One solution is to insert a shaped block of floral foam into the neck so that the foam is wedged tightly and protrudes from the top. Insert the stems into the floral foam, angling them outwards and downwards as well as upwards, to hide the mechanics and the thinnest point of the neck. Straight-sided narrow-necked containers have a natural elegance, but again, a piece of floral foam protruding from the rim increases options enormously.

PAINTING POTS AND PILLARS

As you will soon realize, the flower arranger has to develop many talents other than those traditionally associated with flower arranging. One particularly useful technique is to give pots, pillars and pedestals a new look.

The idea is far from new, for the Greeks, Romans and Victorians were all captivated by marble finishes. Spend some time looking at different pieces of marble and you will be amazed at their beauty.

The idea of owning pots and pedestals that look like marble, stone and terracotta, yet can be transported easily from one place to another, is appealing, and not difficult to put into practice. To make a pedestal or urn resemble stone is quite simple, but it does take time. However, the finished result should be ample reward.

CREATING STONE FINISHES

Many efforts at painting pots look just like that – pots that have been painted! If you want to avoid that pitfall, a good way to begin is to have a look at the real thing, or even photographs of stone pots. Immediately, you will realize that stone is not made up of just one colour but many different ones. Lichen, moss, rain, snow and even grime all have their part to play in the finished texture and colouring of a piece of stone, so just buying a tin of grey paint and hoping for the best will not suffice. In fact, there may be no need to buy paint specially for this job at all, as you could find that you've already got everything you need – unfinished tins of paint in almost any colour will be useful, and even children's powder paints are suitable. Plastic or fibreglass pots, urns, statues and busts all benefit wonderfully from this decorative treatment.

Start by ensuring that the pot you wish to decorate is clean and dry, then cover it with a single coat of matt emulsion and leave to dry. Use black if you want a dark finish, and white for a lighter effect. Then roughly paint the surface with a masonry paint. Choose one that will give a rough-textured finish, then allow to dry. Next, dip your brush into first one colour and then another, such as brown, green, blue or even orange, and gently paint the roughened surface. Don't slap the paint on but simply draw the brush over the surface to leave a faint residue of colour and allow to dry. Then, choosing the grey, beige or whatever stone colour you require, gently paint the whole of the pot, leaving some of the colour showing, and especially a little black in the cracks. Leave this until it is almost dry, then with some drab-coloured paint carefully pull the brush over the surface of the pot – it will just touch the raised parts

of the paint and create a very realistic stone finish.

If you don't get quite the right result first time around, try again until you do. Each layer will give you another dimension and help build up cracks and textures that will add character and conviction to the finished pot. If you want to make pedestals and urns look very old and cracked, you could even paint in the cracks and moss, but this isn't really necessary!

Incidentally, if you are holding a reception in your garden and intend to buy real stone urns, especially for the event, you should ideally buy them several months in advance. You can then paint them with natural yoghurt to encourage the growth of mould and moss. This stops them looking obviously newly-bought, and with luck they will look as if they have been in your garden for years by the time of the party.

CREATING A TERRACOTTA FINISH

A terracotta finish is worked in almost the same way as a stone one, but you must omit the rough textured masonry paint because terracotta is smooth. However, the black base and undercolours are still necessary. Paint labelled 'terracotta' often bears no resemblance to the real colour at all, and better results can be achieved by mixing up a variety of paint colours. Keep an old terracotta flower pot nearby to act as instant colour reference. Once the undercoats of colour are dry, you can add a light touch of drab paint to give the lovely bloom found on real terracotta.

This is a collection of pedestals, bases and pots, all of which have been given special decorative finishes that have transformed their original plastic and wooden appearances.

CREATING A DECORATIVE FINISH

1   Paint the object to be marbled with black eggshell, flat oil or undercoat, and leave to dry. Make up a glaze of paint and white spirit and dab it over the surface.

2   Now flick white spirit over the wet glaze to open it up. Then dip a piece of crumpled newspaper in a white glaze and dab it on the black ground.

3   Now draw in the veins on the marble. This can be done by pulling a feather, dipped in oil paint, over the surface or, as shown here, by drawing in the veins with a wax crayon.

4   Diffuse the veins by drawing a large soft brush over them. Once you are pleased with the result, allow to dry thoroughly. Apply one coat of clear gloss varnish and two coats of clear matt varnish, leaving each one to dry before applying the next.

CREATING A MARBLED FINISH

This is very impressive but equally easy to create. Once again, the more trouble you take, the better the result will be. There are several types of marble, all of which are simple to make but will vary slightly. If possible, do look at the real thing because that will help you greatly.

The marble illustrated in the step-by-step photographs is known as black serpentine marble, and is a useful colour for setting off flowers and foliage. Start by ensuring that the object to be painted is clean and dry, then paint it with black eggshell, flat oil or undercoat and leave to dry. Squeeze a very little emerald oil paint on to an old saucer, and mix in a little raw umber and black, to dirty the colour. Then mix in white spirit, at a ratio of 1:2 parts to make a glaze. Brush this over the whole object, then dip a stiff brush into the white spirit and flick it over the paint. Don't use too much or the paint will run. The aim is to leave little spots on the surface, which will open the glaze to reveal the black below – this is known as 'cissing'. Then dip a crumpled newspaper in a white glaze (made from white oil paint and white spirit mixed up in a ratio of 1:2) and dab it sparingly on the black ground.

To make veins, take a fine brush or feather and dip it in white oil paint, then gently let your hand pull the paint over the surface, twisting the brush or feather as you go. Alternatively, you can use a wax crayon. All marble veins run diagonally and should have the feeling of a meandering river, occasionally with a small tributary.

When you come to draw the veins don't get carried away, as too few veins are better than too many! Allow the finished object to dry thoroughly before touching.

This fragile paint surface must now be varnished, not only to protect it but also to create the characteristic sheen of the real thing. Apply one coat of gloss varnish followed by two coats of matt varnish, allowing each coat to dry thoroughly before applying the next. If you wish the marble to look very old, mix an ochre tint into the final coat of varnish, but do make sure that you use it very sparingly.

MARBLE PEDESTALS

Marble pedestals are extremely useful, and the only thing better than one marble pedestal is two! You can, of course, experiment with other marble colours and finishes and they can be used on anything – plastic urns, china pots, wooden bases, and so on.

A good alternative to a pedestal, and one with which it is easy to work is a box with an inbuilt stand. These look good whether painted as stone or marble. If painted with a stone finish, they blend in well with church arrangements. These boxes are of a useful height but can easily be made taller still by placing a container on top of the box. A plastic tray filled with simple mechanics is usually adequate. They make a very pleasing alternative to the seemingly inevitable wrought iron stand.

5   *To make a stone finish, pull some drab-coloured paint gently over a painted biscuit tin. This is used in the design for the buffet table in the wedding marquee (see p.162).*

BUYING AND PICKING FLOWERS AND FOLIAGE

When buying flowers or foliage, it is always a good idea to choose a reputable florist. The flowers here may be expensive, but you will still get value for money. The shop should be clean and smell of fresh plant materials, not stale water. The buckets holding the materials should also be clean and well displayed. A scruffy, dirty shop is not a good recommendation for the quality of its flowers.

It is a fact of life that for the most part you get what you pay for, and flowers are no exception. The good florist will have his reputation to maintain, and to sell poor quality flowers that are past their best will not be to his advantage. For the most part, the flowers bought from a stall or barrow will not be stale, as the stall-holder usually buys only enough flowers for each day. He lacks space to keep unsold flowers, so in general the standard of fresh flowers from this source will be good. The disadvantage with the stall-holder is that he will have only the flowers that you see, and it will probably not be possible to order special flowers or colourways from him; for these you will have to go to a florist.

WHAT TO LOOK FOR

Fresh flowers should be crisp and firm, and foliage should not droop or flag. Perfumed flowers are always at their most fragrant when very young. Tulips and daffodils squeak or rustle when fresh, and the eyes of all-year-round chrysanthemums should be mainly green with just a little fringe of yellow showing. If the eye is completely yellow then the flower is past its best. Flowers belonging to the stock, larkspur and chrysanthemum families should not have been stripped of their foliage (which may indicate that the flower is fading fast and the tell-tale signs have been removed), and if the water smells stale when they are removed from the bucket, you would be wise not to buy them.

Do not be persuaded to buy tired flowers, hoping that you will be able to revive them at home! There are some useful first aid remedies – warm-to-hot water, for example, will sometimes effect a revival, and a thermos flask of hot water should form part of your equipment. Such measures, however, are for emergencies only and won't rejuvenate flowers that are close to death. Prevention is better than cure.

If the florist is well known to you, you will be able to leave your flowers or foliage order with him, confident that he will fulfil your special needs and knowing that if a certain flower or foliage is not available, that he will be able to substitute another equally suitable one in its place. The florist will have

conditioned the plant materials, and for the most part all you will need to do is to clip the stem ends at an angle and give the materials a drink before they are arranged. If, for any reason, the flowers have been out of water for an abnormally long time, then it will probably be necessary to recondition them. One can certainly tell if roses have been given the boiling water treatment, and if they haven't had this particular treatment it is well worth the effort. If the flowers are intended for an extra-special event and will have to last for a long period, it is sensible to double up on all the conditioning. It is always better to be safe than sorry.

PICKING FRESH FLOWERS

Picking from the garden or the countryside is best carried out in the early morning, when the dew has left everything very firm and fresh. The alternative picking time is late in the day, when the materials will have made good food reserves through the sunlight hours. If it is raining, it will not matter when you pick, though it will not be the most comfortable of exercises.

It is important to pick carefully, both for the continued well-being of the plant and for the material that you are collecting. Good flower scissors or secateurs will ensure that you leave a clean cut, and the stem will not be torn and damaged. A picking basket in which to place the flowers is a good idea, but it is even better to place the flowers directly in a flower bucket. If you can be bothered to recut the stems under water at an angle, you will reduce the risk of an airlock. Once home, carry out all the usual conditioning treatments, and allow the materials to have a good long drink before they are arranged.

A good florist will be prepared to order special flowers or varieties for a regular customer.

CONDITIONING FLOWERS

Anyone who comes home from the florist and arranges their flowers straightaway will surely be disappointed. Even if the flowers are at their very best, they will be short-lived unless they are conditioned first. Conditioning is very important – there are some flowers that naturally survive longer than others, but all benefit from the appropriate conditioning treatment.

The first thing to do is to clip the ends of each stem at an angle of 45°, then place them in a bucket of cool tepid water, preferably overnight, but for at least two hours if time is short. Always remove any leaves or buds below the water line.

Most flowers will need no other treatment, but there are exceptions. Plants with woody stems benefit from their ends being hammered before being given a long cool drink. Blossoms such as lilac last longer if most or all of the foliage is first removed. Poppies, euphorbias and similar flowers contain a milky fluid which flows from the stems when cut – dipping them in a little boiling water for 30 seconds will seal the wounds, allowing the flowers to continue taking up water. Roses also benefit from the boiling water treatment, especially if their heads have dropped. When using boiling water always protect the flower heads with a tissue or cloth to prevent scalding. Singeing or burning the ends of such flowers as poppies is equally efficient.

REMOVING AIR LOCKS

The reason for this seemingly drastic treatment is to remove the air lock created by the plant during its time out of water: the plant will have sealed the end of its stem to prevent further loss of moisture. The air lock forms behind this seal, so clipping the end removes the seal and air lock and allows the plant to continue taking up water. The hot water will remove some of the air and allow the plant to drink freely. The one real exception to the boiling water treatment is any flower produced from a bulb: long cool drinks fulfil their needs.

Tulips have a will of their own, continuing to grow and move in every direction imaginable even when they have been cut and are part of an arrangement. They also have an alarming habit of flopping very easily. Always buy the firmest and crispest tulips you can find, then trim the stem ends and firmly wrap them in tissue paper or newspaper before placing in cool water for a long drink. Pricking just below each flower head with a darning needle will also help. Some people advocate adding a little cold-water starch to the conditioning water, but this is not a foolproof remedy.

Foliage, and such plants as euphorbias, love a bath and enjoy being submerged overnight. The exceptions are all plants with grey furry leaves – these hate getting wet and will show their displeasure by their bedraggled appearance, which cannot be remedied, by the way. Using the bath for soaking plants is very handy, but it can annoy the family! If so, an old zinc bath will solve the problem.

Some flowers, such as lupins, delphiniums and hollyhocks, have hollow stems. These tend to dry out quickly, after which they will not take up water at all. To rectify this, the stems must be inverted and filled with water, then plugged with cotton wool or soft tissue. Carefully holding the plug in position, replace each flower in the bucket for a long drink in deep water. Sometimes these flowers are very tall, in which case you will find that you must stand on a chair or steps to fill them.

Other flowers that require extra care are listed overleaf, and I have also included a list of the flowers and foliage that I consider to be of particular value to the arranger.

PET CONDITIONING REMEDIES

Suggestions for prolonging the life of cut flowers abound, and everyone has their own pet theories. You will hear recommendations for lemonade, sugar, aspirin and even gin, but there is no clear proof that any of these ideas work. If you have conditioned your flowers properly then all should be well. Besides which, it does seem an awful waste of gin!

Often, flowers are sent with a packet of proprietary flower food, which you might as well use, just in case. Checking that the floral foam is still damp or the water in the container fresh and topped up, with an occasional spray to the flower heads and foliage, is usually all that is required to keep everything in order.

The benefits of proper conditioning of plant material are amply illustrated by this tall pedestal. Assuming that the arrangement is kept topped up with water, the life of these flowers and foliage will have been prolonged, ensuring that they continue to look attractive for as long as possible.

1   Some flowers will live longer if given the boiling water treatment. Fill an old can or pot with boiling water to a depth of about 2.5cm (1in), and place the material to be conditioned (having first protected it with a cloth or paper) into the water. Wait for just under a minute, then place in cool water for at least two hours.

2   Singeing stems needs a little care as some of the materials to be conditioned contain a milky fluid that is an irritant. Protecting the flowers with a cloth or paper, hold each stem end over a gas flame or lighted match just long enough for it to be sealed. Then give the flowers a long cool or warm drink.

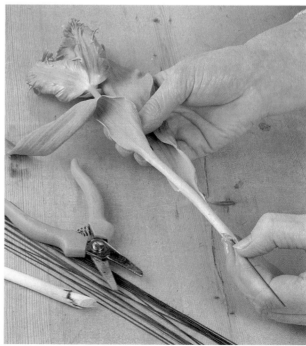

3   Pricking the stem of a tulip with a fine darning needle, just below the flower head, will help to keep the stem straight and stop it drooping once it has been arranged.

4   Internal wiring is a useful aid for hyacinths, tulips and the like. Gently thread a stub wire through the stem and into the flower head. You will need a thin stick to support such flowers as amaryllis, delphiniums and hollyhocks; gently feed the stick into the stem until it feels secure.

5 *Hammering woody stems ensures they will take up sufficient water for their needs. Some people prefer to clip the stems at a 45° angle, which is fine if only a few stems are needed, but when preparing vast quantities it is more convenient and quicker to hammer them.*

The few pieces of equipment needed for conditioning flowers and foliage are just as essential as your mechanics. It is especially important to take them with you when you arrange flowers away from home.

PROLONGING THE LIFE OF CERTAIN FLOWERS

Although not strictly conditioning, there are some helpful ideas that can be used in certain situations. For instance, you may need to keep your flowers for a while before using them. If you are careful, the deterioration of such flowers as roses, tulips and carnations can be delayed for nearly a week. To do this, condition the flowers in the normal way and then seal them in foil or polythene before gently placing them in a refrigerator set at 5.5°C (42°F). Peonies and gladioli can be left untouched on a cold dry floor for two or three days, then, when you wish to use them, you can just cut the stems at an angle and place them in tepid water.

TRANSPORTING FLOWERS

Travelling with flowers is an art in itself. It is also a very important part of the work of the flower arranger. Some journeys will take several hours, so the large flower boxes are indispensable. These usually have small holes in the sides. The box must be lined with enough thin polythene sheeting to cover the base and sides. Layers of crumpled tissue paper are then placed in the box with the flowers carefully arranged around the tissue so that it supports the flower heads and prevents them moving in the box. The flowers should then be sprayed with a fine mist of water, and covered with a layer of tissue paper and another of polythene before the box lid is replaced. A word of warning – do not leave the boxes in a closed car in the height of summer, or you will cook the contents!

As one last recommendation, always top up the container with water when you have finished your arrangement, because flowers drink very readily when first arranged. Then give a fine misting of water, and you can look back with pleasure.

FORCING FLOWERS

In spring we are often overwhelmed with blossom and flowers, yet earlier in the colder months we may well yearn for a branch or two of colour. Flowering currant and forsythia are good for forcing. Choose the branches with the fattest buds, split or hammer the stems and scrape away about 5cm (2in) of bark from the end, then place in warm water in a light position. In a week or maybe two, the flowers will be out and you will be delighted.

CONDITIONING TIPS FOR FLOWERS AND FOLIAGE

Many flowers and foliage can be conditioned in the ordinary way, but this is a list of the plant material that needs extra care if it is to look at its best when arranged. If you will be picking the plant material yourself, you will gain the best results if you gather flowers and foliage either early or late in the day. After soaking the plant material, allow it to drain on newspaper before arranging.

Alchemilla mollis	Normal conditioning. Cut stems under water if desired.
Alstroemeria	Normal conditioning. Cut stems under water if desired.
Althaea (hollyhock)	Dip ends in boiling water. Give long drink in deep water.
Anemone	Dip ends in boiling water. Give cool drink. Prefer water to oasis.
Astrantia	Normal conditioning. Cut stems under water if desired.
Azalea	Hammer woody stems. Scrape bark back a little. Give long drink.
Begonia rex	Dip stems in boiling water for 30 seconds then submerge in cold water. Dry and use with as much stem in the water as possible.
Bergenia	Submerge in water.
Camellia	Hammer stem ends. Give long drink.
Chaenomeles	Hammer stem ends. Give long drink.
Choisya ternata	Hammer stem ends. Give long drink.
Chrysanthemum (all-year-round)	Normal conditioning. Cut stems under water if desired.
Clematis vitalba (old man's beard)	Dip stems in boiling water. Give long drink. Does well when leaves are glycerined.
Cobaea scandens	Normal conditioning. Cut stems under water if desired.
Corylopsis	Hammer stem ends. Give long drink.
Delphinium	Fill hollow stems with water then plug with cotton wool. Give long drink.
Dianthus (carnation)	Cut above or below joints on stems. Give long drink.
Dicentra spectabilis	Give drink of warm water.
Digitalis (foxglove)	Give drink of warm water.
Elaeagnus	Hammer stem ends. Give long drink.
Eremurus	Normal conditioning. Cut stems under water if desired.
Eucalyptus	Normal conditioning. Cut stems under water if desired.
Euphorbia	Scald or burn stem ends. Give long drink. Take care when handling the stems as their milky sap is a strong irritant.
Forsythia	Hammer stem ends. Give long drink. Does well if forced for early flowering.
Garrya elliptica	Hammer stem ends. Give long drink.
Gladiolus	Normal conditioning. Cut stems under water if desired.
Hedera (ivy)	Soak in water.
Helleborus	Dip stems in boiling water. Give long drink. Prick below head.
Hosta	Soak in water.
Hydrangea	Dip stems in boiling water. Submerge whole stem, including head, for an hour or two.

Laurus (laurel)	Soak in water.
Ligustrum (privet)	Hammer stem ends. Give long drink.
Lilium (lily)	Give long drink. Remove the stamens as their pollen can stain.
Malus (crab apple)	Hammer stem ends. Give long drink.
Matthiola (stock)	Strip foliage below water line.
Moluccella	Normal conditioning. Cut stems under water if desired.
Myrsiphyllum asparagoides (smilax)	Normal conditioning. Cut stems under water if desired.
Neillia	Hammer stem ends. Give long drink.
Nicotiana (tobacco plant)	Give drink of warm water.
Ornamental cabbage and kale	Normal conditioning. Cut stems under water if desired.
Paeonia (peony)	Normal conditioning. Cut stems under water if desired.
Papaver (poppy)	Pick when the colour is just showing in the bud. Burn stem ends. Give long drink.
Philadelphus (mock orange)	Remove most or all of leaves. Hammer stem ends. Give long drink.
Phormium tenax	Normal conditioning. Cut stems under water if desired.
Physocarpus opulifolius	Hammer stem ends. Give long drink.
Polygonatum (Solomon's seal)	Normal conditioning. Cut stems under water if desired.
Prunus	Hammer stem ends. Give long drink.
Rhododendron	Hammer stem ends. Give long drink.
Ribes (flowering currant)	Hammer stem ends. Give long drink. Forces well for early flowering.
Rosa (rose)	Dip stems in boiling water. Give long cool drink.
Sorbus aria (whitebeam)	Hammer stem ends. Give long cool drink.
Spirea × *arguta* (bridal wreath)	Hammer stem ends. Give long cool drink.
Stachyrus praecox	Hammer stem ends. Give long drink.
Symphoricarpos (snowberry)	Use the berries. Strip the leaves.
Syringa (lilac)	Hammer stem ends. Give long drink. Remove all foliage.
Tellima grandiflora	Dip stems in boiling water. Give long cool drink.
Tiarella	Soak the leaves.
Tulipa (tulip)	Prick stems below the head with a fine needle. Wrap in newspaper and give a cool drink.
Viburnum	Hammer stems. Give long drink.
Vinca	Dip ends in boiling water. Submerge in cold water.
Weigela	Hammer stems. Give long drink.
Zantedeschia aethiopica (arum lily)	Give long drink up to neck. Submerge leaves.
Zinnias	Give long drink.

DESIGN PRINCIPLES

Flower arranging is a wonderful excuse to give free reign to your individual creativity and colour sense, and you know best the colours and shapes that will complement the decor of your home. At the same time, if you are to arrange flowers with confidence and pleasure, it is useful to have a few guiding principles in mind. These are not rules and regulations, for this would immediately impose a sense of restriction, but they do give a framework within which you can experiment and try out your own ideas.

When setting out on any task, whether it is embroidery, gardening, cooking, or some other skill, one usually has an idea of the finished project, and so it is with flowers. To have a general design in mind before you begin will help to ensure that the end result is successful. The idea cannot be determined in detail, as no two flowers are alike and no two pieces of foliage flow in an identical way, but the basic design principles of proportion, balance, colour, visual depth and interest, contrast and harmony, apply to flower arranging as to other art forms.

Materials, including fruits and nuts as well as foliages, have been wired and laid out on a work table, ready to be combined into a Christmas swag.

BASIC OUTLINES AND STYLES

Flower arranging has changed and developed over the centuries, from the simple basket of flowers depicted in a Roman mosaic, through the symbolic Madonna lily that appears so often in early Renaissance paintings and the mass dried bouquets beloved of the 18th-century American Colonial styling, to the great variety of styles recognized today. Most flower arrangements fall into one or other of the six basic categories of style listed here, but in each of these the use of scale, colour and texture provides an immense variation, with ample scope for creativity.

LINE ARRANGEMENTS

These may be either vertical or horizontal. Vertical arrangements have a strong upward movement and may take the form of a tall, narrow triangle or a simple line of flowers about twice the height of the container. Often, flowers with bold shapes are used, such as iris, arum lily or bird of paradise flowers. The stems of a vertical arrangement originate from a central point.

Horizontal arrangements are often used for table or windowsill decoration. The focal point is towards the centre, and stems radiate in all directions from this area.

Vertical arrangement: stems originate from a central point at the base of the arrangement.

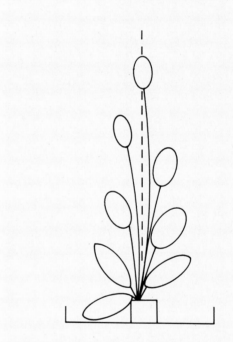

Horizontal arrangement: stems radiate in all directions from the centre of the arrangement.

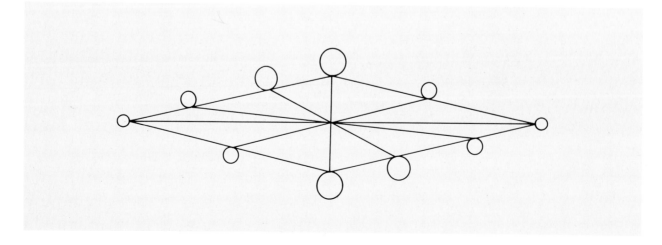

TRIANGULAR ARRANGEMENTS

Typical of this style is the traditional massed arrangement where there is a clear triangular outline but flowers and foliage are closely packaged within this, leaving little internal space. The triangular shape may be equally balanced on each side, or asymmetrical, with one point of the triangle extending further than the others.

A variety of size, shape and texture in the flowers is used. Stems radiate from a central point, usually with paler and smaller flowers at the outer edges graduating to larger, deep-coloured blooms at the centre, the point of focal interest. All components should contribute to a harmonious effect.

The height of the arrangement should be about one-and-a-half times the height or width of the container (whichever is the greater) and the sides about two-thirds of this length.

ALL-ROUND ARRANGEMENTS

This is the description of arrangements in which there is a circular or oval outline and a balanced and similar appearance from all sides. All stems should appear to radiate from a central point. A formal table centrepiece which will be seen from all sides should be designed in this way.

MODERN OR FREE-FORM DESIGN

These designs are much influenced by Oriental styling in the economy of material and use of space. Stems radiate from a central point and the outline is strong and interesting, giving a sculptured effect. Only the minimum of material necessary to the design should be used. The effectiveness of the design often relies on contrasts of texture, form and colour.

Triangular arrangements: create the basic form and gradually fill in with materials of varying lengths and sizes.

All-round arrangements: all stems should radiate from a central point both vertically and horizontally.

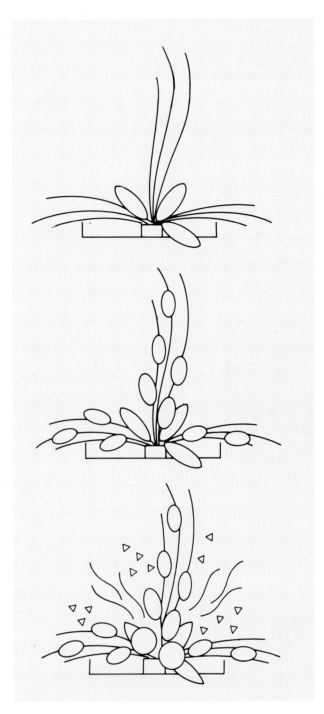

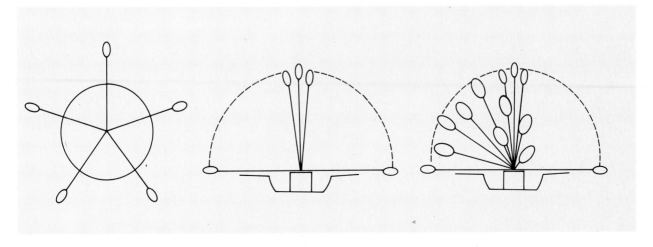

41

CRESCENT ARRANGEMENTS

The crescent may be symmetrical or asymmetrical, the focal point being created at the base of the main stems.

A stemmed container such as a candlestick or figurine provides an elegant base for an inverted crescent or a double curve in the form of an S-shape, known as the Hogarth curve. As with the traditional triangular arrangement, increasing weight and darker colour towards the centre of the design gives a balanced and rhythmic effect.

LANDSCAPE DESIGNS

Landscape is the term applied to arrangements which represent a natural setting, such as the countryside, the seashore, moorland or a garden. A base of slate or unpolished wood is often used with the container hidden from view. Scale is of the utmost importance, and simplicity and restraint in the choice of flowers and foliage materials are essential.

Crescent arrangements.

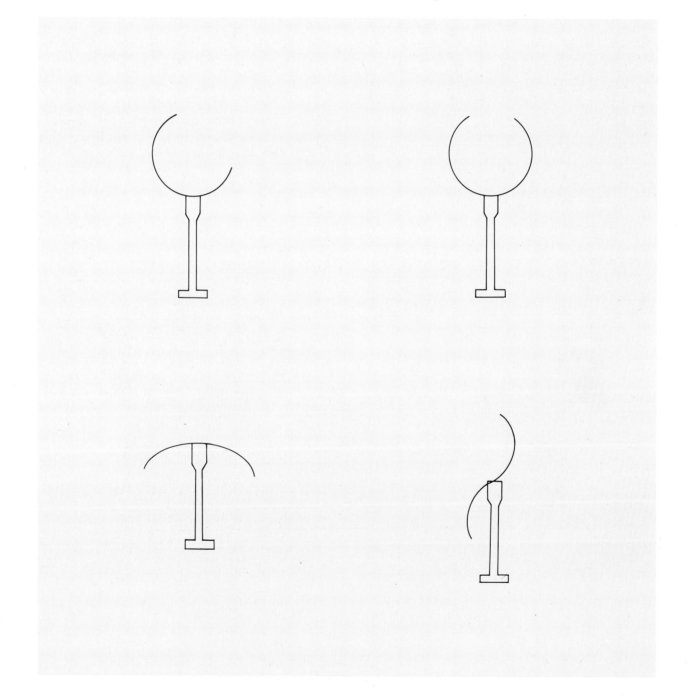

COLOUR

Colour is probably the only element of flower arranging that some people ever notice, as it is more important to them than texture and shape. Colour does give the greatest pleasure, and the endless combinations and contrasts can be very stimulating. In fact, colour is to the flower arranger what the palette is to the artist. Creating opportunities to stun or fascinate, to calm or thrill – such is the power of colour, and when used with imagination and style the results can be unforgettable.

Beautiful as flowers are in themselves, it takes a little consideration to be able to display them to their best advantage. Some people have a flair for using colour and creating amazing arrangements, but not everyone is blessed with this ability, in which case they may need a few pointers before they can create special effects.

a colour wheel

THE RELATIONSHIP OF COLOURS

A colour wheel is a great help in choosing colours, because it clearly shows the ways in which flowers can work together or oppose each other. Look carefully at the outer band of the colour wheel, which shows the distinct colours called pure hues. These are red, orange, yellow, green, blue and violet. A tint is made by adding white to a pure hue, and a shade is created by adding black. To make a tone, you mix black and white together to make grey, then add it to a pure hue.

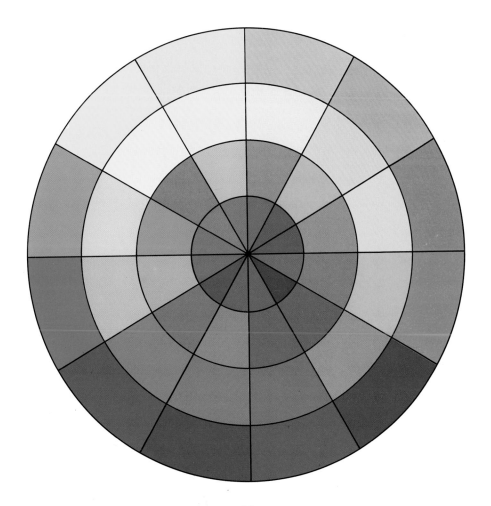

Colour Schemes

Colour schemes using tints, tones and shades are described in several ways. Monochromatic colouring consists of tints, tones and shades of one colour. Analogous or adjacent colouring is the use of two or four colours that are closely related on the colour wheel. Complementary colouring uses colours that are directly or approximately opposite each other on the wheel. Triadic colouring uses three colours that are equidistant on the wheel, while polychromatic colouring is the use of many colours together.

Other dimensions are also helpful. Light value – or the amount of reflected colour – is called luminosity. Colours to which white has been added (tints are in this category) are more easily visible in dull or dim surroundings. Weight is yet another dimension, using tints and shades, that gives a sense of lightness or heaviness that is useful to the balance of the design.

The final group to be mentioned are the neutral, or achromatic, colours of black, white and grey. All other colours are chromatic. In reality, there are no plants or flowers that are completely true in colour, and black tulips will always have a blue-black appearance while white flowers encompass a multitude of variations.

Creating Atmosphere with Colour

Colours also have the ability to create warmth, as in the case of reds and oranges, or coolness, as in the case of blues and greens. With this in mind you can use colour imaginatively to produce some very sensitive designs. In addition, colours can give a sense of movement: oranges and reds appear to come forward, blues recede, yellows elevate and violets diminish. Green, however, remains neutral. The use of the illustration of movement in colour is

The pink tints and tones of the tulips, carnations, pinks, and antirrhinums in this arrangement make it a monochromatic scheme.

fascinating, and well worth remembering when creating a design.

BACKGROUND AND HARMONY

Colour cannot be isolated from its surroundings, for the background will always have a profound effect on the colours you choose. Varying the backgrounds to a single design will aptly illustrate this point, and will show you another reason why arranging flowers *in situ* is so very important.

Harmony is probably the most elusive quality to obtain in an arrangement, and is very much a matter of personal preference (as is most of flower arranging!) because no two people evaluate colour harmony in the same way. Quite simply, the effect must be pleasing to you – and hopefully to others who will view your arrangement as well.

While remembering, then, that the pleasure in harmony rests entirely in the eye of the beholder, here are one or two guidelines that may be of help. Firstly, using flowers and plants of equal colour

weight will not always be effective, and graded colourings, such as deep coral through to apricot, can give a much more pleasing effect than when flowers of a single colour are used. Bright patches of colour should be used carefully, as dotting gaily-coloured flowers through an arrangement can create a very irritating effect. Colour grouping is usually better when you choose one dominant colour and then use variations of it. White flowers should be used with care, and arranging them in flowing lines will prevent them looking stark or strange. Good harmony shows coordination, symmetry and compatibility, as well as the sense of the arrangement being a complete whole.

The sharp, bright and fresh yellows and oranges of the ranunculus, tulips, antirrhinums and marigolds of this analogous arrangement make it an ideal choice for a breakfast table decoration.

OTHER DESIGN ELEMENTS

The colours may be the most immediately noticeable element in a flower arrangement, but other factors have an important part to play in creating a pleasing effect.

TEXTURE

Flower arrangers consider surface texture in terms of rough or smooth, silky or velvety, dull or shiny, all of these qualities being intensified by light. Colours are selected for their relationships, textures for their contrasts. As well as the surface textures of petals and leaves the overall appearance of a flower, or a stem of foliage, can have a textural effect. Chrysanthemums appear rough, for example, although the individual petals are smooth and silky.

FORM

Plant materials have a great variety of shapes but it can be helpful to fit them into broad categories. Round shapes, for example, are common – the dahlia, rose, carnation, chrysanthemum and many other flowers are essentially rounded in form. They can be used either as single or as massed elements in an arrangement.

Pointed shapes, or spikes, occur in multiple flower stems, such as the gladiolus and bells of Ireland. These contribute height and linear emphasis to an arrangement.

Intermediate shapes vary from the small Michaelmas daisy to the elegant lily. They provide a link or transition between round and pointed flowers, which encourages harmony in a group of mixed flowers.

These forms enhance an arrangement because of their differences. In a massed arrangement, all three shapes are used. In a free-form or line arrangement, one shape may be contrasted with another. Repetition of a single form provides sense of rhythm in a design.

SPACE

Space between the flowers and within the outline of a design is an important element. In free-form arrangements, space is a particularly positive and integral design element.

The space around an arrangement is also significant. The size and shape of an arrangement is dictated by the space available in the final setting. The space within and around the arrangement should influence the design from the very start and this is closely related to the scale of the setting and the plant materials.

BALANCE

There are two elements of balance in flower arranging: the physical balance is important – the arrangements should be secure and stable – and the visual balance of the overall shape and style of the arrangement. If the weight is at the top because large flowers have been placed too high, the appearance will be top heavy. Similarly, a base that is too large or too deep will give a bottom-heavy look to an arrangement. If the arrangement is not planned on a natural axis, it will appear to lean over to the left or right.

Imagine a vertical line through the centre of the arrangement: a balance on either side of this line is not made only by symmetrical placing of materials. A mass of flowers on one side of the line, for example, can be balanced by a more open but extended arrangement of materials on the other side.

Colour, form and texture all contribute to balance. If similar materials are grouped together in one area and contrasted with those in another, there is no linking element which can balance the design visually.

SCALE

This is dictated by the relative sizes of every component of the arrangement – base, container, flowers and foliage must all relate to each other in scale. For example, a dahlia would be too large for a specimen vase, a snowdrop too small for a pedestal arrangement, to illustrate the extremes. Careful grading of flower sizes creates a good effect in either a massed arrangement or a linear style. The arrangement must also be in scale with its setting, so that it appears neither too large nor too insignificant against the surroundings.

PROPORTION

In simple terms, this is the amount of each individual component. A traditional massed arrangement, for example, should be in the proportion of one-third container to two-thirds flowers. A tall vertical arrangement should stand at least as high as the length of the container.

Texture, shape and colour must also be proportionate. A good arrangement does not have too much of one element. In modern styles, the economical use of just a few flowers creates the impact, while in mixed arrangements, a good distribution of large, medium and small forms, linked colours and contrasting textures produces a successful result.

RHYTHM

The arrangement should be constructed so that the eye can run freely over it. Repetition of colour, form and texture, gradations of size and radiating patterns all create a fluid, rhythmical effect, as do strong, flowing curves in a free-form design.

This harmonious design of lilies, lilac, guelder roses, sweet peas and eucalyptus has been created to please the eye. Its coordination, rhythm, pleasing proportions and compatibility with its surroundings give an extremely comfortable feeling.

47

CREATING THE OUTLINE OF AN ARRANGEMENT

The basic outline of an arrangement is usually made from the finer plant materials or the lighter-coloured flowers. To determine the height of the arrangement, you should make the tallest stem about one-and-a-half times the height of the container. Set towards the back of the design, thereby giving the arrangement greater depth.

You usually need five or seven stems to make the outline of a basic shape. Following the first placement, add two secondary stems, in positions of approximately five o'clock and seven-thirty. These should follow the line to the focal point, but not actually end there. A useful tip to help you achieve these important positions is to place them underarm.

The next two pieces should come from the back slightly towards the focal point at ten o'clock and one-thirty, and should be shorter than the tallest stem. It adds greatly to the design if the outline stems are slightly varied in length. If using seven stems as the outline then, coming from the back of the design at nine-thirty and two-forty-five, bring your stems in towards the focal point. The largest leaves and flowers, or sometimes the brightest, are normally used as the focal point, and the transitional materials (those which are less heavy) will help the design to blend together happily. Foliage, and perhaps some flowers, must be placed at the back of the arrangement. A particularly important placement, which always creates a sense of stability, is a leaf or bud positioned behind and slightly to one side of the tallest branch, but still aimed at the focal point. This spacial placement must always be shorter than the first stem.

Of course, you do not have to follow these outline ideas to the letter, but they do help to create the right feeling in an arrangement. However, experience will soon make these placements second nature to you. One important point to bear in mind is the shape of the flowers or foliage you are using. For example, if a stem inclines to the right then it is best to use it on the right rather than try to coax it to the left in your arrangement, as it will never look happy. In this simple design, try to ensure that the outline stems look natural, and are not sticking out like wings about to take off! You should also particularly notice the depth gained by placing pieces at the back of the design. This has the effect of taking one's eye through the arrangement, before it comes to rest again at the focal point.

MAKING A SYMMETRICAL DESIGN

1 *A smaller block of wet floral foam is placed in front of a large one, both being tapered into a shallow bowl that in turn fits the mouth of the pedestal. They are then covered with wire netting that is wired into place.*

2 *When the mechanics are in place, begin to create the basic symmetrical outline with foliage, thereby determining the size and shape of your finished design.*

3 *Now build up the arrangement by adding more foliage and some of the flowers.*

4 *Add the rest of the flowers, taking care to maintain the symmetry of the arrangement without allowing it to look dull or predictable.*

49

MAKING A HORIZONTAL DESIGN

1 *It is always best to work* in situ. *Assemble the mechanics – here, two pinholders were placed in the bottom of a low dish and a block of wet floral foam was then held in place with green tape.*

2 *Arrange the basic outline with the foliage. The length of this arrangement has been extended to echo the outline of the dining table, while keeping the top foliage very short.*

3 *Now fill in the outline with the flowers, allowing the outer flowers to trail on the table and hide all the mechanics.*

4 *The elegance of the finished arrangement is accentuated by the formality of the table setting.*

FACING ARRANGEMENTS

Many arrangements are designed to face one way. The mantelpiece design shown here was assembled in a long trough-shaped vase that fitted the width of the mantelpiece. Blossom, lilac, lilies, 'Evelyn' spray roses, hydrangeas, eucalyptus, ivy and silver pear foliage were used.

The most important point to remember when creating an arrangement on a ledge of any sort is to keep the balance correct. For example, you should ensure that you don't have a lot of heavy flowers that jut too far out of the front of the arrangement, as this could overbalance the whole container. To prevent this happening, place such items as the lilac towards the back of the arrangement and cut the ones to be used at the front quite short and close to the vase, as has been done in this arrangement. Trailing ivy placed along the top of the mantelpiece and down the front helps to link the arrangement with its surroundings and to soften the lines of the mantelpiece itself.

MAKING A FACING ARRANGEMENT

1 *Look closely at the way in which the stems all point towards the centre of the bowl in this photograph, making this the central point. As this is a facing arrangement, the foliage starts approximately three-quarters of the way back in the bowl.*

2 *Add more foliage – moluccella was used here. When working with foliage of this type it is important to position it near the beginning of the arrangement as it has such dominant shapes.*

3 *Then add the ferns to fill in the outline, followed by* Euphorbia marginata, *to fill in the centre of the arrangement. Look at the different shapes and textures of the foliage used – the greater the variety, the more interesting the arrangement will be.*

4 *If you are using flowers with weak yet thick stems, such as the hyacinths shown here, position them after the foliage. As they are also relatively short they can be used to give a focal point to the arrangement. You can then add other flowers as you wish.*

MAKING AN ASYMMETRICAL TRIANGLE

1 *Place a block of wet foam in a shallow tray, then cover with wire netting and wire it in position.*

2 *Create the basic outline with foliage, making one side longer than the other.*

3 *Build up the asymmetrical shape with a variety of foliages.*

4 *Fill in the shape with the flowers, allowing the flowers in the longest side of the triangle to trail, thereby softening and accentuating the outline of the arrangement.*

MAKING AN INVERTED CRESCENT DESIGN

1   *Choose a shallow vase for this design. Place a block of wet foam in the base of the vase, then cover it with wire netting and wire it in place by wrapping it around the sides of the vase. The wire will be hidden by the flowers.*

2   *Add the flowers and foliage. Place the shorter material in the centre to keep the overall shape, and choose flowing stems to create the downward curves at the sides.*

3   *Fill in with more flowers. This design is always elegant and allows one to use the minimum of plant material to the maximum effect.*

MAKING A HOGARTH CURVE

1   *Place a block of wet foam in a vase and tape it in position. A tall, simple vase, such as the one shown in the photograph, will help you to create this design more easily.*

2   *Now begin to create the outline. It is very important to use suitable plant material, because stems that have a natural curve will ensure the flowing lines of the finished design.*

3 *Continue to build up the design with foliage and flowers, still following the natural curves of the stems.*

4 *Complete the design by adding a few more flowers until you are pleased with the finished result.*

MAKING A PEDESTAL DESIGN

1 *Ensure that the mechanics for a pedestal are firm. Create the outline with seven stems.*

2 *The lowest stems are more easily placed in the arrangement underarm, and this also creates a more natural flow. Try placing the stem into the design both over and underarm and you will find that the latter is a considerable improvement.*

3 *It is important to pay attention to the back of the pedestal, as it may well be visible. This photograph shows the back of the design and the way the mechanics have been hidden from view. Notice the stems flowing backwards, thus giving greater depth to the design.*

4 *The finished pedestal, after the addition of pink peonies, white ranunculus and green guelder roses.*

USING FLORISTS' TUBES

1 *Quite often, when creating a large arrangement, insufficient tall foliage and flowers are available and tubes have to be used to increase the height of the existing material. Sometimes the height of the tubes will be adequate, but if not you can extend them by wiring green garden bamboo sticks to the sides of the tubes. Position the tubes in the arrangement before adding the flowers and foliage, as you will find it difficult to insert them afterwards. Make sure that they are firm and not wobbly before you start, as this precaution will save you a lot of trouble later on. To be really safe, extend each tube with two sticks.*

2 *Using the longest pieces of foliage, make your basic shape around the outside, through the middle and down over the front. It is always better to create an arrangement of this size in situ, as you will be able to judge how high and how wide the arrangement should be, according to its surroundings.*

3 *Fill in the rest of the shape with foliage, arranging it lightly around the edges and making it denser towards the centre. Here, amaryllis have been inserted. Because of the thickness of their stems, they needed to be placed in the tubes — wire netting would have split the stems. Lilac, cow parsley and longiflorum lilies were added, to complete the arrangement.*

60

MAKING A CONICAL DESIGN

1   To give this design balance, both visually and literally, you should use a heavy vase with a pedestal base. Build up a pyramid shape with blocks of wet foam, but do not make the pyramid too high, as the taller it is, the more unstable it becomes.

2   Trim the corners of the foam with a knife to give a smoother base on which to work. Tightly cover the pyramid with wire netting, then secure it to the vase handles with black reel wire. Push green garden sticks deep into the foam blocks to anchor them together, then trim the ends flush with the netting.

3   Push 18-gauge stub wire through all the fruit and vegetables. Small pineapples, fennel hearts, apples, halved melons, grapes, plums and star fruit were used here. Wire the fruits from different angles to create the maximum interest. For such heavy items as pineapples, you should use green garden sticks instead of wires.

4   When assembling the design it is best to start with the biggest pieces, as they will form the basic shape. The pineapples, grapes and then the melons were fixed in place before the design was filled in with the smaller fruits. It is not necessary to use a great many flowers and foliage when working with this amount of fruit and vegetables.

61

WIRING FLOWERS AND FOLIAGE

The wiring of flowers plays a very important part in the techniques of floristry, as opposed to flower arranging and if you will be creating bouquets, posies, head dresses and the like for a wedding, you will need to know some basic floristry skills first.

Sometimes people who have a great love of flowers find it hard to accept that wiring is necessary at times. However, flowers that are to be worn or carried must be moulded into an acceptable shape, and this is where wiring comes into its own. Replacing a stem with wire enables it to be coaxed into a shape that can be used as part of a posy, bouquet, corsage, buttonhole or head dress – something that would never be possible with the natural stem of the flower.

It goes without saying that the wires must be as inconspicuous as possible, and the finished work lightweight and comfortable to wear and hold. There are many gauges of wire available, but one should always choose the finest gauge that will hold the flower firmly in position. The greatest care should also be taken when handling the flowers and foliage because they can easily be bruised through rough treatment.

THE TYPES OF WIRE

The wires used for spray work are sold as stub wires in the standard imperial gauges of 20, 22 and 24. (The higher the number, the finer the gauge.) These numberings are gradually being replaced by metric measurements, in which case they are sold as 0.90mm, 0.71mm and 0.56mm respectively, and the rule is that the *lower* the number, the finer the wire! You may find this difficult to remember at first but you should soon adjust.

Silver wire is available in reels of varying thicknesses, and also in lengths of approximately 180mm (7in). It is often much easier and quicker to work with these cut lengths, and 0.38mm (28-gauge) and 0.28mm (32-gauge) wires are the most useful sizes. For convenience, and to avoid confusion when you are busy, keep each gauge of stub wire in a different, clearly marked, container that will stand up properly. It is essential to store the wires in a dry place to prevent them from rusting – a rusty stub wire will stain first your hands and then the plant material quite disastrously. Nevertheless, a rusting wire can be used to advantage in floristry, because when a wire comes into contact with the sap of the stem it will soon go rusty, therefore holding the stem and the wire together very securely. However, this must not be allowed to happen until the stem has been taped.

STEM TAPES

These are used to cover wires and are available in several colours and quantities. One of the most popular on the market is a slightly sticky tape which the novice will find easier to hold than the rubbery gutta percha, which is used most often. The sticky tape also keeps better – gutta percha just crumbles away after a time. Unfortunately the tape is only sold in one width and very often narrower gutta percha is preferable, especially when using silver wires for such floristry work as corsages and head dresses.

The tape is usually cut in half by hand, but this is a very laborious task. Help is at hand, however, in cake decorating shops! Sugarpaste flowers require extremely narrow stem tape for their very fine stems, for which you can buy a three-bladed stem cutter. This will also solve your problem with the sticky tape. Remove the two outer blades, leaving just the central one, and you will be able to cut tape to the exact size for covering silver wire stems for spray work. The time and effort saved by this little gadget more than justifies its inclusion in any list of floristry equipment.

Ribbons often provide the perfect finishing touch, and some paper ribbons are widely used. However, real ribbon is available in numerous lovely colours, widths and qualities. It may be expensive but the difference it makes to the end result is often worth the extra expense. In fact, a lesson you will quickly learn about floristry is that you get the best results only by using the best material available, thereby enabling you to produce work of which you can be justly proud.

Spray Work

Here is a list of flowers and foliage that can be successfully wired for spray work:

Alchemilla	Lily
Alstroemeria	Lily of the valley
Cyclamen	Nigella
Carnation	Orchid
Erica	Pittosporum
Eucalyptus	Ranunculus
Euonymus	Rhododendron
Freesia	Rose
Geranium	Senecio
Gladiolus	Spray carnation
Hedera	Stephanotis
Helleborus	Tradescantia
Hyacinth pips	

Before using either flowers or foliage, it is important that both have been properly conditioned (see pages 32 – 37) to improve both their appearance and performance. Remember that once the plant material has been wired it will not be in water or foam, and will have to stay looking good for at least a day. Conditioning for several hours is therefore necessary, during which time the material should be kept in as cool a place as possible (but not the fridge). The flowers will be crisp and firm but quite brittle, and their stems will tend to snap more easily (more often than not in the wrong place!), so handle them as carefully as you can.

If you will be picking your material from the garden, then do so preferably early in the morning or late in the evening. Take a bucket, half-filled with water, into the garden with you and place each flower or piece of foliage in it immediately after cutting. This will ensure that the plant material has no chance to droop.

It is very important to choose mature leaves for floristry, since to use young foliage will be to court disaster – the material will bruise very easily and probably disintegrate when wired. It is a waste to pick and condition plant material that cannot be used, and better to leave it on the plant for future use.

The flowers that have been mentioned are the more usual ones chosen for spray work, but don't be afraid to experiment with other flowers too – not, of course, on the day itself. Try out the proposed materials a few days before the event, and if your experiment is successful you can carry on. If not, then you will have time to review the situation and find a more suitable alternative. It is only by experimenting that discoveries are made, so don't be hidebound!

Technical Floristry Terms

Like any other trade, the floristry business has several specialist terms to explain various techniques and items. Here is a list of the most frequently used terms, and their explanations.

Binding This uses silver reel wire to hold the leaves and wires in place.

Guttaring The process by which the wires are covered with tape. As well as the eponymous gutta percha, other sorts of tape are also available.

Leg mounts The wires that are attached to the flower, pips, etc. They vary, having double, single, extended and even false legs. The latter is used when the wire replaces or extends the stem.

Pips Individual flowers taken from a flower such as a hyacinth.

Spray or corsage An arrangement of flowers worn on the shoulder of a coat or dress.

Stitching leaves The process of wiring leaves.

Wiring down Inserting the wire into the head of the flower and then wiring on the inside or outside of the stem for support.

MAKING A CORSAGE

1 *Wire and then tape the individual flowers and foliage.*

2 *Build up the shape of the corsage, taping the flowers together.*

3 *When the corsage is completed, tape the stem tightly then finish off neatly. Make sure you attach a safety pin to the corsage ready for wearing.*

To wire a single Singapore orchid, detach it from its stem then push a wire through the base of the flower head, keeping one leg of wire much shorter than the other, and twist the longer wire around the shorter one. Bind with stem tape. To make a spray, wire up each orchid individually then tape them together.

Hyacinth pips can be wired together to form a spray that adds interest to a bouquet. Bend over the top of a wire to form a crook, then push it down through the pip until the wire loop is hidden. Now push further pips up the wire and bind the remaining wire stems with stem tape.

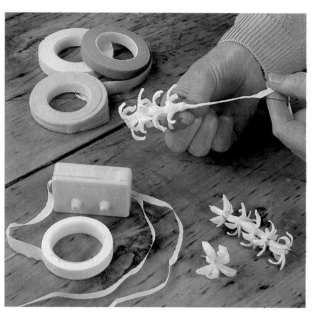

To wire an ivy leaf, keep the back of the leaf uppermost and, about three-quarters of the way up the leaf, push a wire through it to make a tiny 'stitch'. Move the wire until there are two equal legs, then bend them downwards. Make one lie against the stem and twist the other leg around the stem and the wire, thus holding it in place. To finish, bind this wire and stem with stem tape.

To wire a lily, cut off the stem until about 2.5cm (1in) remains, then carefully push a thick wire up the stem, and bind tightly with stem tape.

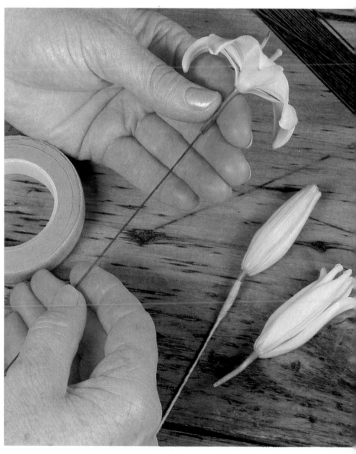

MAKING A BUTTONHOLE

1 *Cut out a small circle of card and make a small cut in the centre. Remove the outer leaves and seed pod of the carnation but leave the stem intact.*

2 *Push the card circle into place as shown, then feed the wire through the back of the carnation. Wire up some ivy leaves.*

3 *Neatly tape the leaves and carnation together. The buttonhole is now ready for use. It will look very elegant and sit easily.*

WIRING A ROSE

1 *Push a thick wire up the stem of the rose then push two wires through the base of the petals at 90° to each other.*

2 *Twist the wires down the stems, then bind with stem tape. To make a spray, tape one rose into the stem of the next.*

FEATHERING CARNATIONS

1 *Carefully separate a few petals from the main flower then wire the bases of the petals together, twisting the wire downwards as shown in the photograph.*

2 *Bind the wire with stem tape to give small, delicate flowers that are ideal for use in bouquets and head dresses.*

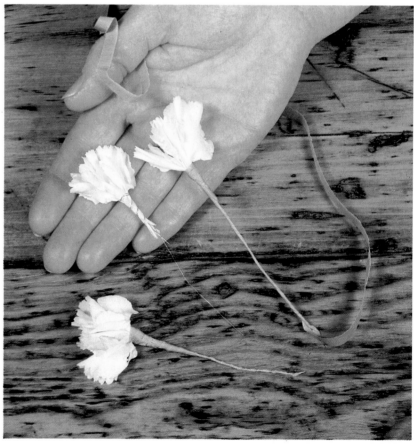

To wire a carnation, cut off its stem until no more than 2.5cm (1in) remains, then push a wire through the base of the flower head as shown, leaving one leg much shorter than the other. Bind the stem and wire with stem tape.

To wire a spray of lily of the valley, wind a length of wire between the bells, then pull it down the stem and bind firmly in place with stem tape.

FLOWERS FOR THE HOME

There are very few houses in which flowers or plants are never used as decorations, and indeed there are very few forms of decoration so varied that they appeal to the most sophisticated and the most simple of tastes. Unfortunately, flowers are often used only for special occasions, and this is a pity, because they can add so much to the quality of life and the ease and comfort of a home.

An arrangement may be used as a focal point to draw the eye away from a problem area, or to light up a dark corner, or it may emphasize your colour scheme, or complement a special piece of china. If your home is in the city, flowers will keep you in touch with the passing seasons – snowdrops in winter, roses in summer, and fruits and berries in autumn. For whatever purpose they are used, flowers bring depth and warmth to a room, which explains why they have often been likened to the living flame of a fire.

An arrangement has been made in a fireplace, with a coordinating design on a tiered side-table. An old black cooking pot was placed in the grate, which was brought forward a little to allow the taller stems of the flowers and foliage to come just above the surround. The flowers used are bold in shape and the design has been kept simple and not overfilled.

71

HALL DECORATIONS

A decoration in the hall is a lovely way to say 'Welcome'. The design does not need to be enormous or stunning; in fact, many hallways are quite narrow and a vast arrangement would be unsuitable.

The hall is, however, an ideal place for plants or a pot-et-fleur design. This combines the advantages of a long-lived design with the opportunity to pop in a few special flowers. If an unexpected guest arrives, for example, a special flower such as a lily or gladiolus can quickly be added to the design to provide a splash of colour or excitement. Two stems of either will be sufficient to last for quite some time if you remove the fading flowers and allow the new ones to open. The pot-et-fleur design really needs to be placed on a table and, if space allows, it will look lovely just inside the doorway.

Some halls are very narrow, and here the ideal solution is the long-neglected wall vase. This is perfect for a trailing ivy or tradescantia, both of which are quite tough and will survive with the minimum of attention while providing a distraction from the football boots, toys and golf bag in the corner. An added advantage is that the plants or flowers are out of harm's way. You can achieve the same effect with a small shelf or ledge which will take a container. One site that should generally be avoided is the table for the telephone – wires, telephone books and fiddling fingers are not conducive to the prolonged good looks of your design. A porch, on the other hand, is a good site, and hanging baskets or stands look very attractive here. Variegated foliages are excellent because they give lovely soft splashes of sunlight at all times. A mirror placed behind the design will double the number of flowers in the arrangement and will help to make the hall seem more spacious. If the hall is a little dark, then pale coloured flowers will help to lighten and brighten it. Avoid reds and blues; they will appear very bright when they are purchased, but these colourings do not show up well in dark places, whereas the cream, white or pale pink flowers will glow.

Planters are a very good idea in the hallway and can be used in many ways. They are usually free standing and fairly easily moved. The Victorians produced some lovely designs and these are once again being produced and seem to blend with almost every type of decor. They are made of wire and are sufficiently robust to cope with the odd school bag swung against them or the keen footballer misdirecting his aim. If there is a planter lurking in your loft, resurrect it, paint it white or deep garden green, and it will delight you.

PEDESTALS

A pedestal arrangement is also useful in the hall and can be arranged as grandly or as simply as the need arises. A fairly sturdy but simple shape is preferable here as the traffic will inevitably move around it and the flowers will quickly become quite tired and battered if the stand is a fragile one. A wooden or wrought iron pedestal is ideal.

A pedestal brings a sense of style to a design, even if it is arranged inexpensively with foliages and berries. Many will have doubts as to their ability to arrange a pedestal design, but rest assured that if you adopt a few basic techniques there is no problem. The one important point to remember when using a pedestal is to allow some of the foliages or flowers to flow over the front or sides; if this is neglected the design has a very cut off feeling, with a definitely surprised air. Silk or dried flowers can be used, and the former combine well with fresh foliages.

Foliages and dried or glycerined arrangements are a good idea for the hall. Glycerined beech or chestnut are lovely, and if you arrange them with old man's beard or orange berries you will create a design which will look charming and will require very little maintenance. Fatsia leaves are another lovely subject to glycerine and these, arranged with preserved moluccella and callicarpa berries, could not fail to please. You will have noticed that these leaves are all fairly large, and these and other materials will give a good design without a lot of fussy small materials. Fresh foliages should follow the same idea in being big and bold, and if there is a sheen on the leaves so much the better. The sheen can easily be maintained with a proprietary leaf shine cleaner, or you can wipe the leaves with a soft, damp duster. Variegated laurels, elaeagnus and similar foliages are a delight to use at any time of the year. Foliages with good autumn colouring, such as mahonia, can be used in their season with elder berries or pyracantha berries to create a very attractive display.

This winter pedestal arrangement has been created with silk flowers and beech, preserved in antifreeze. This is an arrangement that will look good for many months with only an occasional dust or wipe with a soft cloth. The design was made in a simple flat dish, with dry foam secured with tape to the pedestal. It is important to ensure that some of the materials flow down over the front to create a better design.

DARK CORNERS

Dark corners in halls and other rooms can often be brightened with an arrangement, either of fresh flowers and foliages, or perhaps of dried flowers. Pedestal designs work well in this context, as do variegated foliages. Dried flowers and foliages can also be most attractive in a dark corner, though in this case a pedestal design may be better avoided, as dried materials are for the most part rather stiff, and lack the trailing qualities demanded by a pedestal.

All dried flower arrangements, in fact, have a tendency to look like surprised hedgehogs unless care is taken to counteract this unfortunate effect by softening the design. Dried amaranthus (love-lies-bleeding), especially in its green form, is useful in this context, as are sprays of nicandra, both helping to soften a design and lend it greater interest and texture.

As has already been said, pale and soft coloured flowers stand out better than bright reds and blues, and in a dark corner it may be wise to consider using bleached and glycerined materials rather than dried. The outline will be very noticeable against a dark background, and a simple, elegant shape will make more impact than a complex design. A few glycerined aspidistra leaves with allium heads will create a wonderful effect, whereas a massed design of dried flowers would simply look fuzzy.

DECORATING WITH DRIFTWOOD

You can make very good designs from driftwood, which is a treasure that every flower arranger should possess. Invariably one hears tales of finding exciting and beautiful driftwood on the beach or on holiday, but most of us end up by buying choice pieces. Driftwood is the description of wood that has been aged in one of several ways: cleaned and scoured by the sea; burnt and bleached by fire; or old pieces that have rotted and been reshaped by the weather and animals, and a good piece of driftwood may be as beautiful as a piece of sculpture.

If you are in woodland and see an interesting piece of wood, there are several dos and don'ts to remember if you want to collect it. Firstly, do check that you are entitled to take it away! If you are, then wrap it in paper and put it into a plastic bag for the journey home. (Anything could crawl out of it!) Secondly, don't leave your driftwood in the house until you have cleaned it thoroughly, for the same reason. You can do this by soaking it in water for several days. Some people use bleach, but this changes the colour, so it is safer to use plain water. Next, give the wood a good scrub to remove any remaining dirt or inhabitants, before allowing it to dry completely.

Driftwood is often best left in its natural state, but it can be polished or coloured with wood dyes. The danger with this, of course, is that you may not like the finished result, and want to burn it or give it to a flower arranging friend who does like it. If you do the latter, then be prepared to see them use it in a marvellous way that will make you furious with yourself at having parted with it!

If you will be keeping your piece of driftwood, take a good look at it from every angle. Once you have found a position you like, set it down on to a base – a simple piece of wood is ideal. Set a flat dish, containing your mechanics, either behind or within the wood, but remember that it always looks most attractive with the minimum of materials, and just looks messy if smothered with flowers and foliage. Nevertheless, a great variety of materials can be used, although driftwood is particularly useful when plant materials are scarce. For example, frosted driftwood with holly and robins makes a delightful Christmas decoration, and a few daffodils or a potted primrose is a charming spring arrangement. Flowering shrubs are natural companions, and camellias and their foliage are a real joy. Decorations in halls and entrances are always a pleasure, and are especially attractive when driftwood is incorporated in them.

Dried plant materials have been arranged in an old copper canal water carrier. A smaller container was placed inside the can. Floral foam was placed in this and taped in place, and the tape was carried over to the copper can. It is important to have a variety of shapes and textures in a design formed with dried materials, or the result will be a little bland.

MAKING AN ARRANGEMENT FOR A HALL

1 *First prepare the driftwood and mechanics by screwing them on to a base, setting them into cement or clamping them in place. Here, they have been pressed firmly on to a special pinholder. Whichever method is chosen, it is important that the driftwood should be secure.*

2 *Create the outline with some well-defined foliage. Here, variegated elaeagnus has been used. Its leaves respond very well to being sponged with water, and perhaps wiped with a proprietary leaf shine, which reveals their marvellous colourings.*

75

3 *Add a few scarlet parrot tulips to create a natural yet striking design that allows the driftwood to be seen to its best advantage.*

THE SITTING ROOM

The sitting room is probably the chief room in the house in which you will want to have flowers. The arrangement for this room must, in general, be easy to live with, as a very brightly coloured or very large arrangement will constantly call for attention and can become an irritant instead of a pleasure.

It is important to decide where the arrangement is to be placed before it is made, and it is sensible to ask yourself about the way in which the room is used from day to day. Flowers placed just where grandfather normally rests his reading glasses or where the children do their homework will simply be in the way. In some cases the television seems to offer the only available space, but this must be one of the worst places possible, for the heat will rise and quickly dry out a fresh design, and silk or dried flowers will become dusty. The windowsill is another often used position, but again it is not really the most desirable spot, bearing in mind window draughts and the difficulty of creating a good arrangement against the light. Both of these ideas are poor options, and it is better to use a space on a sideboard or table. Even a relatively tall cupboard will be infinitely better, both from a practical point of view and with regard to the appearance of the design.

Flowers for the sitting room, for everyday, should complement the colourings in the room and fit comfortably into the surroundings. Too many arrangements will give a spotty feeling and no single arrangement will give the good effect. Simplicity is the key, whether the arrangements are vast or petite. Overfilled or crammed vases, besides being an unnecessary extravagance, will not show the flowers or foliages to their best advantage. One main arrangement, with a small subsidiary to emphasize the colour or effect, will be far more impressive than a host of vases dotted all over the room. Similar flowers and similar colourings are important here, to give a feeling of unity and to create a satisfying sense of harmony.

CONTAINERS

Even if you use the same vase most of the time, it is best to choose one that offers scope for various types of design. Bases can add to the design by helping to lift the vase or dish, and if they are covered in material they may continue the scheme of the room or the flowers. If there is any doubt about the ideal choice of colour, a soft neutral beige or grey will always be useful.

A base has the added advantage of protecting the furniture to some extent. However careful you try to be when topping up with water, there are times when a leaf syphons water over the edge to the surface below, and unless the drops are very quickly wiped away, ugly water marks will remain. There are some remedies for these, but it is simpler to take precautions in the first place.

FIREPLACE ARRANGEMENTS

A side-table may not be the best place for a summer arrangement. The fireplace is generally the focal point of a main room, but in the summer it is often just a dark yawning hole. Flowers and foliages can help to give a softer touch here, and one idea is to position a large, trailing design on the mantelpiece. Another is to use the empty grate itself. Fireplace designs are not very practical for a party, when guests tend to stand, particularly if the room is crowded. The flowers will not be seen by anyone, and invariably guests use the fireplace, quite unthinkingly, as an ash-tray, even if your best floral design has been placed there. For everyday, a design in the grate can be very pleasant, however, and you will find that your eyes wander over the materials with pleasure as you sit to chat or watch television.

The container for an arrangement in a fireplace needs to be fairly capacious and heavy – an old iron cooking pot is ideal, and if it is black, so much the better. Basic mechanics will need to be either wire netting with a pinholder or floral foam and wire netting, both firmly attached to the pot. An outline is important with such a dark background; think of the still life paintings of the Dutch school. In this type of floral design, the outline should be beautiful and should set the scene for the heavier materials used in the centre. For this reason, it is best to create the outline first, using the lighter, finer materials, after which you can position the more dramatic flowers and foliages at the centre. Flowers will be better here if they are somewhat sculptured in shape; peonies or hollyhocks would be striking, for example, and the materials used as the infill could be delphiniums or Canterbury bells.

Good foliages and berries are very striking against this kind of dark background, and fatsias or bergenia leaves will give a bold base. The arrangement does not have to be centred in the grate, and you will often find that the effect is less overpowering and perhaps a little more original if the design is set to one side or the other. Arrangements with driftwood are very suitable for this type of situation, and if you incorporate ferns or similar plants you will evoke a very cool and restful atmosphere. Ferns arranged with foliages are also lovely and are a perfect foil for each other, creating designs that are sculptured and architectural.

The design shown here, which combines driftwood with ferns, was intended to create a cool calm atmosphere during a period of hot weather, when the interior of the average house can often feel stuffy and oppressive.

This fireplace design was made with a large flat slice of wood as a base. Driftwood was placed near the front, and a plastic dish holding floral foam, taped in place for security, was positioned behind it. The ferns for this type of design should be arranged to look as natural as possible, so it is advisable to group the fronds according to type, as if they were growing in a woodland setting. Two growing ferns were placed at either side in pots, to ensure a long-lasting design.

TIERED TABLES AND STANDS

A tiered table, of the sort that used to be called a 'What-not', is a marvellous piece of furniture for the arranger. It leaves space for all the paraphernalia of everyday living and also a top ledge for a flower design, incidentally at an ideal level. Old ash tray stands are also very good for arranging purposes, especially if they have two shelves, and now that so many people have given up smoking these pieces of furniture are readily available and are quite inexpensive. If they appear a little tatty, this can be easily remedied with a sanding and revarnishing or painting. The top shelf usually holds the metal ash tray and this takes a round of floral foam firmly taped to the stand, in which you can create a design. The choice of shape is again affected by the moment, but the stand affords the opportunity to make your design large or small – either will look in proportion. A little posy topknot may be as attractive as a large flowing arrangement; the choice is yours.

MATCHING DESIGNS

Matching designs can look very attractive at each end of a mantelpiece, but often the two arrangements are made to match exactly, leaf for leaf, flower for flower, even to the extent of reversing the designs as though they are mirror images. This is a disappointing way to arrange flowers – all the lovely spontaneity of plant materials is lost and the whole takes on a very factory-made appearance. It also tends to be dull, because once you have looked at one design there will be little need to look at the other. Uniformity has a very important part to play in many things, but if you vary the angle of a leaf or flower in the designs, even though you may use identical flowers and foliages, you will create greater interest, and at least both arrangements will be enjoyed in their own right. There must always be the element of surprise.

Flowers offer a useful means of creating differing moods and atmosphere. Here, two designs have been made in the same containers, but with different colourways, one designed to blend with the decor, and the other to attract attention and create a focal point.

KITCHEN FLOWERS

Flowers and plants are a joy in the kitchen, and if you regard them as a necessity in other rooms, then this outlook applies equally here, for in most homes the kitchen is where everyone tends to congregate and swop news of the day's events. You, or you and your partner together, are likely to spend a lot of time working in the kitchen, so it is a place where an arrangement of some kind will give a great deal of pleasure.

Naturally, the design does not have to be an elaborate, formal construction, for this would appear out-of-place, but even a simple vegetable arrangement of a cabbage, cauliflowers and a few carrots in an old mixing bowl can look very appropriate. The wonderful, sculptured shapes of the vegetables are a delight, and when you have enjoyed it visually to the full, then you can eat your arrangement, and savour it with the palate. Even a simple pot of berries or leaves, perhaps collected while you walk the dog, can be placed on the windowsill to catch the eye.

A planted bowl or trough on the kitchen window ledge is always a good idea, especially if herbs are included. Chives, parsley and various other herbs which are always needed for cooking or as a garnish will grow quite happily together. Steamy conditions do not suit all herbs or small plants, but your local garden centre advisers will be able to assist you with your choice. The best way to assemble a window box of this type is to leave the plants in their pots when putting them in the container, so that if one or two seem unhappy then they can be replaced without difficulty. Alternatively, they can be planted in individual little plastic bags (allowing, of course, room for watering).

It is also lovely to make space in your kitchen for some bulbs in a planter, so that you can enjoy watching them through the cold winter days. If the space is very limited, then bulb glasses are a lovely idea – there is even one that is designed to take an acorn.

A swag of vegetables or fruits, combined with wheat, mushrooms or other fungi, can look particularly effective in the kitchen. Such arrangements are surprisingly long lasting, and if made on a raffia plait – those from a garlic swag are very useful – they are fairly easy to make. It is a good idea to ask the greengrocer for the raffia plaits that remain after the garlic has been sold, even if you have to buy the last few garlics in order to be given the plait.

Many kitchens have high ledges or cabinets at the top of which is a great deal of wasted space, apart

A trough of pretty or useful growing plants is a lovely way to brighten up the kitchen windowsill. The plants may be chosen simply to echo the kitchen theme, like the ornamental cabbages seen here (above), or you may select plants for their practical culinary uses, like the thyme and chives in the trough on the right. Here, small pots of flowers, which can easily be replaced with others when the need arises, were added to the design to provide colour. Whatever plants you use, make sure that the planter is sufficiently deep to take a layer of broken crocks at the bottom, for drainage, and to allow room for the plants to thrive.

from the odd saucepan. Here, trailing ivies and ferns look very attractive. Foliage plants such as tradescantias are very tough and will endure quite hot, steamy and draughty conditions. All of these plants look lovely when they are allowed to trail a little – not too wildly – over the shelf, or you may choose to limit them so that they just peep over the edge. If there is some light here, they should be able to survive perfectly well. In fact, kitchen plants have a tendency to flourish and become old friends, despite the fact that they are often neglected.

BEDROOMS AND BATHROOMS

Bedrooms are often starved of fresh flowers, but even if you can't keep arrangements in all the bedrooms all the time, they still make a way of saying 'Welcome' to a guest, or perhaps 'Good luck' to a child who is facing an ordeal such as an exam.

Unusual flowers will please a gardener and those with a lovely perfume will be appreciated by everyone, perhaps with the exception of a hay-fever sufferer. The old-fashioned hospital rule of removing flowers from the bedroom at night is not necessary, for the small amount of oxygen that the little arrangement will use up will certainly not cause any problem. Younger guests love an arrangement made in a toy, which can become a going home gift later – a small engine or car never fails to produce wreaths of smiles and sets the visit off to a good start. The older guest is equally delighted with a small posy or buttonhole flower, which he or she can wear at dinner.

BATHROOMS

Bathrooms are another area of the home where it is pleasant to have some decoration, and air plants must have been designed for busy people to use in this situation, for they need practically no attention other than admiration. Shells are marvellous for bathroom arrangements, and echeveria and other similar types of succulents are lovely here. Ferns and ivies also seem to enjoy the bathroom atmosphere, and even the smallest room can be brightened by a planted wall vase or flowers growing on a simple ledge. Flowers are not as happy in the steam, but you may find that silk plants or flowers survive very

A straw box makes a pretty container for dried flowers preserved in silica gel. The colours will eventually fade, but soft browns will still look attractive with the box colouring. Again, the flowers are held in a square of foam, dry this time, taped to a dish placed inside the box.

This fresh flower arrangement was made in a white china container to which a small block of floral foam was taped. Small delicate flowers, including some unusual ones from the garden, were arranged very simply to create an informal, friendly feeling.

well; these just need an occasional blow with the hair dryer to keep them free from talcum powder.

Plants in the bathroom can help to solve the shortage-of-foliage problem for many, as the conditions encourage a fast rate of growth, and this enables you to pick lovely pieces to arrange. Again, a garden centre expert will be able to advise you on the best plants to buy – probably those with a tropical flavour. If your bathroom is of vast proportions then a planter is a delightful idea; the plants can be allowed to cascade down over the ledges, and you can include a few flowers for special occasions.

SICK ROOMS

Rooms used by an invalid, either young or old, are always made more cheerful and hopeful by flowers or plants. This is a time when fresh flowers and plants – living and growing – should be used.

Arrangements and plants change, fade and die, like all living things, and to give a silk or dried arrangement just because it is practical is a little dull. To be faced with an unchanging and static design, however beautiful, is rather monotonous for those confined to bed. Fresh materials will bring a part of the garden into the room. A plant can be put in the garden at a later date, and nothing could be lovelier than bulbs, which will develop and give great pleasure. This is an occasion when perhaps more than at any other time the recipient will have many hours to look and enjoy.

It is always lovely to have arrangements in bedrooms and bathrooms. The bathroom arrangement has been made in a soap dish and uses simple flowers, chosen to pick up the colouring of the wallpaper. The flowers are held in a small square of floral foam, taped to the dish and carefully covered with ivy.

84

DRIED FLOWERS

Dried flowers have an invaluable part to play in winter arrangements. Even if you have some fresh flowers, it is pleasant to fill odd gaps around the house with dried arrangements or to combine dried flowers with fresh foliage. In any case, fresh flowers tend to die very quickly in dry, centrally-heated rooms, but these often provide the correct atmosphere for the dried variety, which tend to become mildewed or to lose their texture in moist conditions.

Dried flower arrangements can become dreary and dull, so it is important to make regular changes. Remove damaged flowers and replace them with new flowers or seed heads; change the container from time to time, and move the revitalized arrangement to a different position.

COUNTRY BASKET

Arching spikes of silvery white artemisia feature heavily in this arrangement. Artemisia is an unruly plant in the garden where its slender stems are often toppled by the slightest summer wind. Artemisia is equally unruly in dried flower arrangements (it quickly wilts when used fresh), but like a wayward child, is charming all the more for this. Its unregimented curves and twists relieve the poker straightness of pink and mauve statice.

There are various stages at which any flower arrangement can be said to be finished, although eventually there is a danger of over-working it, so

Circular tables call for all-round displays, and a basket of dried flowers is a tried and true solution. An informal arrangement, such as the one shown, is also a token of hospitality, and is particularly welcoming in an entrance hall or living room.

that it loses its freshness. In this arrangement, ribbons of toning pink or mauve could be worked round the handle of the basket, or small bows tucked into the arrangement. A small wreath, encircling the base of the basket, could be made of statice, artemisia and phalaris, to continue the floral theme downwards and also visually widen the rather narrow base of the basket in relation to the spread of the dried flowers.

FRESH FOLIAGE AND DRIED FLOWERS

Whatever the size of a garden, there is usually more foliage available than flowers. When there are no fresh flowers at all, as in the depths of winter, garden foliage and dried flowers make a splendid combination.

Cineraria, or silver leaf, is a sun-loving semi-hardy shrubby perennial, but is often grown as a half-hardy annual. It is worth leaving a few plants in the ground over winter, as a source of cut foliage. There are various cultivars, including 'Silver Dust', with silvery, ferny leaves; 'White Diamond' and 'Ramparts', both with deeply cut foliage.

To prevent wilting, the tips of the stems were inserted, immediately after cutting, into boiling water for a few seconds; they can also be singed over a flame. The prepared stems were then placed in a deep container of water for several hours, to complete the conditioning.

The old ginger jar used for this arrangement is half filled with water. This meets the needs of the cineraria, while the dried flowers – sprigs of pink heather and deep pink xeranthemums, both on natural stems, and silvery blue echinops, on wired stems – are inserted so their stems rest above the water line. An unconventional approach and a fiddly task, but it allows the foliage to remain fresh while the dried material remains dry, and can be used again and again.

Fresh heathers, such as the winter-flowering cultivars, could be used in a similar arrangement, and left to dry naturally with their stems in the water.

For a colour scheme based on blue and silver, dried cornflowers and lavender could replace the xeranthemums and heather. For one based on yellow and silver, use African daisies and cluster-flowered everlastings.

Other grey-leaved garden shrubs that could be substituted include the hardier *Senecio greyi*, more correctly *Senecio* 'Sunshine', with its tough, rounded leaves, white felted underneath; and lavender cotton, with its finely divided, thread-like foliage. The senecio needs its woody stem hammered before being immersed in water; lavender cotton should be prepared in the same way as cineraria.

This little arrangement was made in winter, albeit a mild one, and instead of evergreens, the thickly felted white leaves of cineraria were used.

SPRING BLOSSOMS

In spring, we are often overwhelmed with blossom and flowers, yet a little earlier in the year we may well yearn for a branch or two of colour to brighten up the house and remind us that warmer weather is coming. Two ways of producing this effect – one using dried flowers and the other silk florets – are shown here.

Both the artificial trees are based on carefully chosen branches, inserted into a base of dry floral foam. Quick-setting plaster could also be used. Less than one bunch of dried pink delphiniums was used in the construction of the dried blossom tree.

The top surface in the container is a layer of sphagnum moss, as is the tiny nest perched in the branches and discreetly wired for stability. Speckled quail eggs complete the spring image; these are available from large supermarkets and should be blown if the display is to be permanent.

The most costly component is the garlanded

Hazel branches and dried delphinium florets were used for this spring blossom tree, but well-shaped branches of other shrubs and different flowers, such as white and pink helipterum, for example, would have been equally effective.

terracotta pot, but even this is a modern replica and not exorbitantly expensive. It also lasts a lifetime, and most people would find it more attractive than its plastic equivalents. In practical terms, the terracotta provides weight and therefore stability to an otherwise vulnerable display.

Once the tree is built, the tiny delphinium flowers, or florets, are attached to the branches using quick-drying glue. It is better to distribute them evenly over the tree, and build up a density gradually, than to thickly cover one branch and then go on to the next. The florets are easier to glue to the point where branches meet than along an open branch.

The possible variations on this theme are numerous: a traditional wooden Versailles tub, either black or white; a simple, undecorated terracotta flower pot, perhaps spray painted to match the flowers; concrete pots, painted to look like old stone; fibreglass containers, made to look like lead; and attractively glazed Chinese pots, all of which are available from larger garden centres. Glazed, decorated indoor containers, such as an old chamber pot, a huge cache pot or soup tureen; and wicker containers, such as a large laundry or log basket, are possibilities, as no watering or drainage holes are necessary.

This single blossom spray is made with groups of large and small silk florets and buds set at the appropriate points of a cherry branch. For a different effect, silk briar roses might be attached to a rose or bramble stem.

ARRANGEMENTS WITH SILK FLOWERS

Silk flowers can sometimes look very artificial and overpowering, but used with discretion they can be most attractive. Although the aim is not to deceive, it is generally best to use silk flowers that are appropriate to the season – there is something mildly disturbing about poppies in spring or Christmas roses in summer.

Two uses of silk flowers are shown here. The vase of sweet peas might add a delicate touch of colour to a bedroom or an occasional table. Fresh shop-bought sweet peas are often rather oversized and sturdy varieties, but the silk ones featured here have the fragile air of the cottage garden types.

Dried flowers tend to be rather muted and even drab in tone, and the addition of a small number of silk flowers, such as the poppies featured here,

A piece of dry floral foam has been wedged into the small modern specimen vase to hold six stems of silk sweet peas.

WILD FLOWERS

can often lift an otherwise dull dried flower arrangement and give it zing. The design has a country atmosphere suitable for a large kitchen, and you might substitute other flowers, such as dahlias or chrysanthemums, at the appropriate times of year.

The outline of this all-round arrangement was made with glycerined pampas grass and dried grasses. Some 15 silk poppies and four silk beech branches were set at different heights and angles and interspersed with poppy seedheads and preserved ruscus.

In view of all the discussion about the environment and endangered species, it may seem wrong to think of using wild flowers in the home, and certainly the days when children could gather primroses or make cowslip balls, according to the season, have gone. All the same, there are still many wild plants that are in plentiful supply and can safely be used without harming the environment.

If you have the opportunity to use wild plants in arrangements, the first thing to do is to arm yourself with a list of endangered species, so that you can avoid the risk of contravening the law. It is also responsible to follow certain basic rules: pick carefully and tread warily, especially where there are bluebells; never pull out the whole plant, or pick rare flowers that rely on seeds for propagation; only pick plants that are growing in abundance in that particular area, and only pick flowers or fruits that you are going to use.

In addition to a list of endangered and forbidden species, it is good sense to have a guide that will enable you to identify any plant that you might choose to pick. In particular, it is important to know which plants and berries are poisonous. Wild bryony is beautiful, for example, but it is safest not to use it in an arrangement that will be placed where children are liable to hold or even just to touch its stems, and ivy is also dangerous.

With these provisos, there are numerous plants that are wonderful for flower arrangers and fit beautifully into domestic or for that matter even into very formal flower arrangements. Cow parsley is a plant that is wonderful to arrange in all its stages and there can be no hesitation in recommending it, for it grows prolifically everywhere. It does, however, need to be conditioned correctly, which is done by burning the ends of the stems before giving your cow parsley a long cool drink. Thereafter, it is surprisingly long lasting, and is beautiful for weddings and christenings. This lovely plant is just as attractive in its seed stage as it is when in flower, and glittered seed heads make the most delightful Christmas decorations. Seed heads is perhaps a misnomer, for it is best to allow the seeds to drop off (make sure that this does not happen in the flower garden). The little stems which are left look like stars once they have been glittered, and are a joy.

Seeds, berries and fruits also provide good flower arranging materials, though they are often overlooked. A spray of blackberries makes a delightful addition to an autumn arrangement. At the right time of the year there is an abundance of cones and pods waiting to be picked. Nuts of all kinds are wonderful in sprays or garlands and a delight in collage. A spray of hips or haws in an arrangement of chrysanthemums is just one of the many delights to be enjoyed in an arranging year.

Old man's beard or *Clematis vitalba* is another flower arrangers' treasure and, like cow parsley, is a delight to use in all its stages, from the flowers to the soft hairy seeds. This glycerines very well and is a lovely subject for a garland for an autumn buffet table design. If you are using old man's beard in its glycerined state, take care that the glycerine does not ooze on to a buffet table cloth – pat the leaves gently with a soft duster to remove any excess glycerine. If a glycerined spray is to form part of a fresh arrangement, it is a good thing to tape the end of the stem, as this will quickly become very soggy in the wet foam and will then become mouldy. If the arrangement consists solely of dried materials and can therefore be made with dry foam, there will be no problem at all.

Considering how difficult it can prove to eliminate weeds from the garden, it is surprising that wild flowers should be so frail, but they are notoriously finicky and it makes sense, if you are intending to collect flowers to arrange, to take with you a plastic pot filled with water. If the stems are woody, they can be wrapped in a plastic bag, but the most important rule with all wild plants is to keep them out of the sun on the journey home. The worst possible place for them will be the back window ledge of the car or the rack on the back of a bicycle.

Once you are home, the materials should be conditioned in the same ways as cultivated plants, and if you take these precautions, you will gain as much pleasure from the arranging as from the picking, and the results will be a delight.

A simple arrangement of wild plant material has been made in an old pewter mug. The dull grey of the mug shows to advantage the old man's beard, picked from a hedgerow. Wire netting has been crumpled into the mug to ensure that the materials hold their positions – most wild flowers are not particularly happy in floral foam.

ENTERTAINING WITH FLOWERS

It is a great pleasure to entertain friends or business acquaintances, especially if the entertainment takes place in one's home. This is not a time either to impress or overwhelm, but to show hospitality of the best kind. A generous budget or a large house are not necessary, but thoughtfulness and a welcoming atmosphere are essential. The entertainment will vary with the occasion, but whatever the event, some planning will be needed, and the tasks of making lists and shopping for special foods or flowers can be almost as enjoyable as the event itself.

Even if guests have arrived unexpectedly, and you must create food for six out of thin air, with the minimum of fuss, this can generally be managed, and the table setting can be completed with a quick arrangement, perhaps of fruit combined with foliage stripped from a houseplant. For more formal entertaining, well-thought-out flower arrangements set the scene and establish the atmosphere – elegant, romantic, exciting, frivolous, dramatic or simply welcoming.

When space is limited and you have a large number of guests, it is worth considering setting up a buffet table in the kitchen, leaving the rest of the house free for guests and keeping the food and drinks where they can most easily be replenished. Here, a trestle table has been covered with a cloth and a tall arrangement incorporating vegetables and fruits attracts the eye away from the sink.

A FORMAL DINNER PARTY

Even though formal rarely implies full evening dress these days, the flower arrangements for a formal dinner party should still complement the smart suits and pretty dresses of the guests, setting the scene for a memorable occasion.

The dining room or perhaps the china, if it is very striking, will often establish the colour scheme. If neither of these provides an obvious theme, then choose a soft colouring. Soft colours always look attractive at night, especially when lit by candlelight. Candles are not essential, but they add greatly to the atmosphere and certainly improve both the flowers and the appearances of the guests.

Having decided on the colour scheme, the next thing is to select the style and flowers. Here it is emphatically not the cost that is important, but the care and perhaps the flair with which the evening has been planned that will make it memorable. Simple, elegant flowers, free from nibbles or marks, are ideal. Soft peach, pink or cream flowers always look good, but this must be your choice. The container should be sufficiently low for the guests to be able to see each other when the arrangement is completed. An ordinary plastic tray is ideal, and if this can be raised a little on a simple base it will help the design to flow down a little, rather than to stick straight from the tray. It is preferable that there should not be a mass of foliage trailing all through the vegetable dishes; it is not a relaxed guest who has to search for a place to put the dish down, hoping that the decor will not be damaged in any way.

A simple horizontal arrangement or cone will look attractive on the table, with the addition of candlesticks at each side or incorporated into the design. An arrangement on a side-table or sideboard is always elegant, if this area is not being used for the china or wine. The colours of the side-table design may match those of the main table. This certainly contributes to a feeling of well-being and planning, but fruit and foliage are so delightful in this setting that it is often preferable to depart from the overall scheme. Lighting on a side-table can create lovely pools of light and shadow, but as with flowers, the effect must be not to overwhelm but to establish a comfortable and convivial atmosphere.

The hall and cloakroom will need some small decorations, and if the guests will be using a bedroom for their coats, then a simple decoration on a dressing-table is a good idea.

The drawing room will also need to have an arrangement, but as the main aim of the evening will be to dine, the dining room is where the most important design should be. If you have conditioned

your plant materials correctly, all these arrangements can be made well in advance, easily the day before, and this will allow you plenty of time to organize and prepare the food and wine on the day. An important point to remember is that you should water the flowers about three or four hours after they have been arranged, as they will drink very readily to begin with. If this is neglected, the floral foam will dry out and the flowers will have no hope of surviving for the following day. Another top-up on the day, and perhaps a light spray, should be all that is needed.

The arrangements are colour coordinated, and some of the flowers used are the same, but each design has been created with a specific need in mind. Pineapples have been included in the sideboard arrangement, with one placed in front so that it can be used for the dessert. The mantelpiece design is in a small glass dish. Trailing materials have been used to soften the effect, but they have not been allowed to hide the pretty fireplace surround. The height has been kept low, so that the materials just peep up a little over the mirror. The table design is slim and tailored, the perfect complement to an elegant dinner party.

CANDLESTICK ARRANGEMENTS

Using a candlestick as a container is a very practical move: it confines the arrangement to a limited area and turns the candle and flowers into a single unit. One charming idea is to incorporate a candle follower and shade with the candle. A candle follower is a metal frame that fits over the candle (it must be the Georgian, straight-sided kind), and then carries the shade, which is made from a metal or stiff card. Once assembled, it creates a very attractive and intimate feeling.

MAKING A CANDLESTICK ARRANGEMENT

1 *Place a special mould on the candlestick, and fit a candle into its holder with the follower and shade. Cut a piece of floral foam to the correct shape, soak it and then press it into the mould. Create the outline with foliage and downward-flowing plant material.*

2 *Add the flowers to the design. Simplicity is the key to elegance, and here the summer jasmine and 'Champagne' roses combine well to give a soft effect.*

3 *The followers give an added dimension to the candlesticks, and the candlelight shining on to the flowers and foliage helps to create an intimate atmosphere that is ideal for a formal dinner party.*

Candlestick arrangements nearly always benefit from the inclusion of downward-flowing flowers and foliage, unless they are very short, in which case a simple garland looks charming. Always keep your flowers clear of the candles, as they can constitute a considerable fire hazard, and always replace the candles when they begin to burn down near the flowers – no matter how exciting you want the occasion to be, watching the flower arrangements going up in flames is too dramatic for most people's taste!

SIDE-TABLE ARRANGEMENTS

An arrangement on a sideboard or side-table is a good opportunity to let your imagination run riot, and the use of fruits and berries is especially effective.

In most cases, the height of the arrangement is unlimited and, unless the surface will be needed for serving or storing the china or wine, then this will also be yours to command. It is best to link the colour schemes for this arrangement with that of the table, but it isn't essential, particularly if fruit is being used. When creating this type of design it is often better to forgo a traditional container and use two bases and a simple tin such as a bread bin, for the mechanics. It will not be seen in the finished design, yet will make life much easier for you when arranging such fruits as pineapples and grapes. Potted plants, for example *Begonia rex* or caladiums, can also be set into the design more easily. Trailing ivy, whether cut or left in pots, is very effective when used to soften the arrangement and blend all the fruits together.

MAKING A SIDE-TABLE ARRANGEMENT

1   *Assemble the mechanics to give a tall narrow design of foliage and flowers, and allowing space at the base of the design for the fruit which will give a sense of solidity. A block of floral foam, covered with wire netting, was placed in a baking tin. On top of this was placed a large florists' tube, filled with netted foam. This was all placed on a large piece of wood.*

2   *Arrange the outline, placing the heaviest fruit first. Hold the larger fruit in place with barbecue sticks and the lighter berries with wooden cocktail sticks, and wire the cherries.*

3   *Once you are happy with the arrangement of the fruits, add the flowers. This design included a profusion of brightly-coloured poppies, which were allowed to fall into their own curves naturally.*

A Supper Party

Several types of arrangement can be used for a dinner party, and while a formal event demands formal flowers, something a little more relaxed is pleasant for other occasions, such as a luncheon, a family birthday dinner or a supper party with close friends.

Here, individual arrangements are a lovely idea and make charming little gifts to take home, especially if single roses or carnations have been used. One idea that can be incorporated with individual place arrangements is to float candles in a dish of water to create an attractively light and informal effect. Even if you have worked all day and then gone to the theatre with friends, you will still have time for this simple arrangement of flowers and candles.

This is the simplest of ideas, but charming. Flower heads, with just a short length of stem, are placed into glasses containing a little water. It is better to fill the glasses a third or two-thirds full – the halfway mark leaves one with a cut-in-half feeling. To continue the theme, floating candles are placed in a shallow bowl at the centre of the table.

Silk water lilies make an interesting centrepiece for a modern glass-topped table and simply styled tableware. No container is required – the lilies rest on their own stems which are bent together to form a circular base.

An individual place-setting decoration has the novel touch of being also a 'place card': the guest's name is written on the water lily leaf with a silver-ink pen.

Dinner for Two

Whatever your age or sex, it is always a
delight to plan a romantic dinner for two.

Never mind if you are accused of being unashamedly
romantic – what could be more flattering? Being
classed as a romantic allows one to get away with
a slightly eccentric approach to life, delighting in
sunsets and dandelion clocks, without being thought
completely mad. Romance is a lovely word, and the
world would be a happier place if there were more
if it around. As always, the ideas here are only
suggestions, to help to set the scene and evoke the
desired ambience, but you know best what will work
for you.

Colour is definitely a key factor in creating the
relaxed atmosphere that you are hoping for. Whether
the plan is to have a supper by the lake-side or a
hamburger in the bedsit, the colouring has to be soft
and gentle, such as creams, or peaches, or perhaps
colours in the brown range. As has already been
discussed, colour has a great influence over our
moods, and while it can be used to uplift or stimulate,
here the aim is to help your partner to feel
comfortable and welcome. There should be that hint
of intimacy that comes with gentle colouring, and
makes a good beginning for any proposed romantic
occasion.

The table-setting needs to be simple, with flowers
and candles ranged on either side. Symmetry is an
important aid in creating an undemanding
atmosphere and a simple, traditional style of flower
arrangement will be perfect. A modern or extreme
style of design will not evoke a relaxed atmosphere,
and after your successful romantic dinner there will
be ample opportunity to show off your expertise in
these fields. Two unpretentious arrangements, with
candles either at the sides or incorporated in them,
will be perfect.

In the arrangement shown here, the candles have
been positioned so that they bring the eye to the
centre of the table, where a low, pretty design has
been made, which itself then twines tendrils and
golden hop flowers through the candlesticks. One
word about creating a design of this type – it is
essential that you should be able to see your partner
and vice versa. It is one thing to sit in flattering
candlelight, your face beautifully framed with
flowers, but nothing could be less conducive to a
relaxed atmosphere than to be obliged to talk through
a jungle-like screen of foliage. It is often a good idea,
in fact, when making this type of arrangement, to
prepare it while sitting down from time to time,
preferably on the chair that you will be using, so that
you can be sure that it is the perfect height. Take
care, also, that your mechanics are secure and you
have not twisted the foliage into unnatural shapes

that will gradually shift. With these provisos, the type of arrangement shown here will create a lovely feeling of intimacy and set the scene for romance.

With the lights dimmed, whether you are in a one-room apartment or a grand dining room, the rest of the world will be invisible and the setting will be the focal point for a night to be remembered forever.

A romantic occasion needs candles and soft colourings to create the right mood. This arrangement has been made in a simple white china container, which has a short stem. This helps the design to flow easily, but if you do not have a container of this type you can place a small base under a dish instead. The flowers must be kept low and space must be left at either side for dishes.

A KITCHEN BUFFET

Party arrangements in the kitchen are always great fun to plan and arrange. The scope in plant materials is tremendous and the selection of cooking utensils for use as containers is an enjoyable task. In fact, it is hard to avoid going to extremes with the wonderful array of vegetables and flowers that are available.

If the kitchen is large enough to dine in comfortably, then it makes a lovely intimate place for a supper party. The table will probably be relatively small, in which case it is a good idea to eat the decor – not the daisies, perhaps, but an arrangement of fruits can be ideal for this type of occasion.

The colour scheme in the kitchen is no less important than elsewhere, but as this is usually a well-lit area brightly coloured flowers will look very appropriate. Vegetables and fruits are also perfect for kitchen decor, and it is always fun to use these for a colour scheme. Candles, again, are effective and look better in simple candlesticks or wine bottles in this kind of setting rather than in Georgian silver. There is no fixed rule about this, of course, but the simple ideas tend to work best in this type of setting. Candle colourings can match either the party decor or the kitchen; dark green candles always look particularly striking, especially in green wine bottles.

A tall arrangement set to the back of the kitchen buffet table will be practical and will create a good design with the stacked plates and dishes of prepared food. There will be limited space, so it is best to make the arrangement tall and simple rather than big and overflowing. This will allow plenty of room for cutlery, napkins and so on. When the guests return for pudding and deposit their used plates at the side, the arrangement will definitely help to distract the eye from this part of the proceedings.

A buffet table in the kitchen offers a very practical way of entertaining, and will save a lot of extra work from the serving point of view. Here, an old wooden milk pail has been used. A container with floral foam firmly taped onto it was placed inside the pail. The pumpkin and aubergines were placed in front and to the side to give colour interest. The design was made quite tall and slim to retain the maximum of working space while still making an impact. Fruit and vegetables have been incorporated into the design with the use of wooden barbecue sticks. The design will divert all the attention to the table, so that the kitchen sink and cooker will not be noticed.

PARTY PEDESTALS

If you are throwing a party and worried that a particular room, hallway or landing looks rather bare, a large pedestal of flowers will fill the space with colour and form, and is often far more effective than several smaller and less striking vases. The designs shown here incorporate many varieties in shape as well as colour.

This type of arrangement looks especially stunning if placed at the head or foot of some stairs, but do make sure that there is enough room for your guests to walk about without fear of upsetting the vase. Furthermore, if you are creating a large arrangement that will be set on the floor, you must ensure that the vase is stable and high enough to give plenty of space between it and the floor.

·The hallway arrangement shown here combines guelder roses, white lilac, yellow lilies, forsythia, white roses, trailing ivy, eucalyptus and white stock.

The strong colours of the flowers in this pedestal arrangement give it added impact and would help brighten up any room.

The mixture of lime green, yellow and white is very spring-like and has a fresh feel.

To form the basis of the arrangement, roll lots of wire netting into a deep vase. Because of its depth, there should be no need to tape or wire the netting into the vase as it will stay in position of its own accord. If you want the arrangement to fit into a corner, you will achieve a much better effect if you can work *in situ*. As with any large arrangement, you should start at the back, placing the first stem as far back into the vase as possible, so that you can then arrange the flowers to fit the space perfectly. To avoid the arrangement sticking out from the wall at the back, you will have to ensure that you build a triangular-shaped back to the design.

A large pedestal arrangement will give a festive air to a bland hallway or landing.

TOPIARY

As a party decoration, the possibilities of using topiary are endless, especially when it is combined with garlands of flowers and foliage. The exquisite shapes of the garlands look magnificent against the dark green foliage of the topiary.

MAKING TOPIARY

You can easily make the basic shape with wet floral foam, but when you plan it you must remember that the finished result will be at least 2.5cm (1in) larger all over, due to the addition of the plant material. Of course, the size of the tree will determine the number and size of foam blocks you will need, but however many you use, they should be carved to the rough shape, staked together with garden sticks and then covered with wire netting, which is tied or wired in place. If the design is large, you must support it with a central cane or stake. Should the design need a trunk, you will have to prepare it in advance.

MAKING A TOPIARY CONE

1 *Cut out a large triangle of wire netting; join the prongs of two sides together to form a conical shape and then fill with moss. Push it on to a broom handle that you have previously set in a tub filled with cement. Wire lengths of box and push them into the mossed cone, always keeping the appearance of topiary.*

DECORATING THE TRUNK

Choose an appropriately sized stick or stake, which can then be covered with ribbon or painted. If you have a little time, you might choose to simulate bark, which gives a better and more convincing finish. It is easy to make, though rather messy!

Smear rubber glue over the surface of the stick, then wrap lengths of cheap soft lavatory paper around it. As the paper dries, which it will do quite quickly, gently squash it and move it around a little to roughen the surface. Then paint the stick with black matt emulsion. When it is dry, mix together a little brown and green emulsion to make a dirty

Lilies and imitation fruits provide a minor variation (right). The urn is plastic, painted as stone.

2 *Here the finished topiary has been decorated with diagonal bands of roses and ribbons, but this is only one of many designs that you could create.*

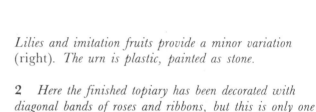

brown, and just brush it over the surface, then use each colour separately to blend a little here and there. Allow this to dry, then dip the brush into drab-coloured paint and wipe almost all of it off on to a rag or paper. Finally, very gently pull the brush over the surface to create the impression of weathered bark. Try again if you don't succeed at first – practice will soon make perfect. Then leave to dry.

Once it is dry, place the trunk in the plastic-lined pot, fill this with ready-mixed cement, then leave it to set. You will now be able to remove the stick, plus its cement base, from the pot or bucket. If the plastic lining has stuck to the cement, so much the better. You can now push the block of wet floral foam on to the handle and secure it in place with wire – you may find this easier if you first whittle the top of the stick into a spike, using a sharp craft knife.

CHOOSING THE FOLIAGE

The type of tree that you wish to make will affect your choice of foliage, determining its colour, shape and size, as well as type. A simple bay tree style is easily arranged by just pushing the pieces into the foam. You can use flowers too – the white all-year-round chrysanthemums can look very pretty – and ribbon bows are also attractive. Privet, or similar foliage is attractive and a variety of foliage can be lovely.

A close-clipped tree takes longer to make, and is best when yew, box or privet is used. An economical way in which to work is to push a stem into the foam and clip it off at the required length, repeating the process until the stem is used up. This is not as slow a process as it first appears, and in fact is a very rewarding task, for a clipped topiary tree can last many weeks or even months.

Pedestals or pillars combine attractively with topiary shapes, even more so when the topiary is spiralled from top to bottom with garlands. Other ideas are just waiting to be created by you!

OUTDOOR PARTIES

There is something very special about holding a party out of doors – if the weather is kind, of course! If you are planning to hold a party outside, naturally the more flowers and interesting foliage that are growing in the proposed area, the fewer arrangements you will need to create.

If you will be holding the party in your own garden and have a lot of shrubs but not many flowers, you can easily create the illusion of plenty of growing flowers. Simply bury bottles filled with water in the ground, leaving their necks just protruding above the earth, and then fill them with such straight-stemmed flowers as phlox, delphiniums or lilies, remembering to include some of their foliage as well. You will gain a much more realistic effect if you bury groups of five or seven bottles in close proximity so that the flowers resemble a bush rather than just single stems.

When arranging your garden for a party it is very important not to leave too much open space, otherwise the first guests, in particular, will feel very exposed and self-conscious, and be reluctant to move away from the sides of the garden into the middle, thereby creating an uneasy atmosphere. You could also arrange little groups of tables and chairs in various parts of the garden, or shade a particularly sunny spot with a large and attractive umbrella.

One lovely decoration in any garden is a stone urn filled with flowers and foliage. If you already have some urns in your garden, you could either fill them with flowering plants or create large flower arrangements inside them. Whichever option you choose, you should ensure that the urns are well-secured in case someone knocks against them or a gust of wind upsets them. If you want to buy some urns especially for your party, ideally you should do so several months in advance, and paint them with natural yoghurt to encourage the growth of mould and moss. This stops them looking obviously newly-bought and with luck they will look as if they have been in your garden for years by the time of the party. Stone urns can be used inside as well as out, and look especially attractive in a church or hall.

A large umbrella in the centre of an empty lawn creates a strong focal point and also brings people into the middle of the garden, especially if you group tables or decorative chairs around it. Arranging garlands of flowers around its edge will make the umbrella look more attractive and interesting. To do this, make rolls of wire netting, containing foam blocks, as you would for an archway (see pages 168–169), ensuring that each one is long enough to stretch from one spoke to the next. Firmly wire the ends of each roll to the spokes and then position the flowers. Wild gypsophila, white campanulas, Doris pinks, *Alchemilla mollis* and lavender sweet peas are here combined to give a very pretty, summery and rather frothy effect.

Very often the base of the umbrella is rather unattractive, but it can easily be transformed with some foliage and flowers. Place blocks of wet foam around the base; cover them with wire netting and then arrange plenty of grasses and a few stems of phlox or similar flowers to hide the base and give an informal effect. Bun moss and pieces of bark will cover up any mechanics that are left exposed, and also help to create additional interest.

In addition to any existing trees in the garden, you can also create your own rose trees that resemble stylized standard rose bushes. Like obelisks, they look very attractive when arranged by the walkway leading to an entrance or used to frame a special feature in the garden. You can make them in any size, although if they are more than 1.2m (4ft) high they should be secured to a wall or some other permanent and strong structure, to prevent any danger of their toppling over. Unfortunately, these trees do not last very long and must therefore be made on the day of the party.

Bare walls are sometimes decorative features in their own right, but you can increase their attractiveness with trays of flowers that are placed on top of the wall or on the ground close by. To make a wall arrangement, wire or tape a block of floral foam to a tray, then create the arrangement *in situ*. You can then let the flowers and foliage trail if they are to be placed on the wall, or make the arrangement taller and wider if it is to be on the ground.

To decorate the urn, it was filled with cow parsley, delphiniums, rubrum lilies and phlox. As stone is porous, it was necessary to give the urn a waterproof lining, so a plastic bowl was used. This was filled with blocks of wet floral foam, and wire netting was stretched over the top of the bowl. The bowl was then placed inside the urn and the two were wired together.

A garlanded umbrella not only looks pretty but can also provide some much-needed shade in hot weather.

EASTER FLOWERS

Even if Easter has no religious significance for you, you can still derive a great deal of enjoyment and satisfaction from celebrating the arrival of spring and the visible rebirth of life, by making the most of the lovely flowers and foliage that will be available.

As with Christmas, it is often the time for a family gathering, and for entertaining, and you will want your home to look particularly attractive and welcoming.

As well as vases of cut flowers and foliage, you can also make a living display of plants, which looks especially effective when arranged in a deep windowsill, as shown in the photograph on the facing page. A mixture of garden plants, including pansies, freesias, ivies, forsythia and various other plants was used here, with moss and pebbles to hide their soil. These plants can be taken out of the garden (or bought from a nursery and planted in the garden afterwards) and planted in individual pots. Cover the windowsill with a thick sheet of plastic to prevent any soil or moisture leaking through, then arrange the plants, in their pots, on the plastic. Pieces of bark, twisted stem or roots can also be incorporated into the display to make it more interesting. Place the tallest plants at the back of the display, and trail some small plants, such as ivy, over the front of the sill to soften the edge and hide any pieces of plastic that might otherwise be visible. Then cover the tops and sides of the post with a blanket of moss, arranging it into tendrils at the front and holding it in place with a few pebbles.

For Easter Sunday itself, you could hide chocolate eggs or bunnies amid the foliage for an Easter egg hunt with a difference.

If you do not have enough small flowering plants in your garden, cover the windowsill with the plastic sheeting and a few plants in pots, as before, then place a quarter of a block of wet floral foam on the sheet and arrange in it a selection of cut flowers and foliage. This will give you the added colour and varying shapes you need to make the arrangement look alive.

All too often breakfast is rather a hurried affair, but during the Easter break you have the perfect opportunity to start the day in a leisurely and relaxed way. Get out your favourite china, make a special effort to prepare some delicious breakfast food and give the table the perfect finishing touch with a pretty arrangement of scented spring flowers. Freesias and narcissi are good choices because they are particularly fragrant and delicate-looking.

This display combines 'Cheer' narcissi, yellow parrot tulips, 'Connecticut King' lilies, white freesias and eucalyptus in a broom basket. The lilies contrast dramatically with the narcissi and the fatness of the tulips, and the white freesias make the arrangement look crisp and fresh, thereby accentuating the yellows and creams. If you removed the white from the arrangement, it would become rather dull and lifeless; equally, if you took out the cream, the remaining flowers would form too sharp and stark a contrast. The eucalyptus was a natural choice because it is soft and dark green – lime green would have been too similar in colour to the rest of the foliage.

The basket was lined with thick plastic and was then filled with wet floral foam – it is virtually impossible to find a container to fit the exact shape of the basket you wish to use. Since both the narcissi and tulips have rather fat and weak stems, you should use a pencil or similar-shaped object to drill the holes in the foam before inserting the flowers. Do this first, then arrange the other flowers and foliage afterwards.

This sweetly-scented basket of yellow and white flowers would get any day off to a good start.

A deep windowsill filled with plants is an unusual but charming Easter decoration.

110

HALLOWE'EN

Hallowe'en is one time of the year when you can really let your imagination run riot when planning the arrangements for a party.

There is tremendous scope for unusual decorations, and the clever use of colours, shapes and textures will help you to create the right atmosphere of mystery, suspense and excitement.

Some effects, of course, are much more involved and complicated than others – if you are feeling adventurous, you could turn an entire room into a witches' coven or a similarly spine-chilling setting.

The main structure might be made from gnarled, moss- and lichen-covered branches, with swags of white, grey and black netting across the ceiling. Use uplighters and shine a garden light through the window to cast reflections against the ceiling. Atmosphere is all in a design like this, so look for anything that will create the appropriate air of mystery – you might use gnarled tree roots, half-broken baskets and even old garden rakes, which take on an entirely new dimension once they are incorporated into this type of design.

A less ambitious, but none the less equally effective, Hallowe'en display is a table arrangement. The one shown here incorporated mushrooms, garlic, heather, 'Champagne' roses, small cabbage leaves, mixed green foliage, broccoli and an artificial dragonfly and lizard.

The arrangement was placed in a basket because it gave a more natural effect than a china or glass bowl would have done. Using vegetables in a table arrangement creates interest at a dinner party and enables you to use any vegetables you have to hand or growing in the garden, although for Hallowe'en they should ideally be greyish and of an interesting shape. For instance, if you were making a similar arrangement in the summer, you could use courgettes (zucchini), tomatoes, radishes and other seasonal vegetables. It is not necessary to use flowers, but foliage is important, as it helps to soften and shape the arrangement.

The mushrooms and garlic should be wired with 18-gauge stub wire so that they stand away from the basket and give an interesting variation in height. The basket itself can be filled with either wire netting or oasis, depending on the strength of the stems of foliage, and possibly flowers, used. Other than the cabbage leaves, the rest of the foliage should be small-leaved and light to counteract the heaviness of the vegetables. If you are using orange or red vegetables you will have to ensure that at least one of the types of foliage is similarly coloured, as this will make the completed arrangement come together. As you will notice, grey foliage was used here, to blend the white of the garlic with the grey of the mushrooms.

When creating the arrangement, you will find it easiest to position the vegetables first, and then the largest leaves (in this case, cabbage). After this, the broccoli and the rest of the foliage and flowers (if used) should be added. In my arrangement, the artificial dragonfly and lizard were added extras, but they are not essential. However, if you have children, you should be able to borrow from them some plastic or rubber spiders, snakes or lizards to place in or around the arrangement.

Garlic, mushrooms and an artificial lizard and dragonfly are the unexpected but effective finishing touches to this table arrangement.

CHRISTMAS ARRANGEMENTS

Christmas is a celebration that affects us all, even if your only problem is to choose a gift for the aunt who has everything.

If it is your turn to be the hostess to your family and friends, then you will want to set the scene so that your home is transformed by the decorations that are such an essential part of Christmas. This is one occasion when children can thoroughly enjoy helping, starting with collecting suitable nuts, berries and seed heads.

Even in the most modern of families Christmas isn't really Christmas without the traditional decorations, and although from time to time there may be innovations, such as an artificial tree, most of us are eventually persuaded to return to the 'real thing'. If you are the Christmas hostess, your family may allow you to introduce one or two novelties, but these still have to conform to the authentic spirit. The occasional diversion may be worth trying, but for this one time in the year the old-fashioned ideas and decorations usually turn out the best.

The Christmas tree is always the focal point of the house, and although there are many varieties of decor, the successful ones generally keep to a theme, such as all gold or all silver. Here again, the traditional ideas are often best, and one of the most

effective ways of decorating the tree is simply to use red velvet ribbon bows and white candles. The candles must be safely secured with Victorian-style holders, which are weighted at the bottom, and they should only be lit when there is an adult in the room. A star or angel at the top completes the tree, and presents underneath afford a welcome splash of colour. It is a good idea to wrap a few empty boxes and leave these under the tree to fill the gap when the real gifts have been taken.

WREATHS

The lovely idea of hanging a welcoming wreath on the front door is an American contribution to the Christmas tradition. Many years ago, Constance Spry, the famous flower arranger, saw Christmas wreaths in America and remarked how delightful they looked, adding that she loved the way American families left the curtains open so that passers-by might see and enjoy the lighted trees. Both ideas (like Christmas trees, which were introduced from Germany in Victorian times) have now become equally part of the British Christmas tradition.

Christmas wreaths help you to share the spirit of the festive season with passers-by. The wreaths shown here and overleaf give just some idea of the immense range of different approaches to this theme.

This pink-toned wreath has been made with artificial materials.

Wreaths vary almost as much as tree decorations, and are easy to make, but if you don't enjoy handling holly you might buy a ready-made wreath and then add finishing touches. A few special Christmas roses added to the design on Christmas Eve will look wonderful in their waxy beauty, with the added advantage, in the case of a door wreath, of being seen at eye level. If you are adding fresh flowers, it is best to buy a moss-based wreath, so that soft stems can be eased gently into position without damage. A moss-based wreath will also help to keep holly, ivy and other foliage fresh throughout the Christmas period.

Other additions, such as cones or nuts, also look lovely, and you will find that a coat of varnish improves the colour greatly. Red ribbons contrast beautifully with the sheened cones and nuts, and make the perfect finishing touch. The snow sprays and glitters that are readily available as Christmas approaches are also an effective idea and show up well in a lighted porch. Lightly glittered holly and ivy look most attractive and have a lovely frosty feeling. If the holly on a purchased wreath has few berries or none, these can be added. You may be fortunate enough to find some berries on a holly bush from which you can take a few sprigs, but if not, then wire on the artificial variety. Choose the best that you can find, so that they can be used again and again. Other berries, such as those of ivy, look beautiful when glittered and introduced into a swag or wreath.

If you are planning to make your own wreath, there are several methods that can be employed to obtain the good result. A basic door wreath is easily made using a copper wire frame, purchased from a florist or garden centre, which is then covered with moss. The moss is tightly bound to the frame with fine wire. The holly, ivy and any other foliages to be used are then wired, pushed into the moss, and securely fastened. When the whole frame has been covered with foliage, the cones, fruits and ribbons can be added. A wire hook is needed to hang the wreath and this can be wired into place – make sure that the wire has passed through the metal frame and not just through the foliages.

A swag can be as effective as a wreath. Here, apples, tangerines, cones and holly have been wired together. A red ribbon bow, with wired edges, completes the design. Three pomanders have been added, with bells made from cone seeds.

Dried apple rings have been glued to a twig base to make a pretty and unusual wreath.

A design made with various nuts and cones has been decorated with a ribbon-twist bow and cane bells with cone clangers.

A wreath of cones can be made on a dry foam base. Remember when buying the base that the finished wreath will be much bigger than the original base. Using a glue suitable for polystyrene, attach the cones, starting with the outer ring of cones, and spacing the cones evenly for a good finished appearance. The wreath of nuts and cones, shown on the preceding page, can be made in the same way, although this one was built up on a simple cardboard circle, which gave a flat surface to which to glue the materials. If you are attaching nuts and cones to a flat surface it is important to use materials of slightly differing sizes to create greater depth and interest – the familiar flower arrangers' principle of recession. Again, ribbons will give a festive feeling.

The circles made from straw, cane and sticks make excellent wreath bases and can be decorated very easily with Christmas baubles or ribbons. There are some very attractive bells made from fir cone seeds and these look lovely with the stick wreaths, being of the same colour and texture; a ribbon bow and the design is complete. The straw wreaths make very good bases for wired materials, though they also look most attractive with a little spray of mistletoe and a simple red ribbon bow.

TOPIARY

Even if the same decorations are used every year – and getting out the tree box is always a fun thing to do – it is also good to have something new to bring surprise and pleasure. Perhaps this year you might add a topiary tree to the general Christmas decor, for example. A topiary tree is always fun and can vary in scale from a table decoration to a large full-scale tree, depending on the need and, of course, the available space. The method for making the trees is similar, in so far as all will require a trunk, fixed in quick-setting cement in a container (a plastic pot is ideal). A piece of floral foam is wired to the top of the trunk – the dry foam should be used for dried materials – and then the chosen materials are inserted into the foam.

A lovely idea is to use the wet foam and decorate it with glittered fruits and dark green foliages that have been glittered round the edges. A large bow tied under the foliage design completes a very attractive decoration for Christmas. A clay flower pot looks most attractive with fresh foliages, but remember to attach a piece of felt to the base to avoid scratches to furniture. A clay pot also gives much-needed stability to the smaller designs; the larger trees will have ample ballast to keep them from being knocked over, as there will be quite a considerable weight of cement at the base. If you use a plastic pot which is not very attractive, it can be painted any suitable colour; alternatively, the tree, plus its plastic pot, can be set into a larger but more attractive pot. Do not make your topiary tree in a valuable container as you will not be able to remove the cement to use the pot in any other way.

Small topiary trees for the Christmas dining table are very pretty and can be decorated with many types of Christmas bauble. Children love to find a wrapped lollipop or two tucked into the tree, and even the grownups can be tempted with truffles, prettily wrapped in clear cellophane.

GARLANDS

Another decoration for Christmas is a garland for the mantelpiece. These are delightful and, like topiary trees, can easily be made in advance. If even a small quantity of pine has been introduced into the design, the wonderful smell of Christmas fills the house as the garland warms with the heat from the fire. It is important to make sure that the garland is well secured and sufficiently distant from the fire to avoid any risk of accidents. In a household with children there will, of course, be a fire guard, and

Several thin branches were intertwined to make this unusual topiary tree. They were fixed in a pot of quick-setting cement which was placed in a basket and covered with moss to hide the cement. The branches were topped with a piece of wet floral foam, held firm with a cap of wire netting. Various ivies were then combined with artificial decorations, the ivy berries being given a light spray of glimmer to add a subtle sparkle. A green moiré ribbon, edged with gold, has been tied to the trunk to complete the design.

A garlanded mantelpiece always creates a very festive atmosphere. Here, a garland of artificial and real materials has been wired together and a ribbon has been *intertwined with the garland, giving a slightly Victorian feeling to the finished piece. A wider ribbon in the same design has been used to make the bow and tails.*

this is a sensible precaution from an adult point of view also. A garland can be made from both fresh or artificial materials, or a mixture of both, and the possible variations are endless. Fresh garlands are particularly delightful, especially if they include nuts, berries and red ribbons. The bells and balls made from cone seeds look very effective with hollies and ivies, all the more so if these are variegated. Christmas, after all, is a time for foliage, and it is fun to use as wide a range as possible – there can be few more evocative and heart-warming sights than a house decorated for Christmas, with the Yule Log burning, lighted candles, and festoons of foliage, highlighted with red ribbons.

There are several methods of making garlands with fresh foliage: you can use a base of foam sausages, wired together, or you can either wire the sprigs of foliage to a rope, or wire them and then tape them together. The latter method is generally preferable, as an individually wired garland tends to hang more naturally and can also be more easily adjusted, but the foam garland will remain fresh for the whole of the festive season. It is preferable to make the garland well before Christmas and then keep it in a cool place, perhaps under a sack in the garden. Do not put the garland in a plastic bag as the foliage will go brown and mouldy. When the garland is needed to decorate the house, you can bring it in and make the final adjustments when you hang it in position. It will be easy to add baubles and so on when the garland is in place.

The new ribbon twist is ideal for garlands and is available in a wonderful range of colours. Although the red and green twist is very Christmassy, it is sometimes more unusual and attractive to match the ribbon to the room colourings. Certainly, if the garland is to include painted and glittered materials, there is a wide range of stunning colours from which to choose. Ribbon twist looks like coloured string and is made from paper very tightly twisted together; this is gently untwisted to reveal a very easily tied and arranged ribbon, which beautifully resembles wild silk. Do not be put off by the initial appearance, which tells nothing of the joys that will be revealed when it is untwisted.

Christmas decorations can be overdone, but all the same, this is the right time to be a little frivolous and have several arrangements or decorations in the room. They should preferably coordinate in some way, even if this is only because the same ribbon or similar materials are used throughout. Somehow, the design idea gets a little lost at this time, and the result can be a rather messy jumble. Planning is again as important here as at any time.

TABLE ARRANGEMENTS

The Christmas hostess will, of course, be as much concerned with the Christmas dinner as with the rest of the plans, and the dining-table arrangement is one that will be very important and will certainly need to be planned and arranged well ahead. It is an excellent idea to create the design so that it can be altered a little by the inclusion of other flowers or baubles for Boxing Day and then for New Year. With foliages being so agreeably good natured, this can easily be accomplished with just a little forethought.

The arrangement must be one that allows the guests to see each other, as this is essentially a time of friends and family reunions and the whole of the entertainment is spoilt if guests can only communicate by talking round, over or through a vastly grand arrangement. The container must be stable, as one that is precariously wobbly will inevitably fall at the worst possible moment. Unless the table is very large, the arrangement really should be of sensible proportions, allowing space for dishes, glasses, napkins and crackers. It is always a good idea to have candlestick designs, using the candlesticks as containers and adding the candles if needed for dinner later. A candlestick is convenient because it leaves plenty of table space and keeps the decorations at a good height, but take care not to make the arrangements too tall or you will fall into the pitfall of forcing your guests to peer through the foliage to see friends on the other side of the table. Pretty garlands round the candlesticks are an attractive idea, and if time is short there are many that can be purchased. Such garlands are, however, very easily made and require a minimum of materials. As candles will not be used at lunch time a small bunch, made to match the garland, can be placed in a candlecup – use the smallest size – which can then be removed to return the candlestick to its proper use in the evenings.

A table arrangement of holly and ivy is decorated with artificial berries and red glittered ribbon. The design is made in a hollow log, with a piece of plastic material, to prevent leaks, lining the inside. Floral foam is firmly wedged into the hollow (do not fill the entire space or it will be impossible to water the arrangement). The design can be used with or without the candle. Cocktail sticks are taped to the base of the candle, allowing it to be removed or put back into the design without disturbing the arrangement or damaging the foam.

FLOWERS FOR CHURCHES

Once you have begun to explore your talents as a flower arranger, you will find that churches and other places of worship offer great scope for creativity. The size and scale of the architecture calls for larger and bolder arrangements than you will generally require for the home, and this may at first seem rather daunting. If you are about to arrange some church flowers for the first time, however, take heart – the basic principles of floral design will still apply, even though the scale may be larger than you are used to.

As with designs for the home, it is worth taking risks and experimenting with new ideas. A major fault with many church designs is that they tend to be predictable and safe – an endless succession of triangular arrangements with chrysanthemums – but there is no reason why you should not try out new ideas. While the result should not look garish, and it is essential to bear in mind the sensitivities and wishes of the priest or rabbi and of the worshippers, it is rewarding to experiment with unusual foliage and flowers and interesting colour combinations.

The glorious colours of the stained glass window were a major factor in the choice of colours for these wedding arrangements.

USING THE ARCHITECTURE

Flowers in the church are always appreciated, especially if they take the design of the church into account. There are times, such as at harvest festival, when a very modern church can happily be overwhelmed with a traditional arrangement but for the most part a church of this type will look and feel more comfortable with a simple design that echoes the modern style.

Similarly, flowing arrangements are normally an appropriate choice for a very old church, but the same building will look stunning with two elegant cones of flowers or fruit adding to the dignity of the architecture. So many times, the same inevitable pedestal triangle is made, almost automatically, week by week, but just as our own homes benefit from a change so, too, do church decorations. A novel idea might not always please, but it will stimulate and inspire other ideas.

Window ledges in churches, synagogues, mosques and the like can sometimes cause problems, especially if they slope down without a level position for your container. You can solve this by wiring a wooden wedge on to the ledge, thereby giving you a flat area for your dish or tray. Remember it is never easy to work against the light, and heavier leaves and flowers will show up best when silhouetted against a window. You can add some lighter sprays to soften the overall effect.

The font is always a lovely position for flowers, particularly for a christening or baptism. Blocks of floral foam can be arranged on the top or sides and filled with flowers for a very pretty arrangement. However, if you will be decorating the building for a christening, you should first check with the priest as you may not be allowed to decorate the font itself, or you may be limited as to size. If that's the case, candle arrangements are a lovely alternative.

Very often, places of worship hold festivals of flowers, so do help out if you are asked. The prime consideration is to ensure that the building will still be visible once the flowers are in place, so don't smother all the architecture with volumes of flowers! It is always a matter of courtesy to consult the priest before creating arrangements in a place of worship that is unfamiliar to you, particularly when you will be decorating the altar – some priests have very definite views on the subject. If flowers are allowed, then ask about their position and size and ensure that you stick to the guidelines.

Many religious buildings have beautiful pillars, and there are some lovely ways in which to decorate them. They are also very useful since they will be visible to the congregation whether they are standing or seated. Swags always look elegant and can be used to great effect on special occasions. Garlands arranged around pillars also look attractive.

Many churches will not allow flowers on the altar, and if so you must adhere to this restriction, but there are other suitable situations that you can choose in place of altar arrangements and these can be equally effective. Arrangements set to either side of the altar, ranged closely to the sides, can make an attractive impact. If the design is successful and the colours and shapes are well chosen, for example, there can be a wonderful feeling of continuity between the folds and patterning of the altar cloth and the flower arrangements.

If the altar is set well forward, it is possible to place arrangements behind it, creating an impression of flowers simply suspended on the altar cloth, and bringing a lovely dimension of space to the chancel. The arrangements will only need to be simple low pedestal designs. Remember with this type of design that it will have to be carefully arranged, because more of the arrangement will become visible as the congregation move up to the altar, and some of the materials must therefore be allowed to flow down and to the sides.

TALL STANDS

Tall, very slender designs arranged at the back and on either side of the altar area will look very dramatic, especially in a modern church. The foliages used here will need to be quite bold, such as laurel or camellia, to create a clean cut effect – this is not a design that calls for fussy arranging. The mechanics will need to be stable and there are several tall slim stands that can be purchased for just this type of design. If you have access to a blacksmith, it is something that can be easily made. If you are

A very beautiful but simple church, with a golden glass window, is decorated for harvest, and here the design, although it is rich in colour and textures, does not overpower the altar. The arrangements have been made in 45cm (18in) plastic troughs containing three large blocks of foam. Pumpkins and ornamental cabbages have been incorporated in the design.

able to acquire a set of such stands, you will be amazed at the number of occasions and the variety of ways in which they can be used. For the most part the stands that are sold have a base into which a tall hollow metal pole is screwed. Little metal dishes are then threaded over the top of the pole and screwed securely in the required position, and the final dish rests firmly on the top, fitting in the hollow of the pole. Additional mechanics can be added to make the arrangements even taller. The great advantage of these stands is that they do not create a heavy design and yet give a good feeling of height and importance.

ARCHWAYS

For special occasions, such as Christmas, Easter or a wedding, garlands make an extremely attractive floral decoration, and a lovely idea for a doorway or porch is a garlanded arch to welcome the congregation. As the porch will not be equipped with nails or supports, it is a help to have a simple wooden surround made. The frame will be covered with flowers or foliage, so the wood can be very inexpensive. An archway of this type will be amazingly versatile – for Christmas, it can be garlanded with evergreen foliage set with holly berries; for harvest festival, you might choose vines, grapes and fruits, and at Easter it could be covered with small posies of primroses or other spring flowers, set into a bower of mosses and foliage, such as pussy willow and catkins.

WORKING WITH PEDESTALS

Pedestals are usually placed by the altar and at the entrance to the building, and usually look most effective if they are all arranged with similar, but not identical, plant material and foliage. This will give the impression of a thoughtful design and form a harmonious link between each pedestal arrangement.

As a rule, the whole of the pedestal will be on view, so you will have to ensure that its back is just as decorative as its front. This will mean you have to take care when planning the outline. A good starting point is the design using seven stems (pages 58–59), taking care to remember the back of the arrangement. Trailing and flowing ivies and branches help to stop the feeling of the arrangement being cut off. Large leaves, such as *Bergenia cordifolia*, are useful for the front, but don't let them hang down too far as they can give the appearance of thirsty dogs! Placing the largest and brightest flowers at the focal point will also help, particularly when the arrangement is viewed from a distance. Once you have worked on these designs you will realize that they are just as easy as those created at home on a smaller scale – they simply need more impressive materials.

It is especially important to arrange *in situ* when working on pedestals for places of worship. So many arrangers opt to do their flowers at home in a vase of their own, and then place or tie it in position when they arrive at their destination. This is convenient for them, but doesn't produce nearly such a pleasing arrangement.

Most types of design can look attractive in a modern church, but here two tall slim arrangements of foliage have been made. These are a marvellously long lasting and effective idea and flowers can easily be added to give more colour if needed. The tall mechanics have dishes set on the poles. These hold foam, taped for security. The foliage is then arranged to create a tall sweep of material, attractively displayed.

ALTARS

Before planning an arrangement for the altar you will have to check that it will be permitted. In some cases a small arrangement that is not too obtrusive is acceptable, although anything larger would not be.

Always try to keep any altar decorations very clean and sharp, as they have to be seen from a distance and if you use dark or coloured flowers they tend to disappear against the ornate nature of the altar cloths.

USING EXISTING CONTAINERS

Most places of worship have their own containers, although occasionally you may despair at some of the pots that are available! If you are stuck with the inevitable brass vase, which usually has flowers just stuffed into it, try placing floral foam and wire netting in the top so that you can create a downward-flowing design. The wrought iron pedestal looks less stark if ivies and similar foliage are allowed to trail

You may be asked to keep the altar arrangements strong and well defined.

down. Large leaves covering the front of the container and a deliberately soft outline will help to prevent the 'surprised hedgehog' appearance of so many of these designs!

WORKING TIDILY

It is essential that you clear up after arranging the flowers in a place of worship, and you will find life much easier if you work with a florists' dust sheet in place, as with luck that will have collected all the rubbish, and all you need to do is pick it up by its handles and depart. If there will be a lot of rubbish, then large plastic refuse bags are invaluable. A dustpan and brush should be part of your usual equipment, but if not, do remember to take them with you on this occasion – if there are any on the premises they are bound to have been locked in the caretaker's cupboard!

MAKING AN ALTAR ARRANGEMENT

1 *As it is important to create this arrangement* in situ, *you must protect the altar cloth with a large table cloth or something similar. Set the mechanics slightly behind the crucifix and then create the outline.*

2 *Continue to build up the design, allowing the lilies to create the form that will be taken. Take care not to distract attention from the crucifix – keeping the flowers low may help.*

3 *Here, the finished design is shown. The gold-coloured roses were chosen to continue the theme and colouring of the altar cloth.*

MAKING A WINDOW ARRANGEMENT

1 *Church windows are often very difficult to decorate because they frequently slope downwards. Here, wooden wedges have been placed beneath the container to make it level and secure. Create the basic outline with light plant material.*

2 *Place the heaviest flowers in the centre of the design to give a good focal point. This arrangement shows off the shape of the window to good advantage without smothering it, while allowing the view to remain visible to the congregation.*

127

MAKING A BASKET ARRANGEMENT FOR A WINDOW

1 *Line an attractive basket with plastic and fill with wet foam, then place it on the window ledge. Create the outline with light plant material.*

2 *Complete the arrangement by adding the flowers. As well as being an interesting window arrangement, this basket can also be taken to a sick member of the congregation.*

WINTER COLOUR

Winter flowers for church decorations are not always easy to obtain from a garden, and if there is a limited budget for church flowers it is often a good solution to use all foliage or foliage with silk flowers.

To use silk flowers all the time would be a little dull, but for the odd occasion the inclusion of silk flowers will help bring some colour into the arrangement.

Foliage arrangements are very rewarding, and once you begin to appreciate them you will soon find that they are often preferable to those massed with flowers. Foliages are so majestic in their shape and design that using them in their own right is a delight. They can be used in several ways: you may, for example, keep to a deep green but select varied shapes to create a simple but elegant design. Laurel might be combined with fatsias and privet. The sprays of privet would show to advantage with the large fatsia hands and with the weight of the laurel leaves positioned simply in a large earthenware jug at the base of the design. This would be far more effective than a vast collection of spray chrysanths packed tightly into a pedestal design. Variegated foliages will also lend themselves to very beautiful designs, the foliages complementing each other with splashes of green and yellow. Variegated elaeagnus is a particularly lovely choice of plant material.

SILK FLOWERS

A foliage design will be very long lasting, particularly in a church, and if it is intended to be used as an arrangement in its own right then silk flowers can be added at will. Perhaps a quick word about choosing silk flowers for such a situation will help. Although it may be tempting to save money, it is important, if you are buying rather than making silk flowers, to choose the best, as some of the cheaper ones are particularly bright (though they are fun to use for parties). You should also select flowers that are usually in season at that time of year. Some of the chrysanthemums are especially good, and if these have been chosen in a soft gold or rust they will be a very useful standby which can be kept for many years. You may add them to a foliage design, as already suggested, but you can also use them to supplement fresh flowers in the arrangement, if needed. If poor silk flowers are bought, the comparison between fresh and silk will be very obvious and will spoil the appearance of the entire design. It is not a question of trying to persuade the congregation that the flowers are real in any way, but from a flower lover's point of view they must appear as good as possible.

One very important thing is to resist the temptation to fold back the wire stems of the silk flowers. This will do much damage to the floral foam and create havoc with the wire-netting if this is being used, especially if the silk flowers are to be taken out to be replaced with others or with fresh flowers. Cut the wire stems as you would cut those of fresh flowers, and if a stem needs to be lengthened at a later date it can easily be rewired.

Even though you may use silk flowers, a design should not be neglected: the foliages will need to be watered and perhaps replaced, and the silk flowers will require dusting unless they are to become definitely scruffy. A soft feather duster may be used *in situ*, or you can remove the flowers and take them home for a blow with a hair dryer, which will greatly improve their appearance. Sometimes a quick steam will make them look better.

Do not use too many silk flowers in a large design, as this will create a very false appearance – a few placed strategically will be far more effective. Large flowers will probably be more useful than small ones in a church and just five peonies, for example, or three poinsettias will always look very elegant.

The arrangements shown overleaf have been made with beautiful variegated foliages, combined with silk poinsettias. A baba mould was used for each design, and wet floral foam was cut into small bricks and then taped securely in position, ready to hold the materials. A similar design will be placed at the other side of the altar and, if desired, all the candle holders could be decorated. It must be remembered, however, that the altar and the cross are the most important and central features, and the idea is to enhance them, not to overwhelm them.

It is important in a design of this type to allow the materials to flow naturally, rather than attempting to manipulate them to another direction. The back of the design must also be well covered.

OTHER ARRANGEMENTS WITH SILK FLOWERS

Silk flowers come into their own in church arrangements, particularly in winter. At other times of year, when there is a wider range in the shops and in gardens, it is generally possible to find appropriate fresh flowers.

Nevertheless, there are still occasions when a design with silk flowers may be just what is required to fill a gap – perhaps because the holiday season has upset the flower rota, or a temporary scarcity of fresh flowers has put them beyond the limits of the budget.

The arrangements shown here are all designed with flowers that can easily be made at home, following the instructions given on pages 216 – 53.

In addition to 7 silk rosebuds and 7 silk roses, this traditional triangular arrangement includes some lovely and unusual fresh foliages – young raspberry canes, branches of flowering currant and tall spears of Phormium tenax.

A low glass dish and half a block of foam form the basis of this strikingly simple arrangement (right). It was made with 30 lilies, 12 lily buds and 9 leaves.

The simple swag below – 5 rosebuds, 3 roses, 10 beech branches, 9 ribbon loops and 2 ribbon tails – requires a lightweight and unobtrusive container such as a plant pot saucer or coffee jar lid. Use a heated wire to pierce two holes in the side and thread wire through them to form a hanging loop. A piece of foam is then fixed to a plastic frog and taped firmly to the container, ready for the flowers.

Fresh gypsophila and cupressus have been used in this arrangement (below right), in addition to 14 nerine florets and wired ribbon bows, so the mechanics used here, though otherwise similar to those used for the swag of roses, require the use of green floral foam. Other medium-sized flowers, such as scabious, or carnations, could replace the nerines.

FESTIVALS

The major festivals provide a wonderful
excuse for a riot of colour. Vibrant yellow
daffodils represent glorious release from the
austerities of Lent. They are not always easy
to arrange, but try placing the heads in
different directions and varying the heights a
little.

Harvest festivals allow a wonderful opportunity, rare
in church decoration, of combining flowers with
fruits, vegetables, berries and seeds. Choose vibrant,
glowing colours for this time of the year – sprays
of berries, *Clematis vitalba*, blackberries, seed pods
and crab apples all add texture and dimension, and
their marvellous colourings and sheens instantly
create the right atmosphere. The autumnal
colourings of foliage are themselves a joy and can
give great pleasure. A lovely altar arrangement can
be made from wheat, lilies and grapes, and a design
incorporating the harvest loaf, wheat, grapes and
fruit is a classic feature in many places of worship
in the autumn.

Christmas is surely one of the most joyous
occasions of the year, when you have every excuse
for creating magnificently extravagant arrangements.
There seem to be two schools of thought as far as
Christmas colour is concerned, with arrangements
being either all-white or all-red. When working with
all-white arrangements, it creates a lovely feeling if
you add a few red berries to the holly – wire on
artificial ones if the holly doesn't have any. There
are many wonderful foliages from which to choose
for added interest, such as elaeagnus and the spotted
laurels. Red arrangements just glow, and deep green
and grey foliages are perfect partners.

*Cauliflowers, beans, tomatoes, peppers, carrots and
mushrooms and a plaited harvest loaf have been
incorporated into this harvest design, together with lilies,
poppies and white daisy chrysanthemums. Dahlias and
Michaelmas daisies would also be very suitable. If
berries are to be used they will last longer if lacquered
first. Lacquering also helps to prevent bulrushes and
fluffy grasses shedding their seeds.*

133

Making a Christmas Arrangement

1   Place a large mould on a candlestick and wedge foam into it. Make the outline of the design with flowing ivy and variegated holly.

2   Very often berries are missing from holly, in which case you can wire on a few artificial ones to help create a festive feeling.

3   Add some red flowers to complete the design (facing page) – red spray carnations were used here. A pair of candlesticks ranged either side of the altar would look very beautiful.

134

WEDDINGS

If you are to be married in a church or synagogue, there may be several architectural features, such as well-placed pillars, that will lend themselves to floral decoration.

Naturally, you should first consult the priest or rabbi, just to check that they have no objections, and in fact they may want to discuss the flowers with you anyway. Do take note of everything that they say, particularly if they mention any restrictions, and abide by what they tell you – it may be your day, but it is their place of worship. This rule applies whether it is you or a florist who does the decorations.

It is important when arranging flowers, whatever the venue, to use the areas that lend themselves to the flowers rather than creating free-standing arrangements that are then dotted about, seemingly willy-nilly. This will ensure that the decorations look much more natural and are in keeping with their environment.

Large arrangements or pedestals are a good way of decorating a church, and are often placed by the steps leading up to the altar or by the altar itself, depending on the size of the building. As you will notice in the main photograph (see pages 120–21) the flowers in the pedestal arrangements were specially chosen to bring forward the colours of the stained glass windows. This is not always common practice at weddings, since the bride normally likes all the flowers to echo precisely her colour theme, but in this case the windows of the church dominated her choice. As the bride's colours were pink and white, we used white, pink and lime green in the pew ends and chose lime green and white to connect them with the pedestal arrangements.

DECORATING PEW ENDS

Arrangements on pew ends are a marvellous way of decorating aisles for a major celebration, such as a wedding, because not only do they look beautiful but also, if you have chosen your flowers carefully, they will release their fragrance as the guests walk past. In fact, it is almost essential to decorate wide aisles and dark wood, otherwise the church or synagogue can look bare and not festive enough for such a special occasion. When planning pew-end decorations it is important to consider not only the shape of the pews themselves but also the width of the aisle. This will dictate your floral design, because if the aisle is very narrow, the bridal procession, as well as the guests, may brush against the flowers and inadvertently spoil them.

It is always best to assemble the arrangement *in situ*, at least until you learn the exact shape and method with which to create them. Otherwise, if you make them on a floor, you will find that large gaps are visible between the foam and the pews when the decorations are hung in position, thereby revealing all your mechanics. If you do have to make them up beforehand, try to work with them hanging from something that is roughly of the same width and height as the pews for which they are intended.

If there aren't any pews in the building in which you will be married, you could instead place florists' trays, filled with flowers, by the sides of the chairs ranged down the aisle. Of course, you will have to ensure that it will be easy for the guests to get in and out of the rows of chairs without treading or slipping on the flowers.

The arrangements shown here are made with ready-made mechanics, but it is possible to use quarter-blocks of wet foam, wrapped in netting and backed with plastic sheeting, securing them to the pew ends with silver wire.

The pale pinks and greens of these pew ends are perfectly suited to their dark wood backgrounds.

MAKING A PEW-END DESIGN

1 *This plastic holder containing floral foam is a proprietary pew-end mechanic that can easily be fitted over the pew. It is re-usable.*

2 *Now add the plant material, starting with the foliage. It is important to ensure that you have obscured all the mechanics.*

138

ALTERNATIVE PEW-END DESIGN

1 *This is an alternative plastic pew-end holder that is used once and then thrown away. It is useful because it can be used in several positions. Here, it is seen in the longest position, ready for a long, slender floral design.*

2 *Now add the foliage and flowers, creating an elegant, draped effect. It is not always desirable to decorate every pew end, as the finished result may look very fussy. To avoid this, you could decorate every second or third pew end for a more restful feeling.*

PILLAR ARRANGEMENTS

Arrangements on pillars or walls are also an excellent idea, as they can be easily seen whether the congregation are standing up or sitting down.

To secure the basket or plaque to the pillar you will have to find an existing nail or hook on which to hang it. Even if the only nail is on the opposite side of the pillar, you will be able to attach a length of wire through the mechanics and secure them in the right position. Alternatively, you may have to suspend the arrangement from the top of the pillar. A plaque type of arrangement should be made a good five or six hours before the wedding, by which time it should have stopped dripping water.

HANGING PILLAR DECORATIONS

1   *This pillar has been decorated with a painted basket that would be equally suitable for a pew end – the ribbons would hook over the pew. In this instance the basket has been painted to match the pillar, but if it were being used for a pew end then it would be preferable to colour it the same shade as the wood.*

2   *Once lined with plastic and filled with wet foam, the basket can be used for a simple but elegant design using the minimum of plant material. If used for a wedding, the ribbons could match the overall colour scheme.*

DECORATING A PILLAR HEAD

1 *Tie 'sausages' of floral foam (see page 160) around the ledge of the pillar and cover the mechanics with a little foliage. This can be inserted before the garland of foam is put in position.*

2 *Complete the arrangement by adding flowers and more foliage if necessary. Here, pretty pieces of trailing ivy help to soften the arrangement and carry one's eye down the pillar.*

CHRISTENINGS

One of the prettiest ways of celebrating a baptism or christening is to decorate the font itself. Of course, it does help if the font is very old or made from carved stone, but even the most angular and modern font can be decorated with a few flowers.

As with all other floral decorations that you have planned for a place of worship, you must discuss your ideas with the priest or minister first, and ask their permission before going ahead with your designs.

To create the arrangement shown below, you should cut a block of wet foam into four, lengthways, cover one side of each piece in plastic and then evenly shape them on top of the font, plastic side down, leaving a gap of at least 30cm (12in) where the priest will stand. Here, we used lavender sweet peas, 'Little Silver' and baby pink roses from which the thorns had been removed, cow parsley and eucalyptus, although you could use ivy instead. First, the cow parsley was arranged to make the overall shape, ensuring that it did not become too wide or trail into the bowl of the font. Then the sweet peas, roses and eucalyptus were added. It is important to make the arrangement on the font itself as this will help you to achieve the right shape and height. If well sprayed and kept in a cool place, this arrangement should last for about two days.

When decorating the font, be sure to leave a space for the priest or minister to conduct the service.

CONSTRUCTING A FONT DECORATION

1 *Arrangements to decorate a font can vary in many ways. Here, packs of foam have been wired to the font and the basic outline created with cow parsley. If you use this, do make sure it has been properly conditioned, otherwise it will droop very quickly.*

2 *Complete the arrangement, keeping to the colour scheme of soft creams and whites that is so suitable for a christening. It is important to give some depth to this arrangement, as otherwise it will look very solid.*

FUNERALS

Once you have become proficient and well-known for your ecclesiastical flower arrangements, you may well be asked to arrange flowers for funerals, and if you've never done so before you could find it a daunting prospect at first. However, there will be no need to worry if you follow these guidelines.

At a funeral there is always a sad and quiet time before the service begins, and beautiful flowers can create a calm and comforting atmosphere, particularly if the coffin or casket has already been placed in the chapel. Two low pedestals positioned on either side can look lovely, especially if they match the colourings of the family flowers. If this isn't practical or possible, you can match the flowers to the colourings in the church instead. An arrangement placed in the porch or entrance is always appreciated (as long as it doesn't get in the way) and can help to lighten what is often a very sombre atmosphere.

You may be asked to make a wreath or floral tribute for the funeral, and this is an especially important commission. The family, in particular, will want it to be a beautiful expression of their love, so it should show sympathy and thoughtfulness, often using favourite flowers or colourings. Ideally, you should also use suitable flowers, perhaps choosing bold ones for a man, more delicate flowers for a woman and small, pretty material for a child. Using interesting foliage is just as important for funeral work as it is for any other type of flower arranging, and it will also help to show that you really care about what you are doing.

MAKING A SIMPLE WREATH

Wreaths can be made in a variety of sizes, using wire frames that are sold ready-assembled. If the wreath is to be very large it can be placed on a stand at the funeral.

Firstly, the frame is covered with moss. This will form the foundation for the flowers, so it is important that it is as firm as possible – if you do not do this, the flowers will fall out.

To cover the frame you will need plenty of moist moss (bought in bags) and a roll of fine green garden twine. Knot the end of the garden twine on to the frame, then take a large handful of moss, place it on the frame and bind it in place with the twine, winding it round and round until it is firm. Do not cut it! Then cover the next piece of wire framework with moss and bind it in place. Continue in this way until the whole of the frame is covered with a firm layer of moss and the wreath is a good shape. Once you are happy with it, secure and cut the twine, then trim off any loose moss with a pair of scissors, taking care not to cut the twine in the process. Pin leaves to the underside, overlapping them to give a neat appearance.

Each flower will have to be wired before being placed in position, and to do this you must make a hairpin shape with stub wire, ensuring that one end is longer than the other. Then hold the flower stem and hairpin firmly, and wind the longer wire around the shorter one two or three times, ensuring that you enclose the flower stem in the wire. The legs will now be the same length and can easily be inserted in the moss. Sometimes the wire can be pushed through the stem before being made into the hairpin and then twisted around the stem.

This wreath design looks lovely when filled with many pretty flowers and unusual decorative foliage.

Strong but sympathetic colours have been chosen for this funeral pedestal, with some trailing foliage to soften the effect.

144

MAKING A WIRED FUNERAL WREATH

1 *Bind some damp moss on to a wire wreath frame, using soft green garden twine, until it is completely covered.*

2 *Pin leaves of* Elaeagnus x ebbingei *around the back to form a neat backing. Bend stub wires into the shapes of hairpins and use these to hold the leaves in place.*

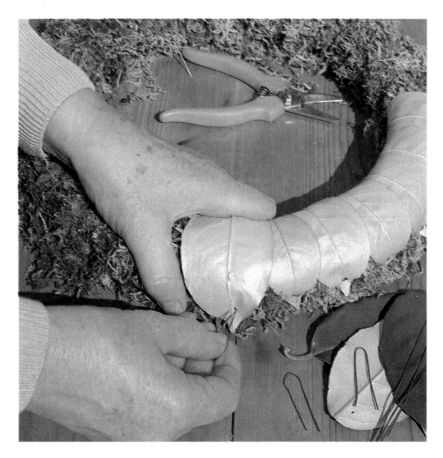

3 *Now begin to wire the flowers for the design and insert them in the moss.*

4 *Complete the design with more flowers. Spray the wreath with a fine mist of water if it is not to be used immediately.*

WEDDINGS AND CELEBRATIONS

It is hard to imagine a wedding, or for that matter any other major celebration, such as a christening or a coming-of-age party, without flowers. They help to set the scene, and their beauty, colour and, possibly, their fragrance contribute towards ensuring that the day is a joyful and memorable one.

Whatever the occasion may be, it is essential to set aside a realistic budget for flowers, and this should be an amount on a similar scale to that allocated for food or drink. Other important considerations include the season, the venue – town or country – and the colour theme. This last may be established by the surroundings, by the sex of the child, in the case of a traditional christening, or by the bride's colour preferences, if the occasion is a wedding. If you decide to use a florist rather than arrange the flowers yourself, you should ask them to visit the venue with you in advance, as they may well have some decorating ideas that had not occurred to you, or be able to suggest ways of camouflaging or drawing attention away from any unsightly areas.

The colours used in these silver wedding decorations for a dinner party are the traditional soft pinks and silver. Silver-coloured plastic candlesticks have been used to show how effective these can be, and the palest of pink candles add a very soft warm touch to the design.

MAKING THE MOST OF MARQUEES

When a major celebration is being held in a private home, a marquee or tent is often erected in the garden, and this can be great fun to decorate. Several types of marquee are available, both large and small, so you will have to adapt your designs accordingly.

For instance, a frame marquee may not have any lining, so that you will have to consider decorating all the metal supports that will be in full view. If the marquee is lined, you will have to know whether the lining will match your colour scheme, and if it has poles you will have to decide whether or not to cover or decorate them. Of course, the style of the occasion will influence your plans to a great extent, but in the main, the higher up you place the flowers, the better they will look. This is especially so if the marquee is supported by poles, because they will act as useful supports for your designs. The entrance to the marquee may also be decorated in a number of ways: with urns filled with flowers; with floral statues, as shown overleaf, or perhaps with an arrangement attached to the frame of the marquee itself, as shown on pages 154-155.

Trees or topiary are very suitable because they bring the garden into the marquee, and look particularly delightful when arranged around the entrance. It is also a good idea to make a special feature of the cake table, dais or buffet table.

When planning the flowers, do remember that it can become quite warm inside a marquee, especially once all the guests are assembled. Heat rises, and arrangements on the top of the poles can suffer considerably as a result. It is therefore extremely important to ensure that all your floral foam has been thoroughly soaked, as there is no way that you will be able to water it once the ladder has been removed. A long-armed garden sprayer is useful if you want to give the flowers a last-minute misting before the guests arrive, but not everyone has one of these. If you are able to use one, do make sure that you rinse it out thoroughly before filling with water. You should also remember to tidy up the backs of the arrangements in case it is such a warm day that the sides of the marquee are removed and your mechanics revealed!

MAKING TWO ARRANGEMENTS OUT OF ONE
Very often a daytime reception continues with further celebrations into the evening, and one lovely way to transform your existing arrangements is to add some candles. Ideally these should be placed in candle-holders before being added to the designs, but you can make do by taping wooden toothpicks to the bases and inserting these into the foam or wire

netting. You can also buy small plastic candle-holders that are then inserted into the foam. However, you must be extremely careful with the candles; ensure that you position them sensibly, and replace them each time they burn down low, otherwise they could be a perilous fire hazard. You will also have to remember to top up all the arrangements and ensure that the foam is still moist if the reception is to continue for some time.

LAVISH EFFECTS ON LOW BUDGETS
One doesn't always have a large budget for the flowers, but there are plenty of inexpensive ideas that will still look very pretty without seeming skimped.

You can add a lot of inexpensive colour with plenty of ribbon bows, perhaps tied around the marquee poles. Garlands always look lovely but they do take time and money, so trails of smilax or ivy are a good alternative, especially if they are held up with ribbons or simple posies. Painted birds are also charming when placed in an all-green tree, perhaps with a large bow tied underneath, and they look much more expensive than they really are! If your budget won't stretch to extravagant and expensive decorations on the marquee poles, wired baskets filled with variegated foliage and flowers (particularly gypsophila) can look just as lovely. To make them, soak the foam or moss thoroughly before placing in the wire baskets; arrange the flowers and foliage, and then hang in place. If you are not allowed to hammer nails into the poles, you can hang the baskets from straps or clamps instead. These may be assembled at the same time as the marquee, or put on the poles afterwards. Sometimes the pole is covered with cloth once the lining is in position, and that could hide your clamps altogether, so try to find out if this will be the case.

The impact of a flower-filled stone urn makes a magnificent first impression for wedding guests. In this design, forsythia, white delphiniums, blue bee, pink and yellow antirrhinums, alstroemeria and blossom were arranged in a large bowl filled with wire netting. This was then placed in the stone urn. The mixed colourings in this arrangement are not only suitable for weddings but also birthdays, garden parties or any other occasions that call for the use of a marquee.

150

DESIGNS WITH STATUARY

A figurine, bust or statue can look extremely elegant in an arrangement, but you will have to plan the design carefully first. The difficulty is to make the arrangement look like a harmonious whole, rather than a floral design that just happens to be sitting next to a piece of statuary, or a complete jungle of plant material through which the figure can barely be glimpsed!

Choose a base that will unite the piece of statuary and the plant material, then find a simple tin which can be placed close to the figure to hold the mechanics and flowers. Fabric figures and flowers seem to combine very well, but the drapes must enhance the arrangement and not look like an accidental placing, so your choice of material is very important. A soft neutral colour is useful, and silk is a particularly good choice of fabric, as it falls into marvellously elegant folds (though sometimes it needs a little help!). You can create a very smart effect if the drape and base are made from the same material.

When working with a piece of statuary, it is particularly important for the design to be created *in situ*, with the figure, base, fabric and container set up ready for the flowers and foliage. Line designs always work well with figurines.

Busts or statues are a marvellous excuse to create a spectacle, especially if they are loosely decorated with soft garden flowers and foliage that appear to be growing through, over, in and around them. Garlands are also enchanting. These ideas can look particularly stunning at parties given in gardens or conservatories or wedding receptions held in marquees.

WORKING WITH STATUARY

1 *When arranging flowers or foliage with any sort of statuary it is very important to work* in situ, *otherwise the design will not feel complete. Here the outline is being created around the figure and stand which have been painted to look like stone. Florists' tubes have been used to increase the height of the arrangement.*

2 *Now build up the design using the heavier plant material. At this stage it doesn't matter if any mechanics are still visible.*

3 *Complete the arrangements by adding the rest of the flowers and making sure you have hidden all the mechanics. Here, two arrangements have been used to frame the entrance to a garden marquee.*

DECORATING THE ENTRANCE TO A MARQUEE

1   *Wrap half a block of wet floral foam in wire netting, making sure it is secure by twisting together the opposite ends of the netting. Thread an 18-gauge wire through the top of the foam block and pull and twist together to make a loop, then, using double lengths of black reel wire, attach the foam to the frame of the marquee.*

2   *Using a mixture of foliage – at least three types – loosely fill in the basic shape. If the arrangement does not look pleasing to the eye at this stage, then it is unlikely to do so later on. You must therefore be happy with this stage before moving on to the next.*

3   *Add the thickest and heaviest flowers first, again making sure you like the effect. Do not put all the flowers just on the outer edge, but place a few in the middle so that the arrangement flows.*

4 *Next add the forsythia, then the double pink tulips, blue bee and finally the roses. Do not try to overfill an arrangement, especially of this type, as the foam simply will not hold. To ensure the flowers stay fresh, spray very frequently and keep the foam wet.*

DECORATING MARQUEE POLES

1 *Decorating marquee poles is fun but not always easy, and it is sometimes even a challenge, because there are so many possibilities. Here, the mechanics have been clamped on to the pole, with wire netting encasing a block of wet floral foam covered with moss.*

2 *Link the moss cages with trails of ivy and similar foliage, allowing them to drape around the pole in elegant curves.*

3 *Now add the flowers, choosing ones that enhance the colours of the marquee. Place them in the balls of mossed foam, arranging them in such a way that they seem to be trailing down the pole with the foliage. Do not use too much decoration or the result could be overwhelming!*

SWAGS AND GARLANDS

Whether they are made from flowers, flowers and foliage or just foliage, garlands can be used in all sorts of exciting and attractive ways and, although they take a long time to make, the finished results are well worth the effort. The way in which a garland is made will depend on the situation for which it is intended.

MAKING GARLANDS WITH WIRE AND MOSS

Fresh flowers really cannot be bettered for garlands, so try to use them whenever possible. To make a garland with fresh flowers, cut a piece of 5cm (2in) wire netting 20–22cm (8–9in) wide (the green plastic covered variety is preferable). Place the wire flat on a table, then arrange sphagnum moss along its length as though filling a cigarette paper. The moss is readily available and is usually sold in plastic bags – make sure it is moist. Fold the wire over and hook its prongs together to seal the join. Then press down gently on the joined side. This will make a garland about 7.5cm (3in) thick, and very delicate

ones about 2.5cm (1in) thick.

Choose fairly small plant materials, such as box foliage or pittosporum, and push it into the frame and moss first, followed by the flowers. If you need longer garlands, they can be made in sections and then wired together. It looks very elegant if the centre of the garland is the focal point, with all the leaves facing in that direction. If the garland will look better when tapered at both ends, simply squeeze the wire netting a little tighter. A drop for the garland can be made in the same way, but you must taper the end carefully and use the flowers and foliage more sparingly than on the garland itself.

Here, a wired garland of flowers and foliage has been looped around a piece of garden statuary – a delightful decoration for a wedding reception or indeed any outdoor party.

MAKING GARLANDS WITH FOAM

An alternative is to make garlands with bricks of wet foam that have been cut into four or eight lengthwise, according to the thickness of garland required. These are either wrapped in fine polythene and joined with sticky tape, or pushed into a stitched tube of polythene. It is best to make lengths of eight or so 'sausages', and you should allow a length of polythene at either end to enable them to be joined together. If a long length is needed, they are tied together with string. Do not cut the string between each block, but take it along each length as this will stop the garland sagging when the flowers and foliage are in place. Once you have made the garland to the required length, it.is quite simple to push the foliage and flowers into the foam through the polythene, and for finer stems it is easier to pierce the foam with a plant stem. If you have any problems, you can make a hole first with a darning needle or wooden toothpick.

All the small pretty flowers look delightful in these garlands, including pinks, all-year-round chrysanthemums, roses and berries. You can also make garlands out of rope, binding the flowers and foliage on to it, but it does tend to twist and is not so effective.

MAKING GARLANDS OF DRIED FLOWERS

Either the moss or foam bases can be used for garlands of dried flowers and glycerined foliage, but I prefer to wire the plant material together piece by piece. Although it takes a considerable time, it produces a much more delicate and elegant design. Dried gypsophila and roses and their leaves all look wonderful when used in this way. Each component is wired individually, then they are taped with gutta percha or stem tape in a suitably toning shade.

Instead of fresh flowers you can make garlands from dried flowers and foliage. To do this, wire each piece of plant material then tape all the pieces together to form a very delicate and long-lasting design. You can use a variety of interesting materials, including berries and nuts.

MAKING A WIRED GARLAND

1 *Cut a strip of wire netting that will be as long as the garland you wish to make. Then cut away the edging to the wire netting and place the moss along the centre of the netting.*

2 *Pull the netting up around the moss and hook the prongs around each other to secure the netting properly. Press down gently on one side to make it a little flatter than the other.*

3 *Decorate the garland with wired foliage and flowers. This is quite economical because the moss helps to make an attractive background.*

MAKING A FOAM GARLAND

1   *Cut wet floral foam into fairly small lengths and place them along lengths of fine polythene sheeting before joining the sides together with sticky tape. Take string along the length, tying each 'sausage' along the row to prevent it stretching, then insert flowers and foliage through the plastic into the foam, first using a darning needle to pierce the plastic if necessary.*

2   *Here the finished garland has been used to decorate a box topiary tree. The garland is held in position with stub wires bent into the shape of hairpins.*

DECORATING TABLES

Wedding receptions are held in so many places that it is almost impossible to cover all eventualities, but here are a few basic ideas that can be adapted in many different ways.

The type of reception that is to be held will determine your flower requirements, and a set wedding breakfast or buffet will take a lot of planning. Less formal receptions call for a different, more relaxed approach. The decoration and position of the wedding cake, always an important focal point, will also have to be considered. It may, for example, be placed either on the top table, or on a table by itself, or as part of the buffet. The bride may want the base of the cake to be decorated with flowers, or she may choose to have garlands around the table, or a floral arrangement placed on the top tier of the cake itself.

CAMOUFLAGING PROBLEM AREAS

Church and local halls are often chosen for receptions, but they can cause many problems when it comes to floral decorations. Usually they are painted in dreary colours and often have very dull furniture. Don't panic if you are faced with a similar situation, because there are several quick and easy solutions to the problem. Most important of all, you should aim to detract the eye from the bad points and focus on the wedding party instead, because they will look good. You can camouflage ugly or plain tables by covering them with crisp white tablecloths, and then placing pretty table decorations on top. In addition, you should make some large and stunning floral decorations that match the colour scheme of the wedding, not the hall. Two big arrangements are usually sufficient, and you can place them either side of the doors, next to the cake or behind the bride and groom if they will be seated. Finally, don't forget that by the time the room is filled with the wedding guests its shortcomings won't be nearly so obvious, while your flowers will stand out marvellously.

CREATING TABLE DECORATIONS

Arranging flowers *in situ* is always preferable, but small table decorations are an exception. Quickly check to determine the size and shape required, then get to work at a small table to one side, out of everyone's way. This is because table decorations should be arranged sitting down – not to give you a rest (although that can be very welcome!) but because you can then work at the angle from which they will be viewed. Another very practical point is that creating the arrangements on the tablecloths themselves could be rather messy, and these simple shapes do not need to be viewed against their background to create the right effect.

USING SILK FLOWERS

While most people think of using fresh flowers for a wedding reception, silk flowers have obvious advantages for the bride who wishes to organize her own arrangements. When the day comes there will be no time even to supervise the arrangement of fresh flowers, let alone arrange them yourself, but silk flowers can be prepared in advance. If the venue is much used, there may not be sufficient time to make elaborate fresh decorations *in situ*, and here again silk flowers may be the answer to the problem.

The centrepiece of the arrangement shown here includes a variety of fresh foliage, which sets off the silk flowers and creates an interesting framework of colour and texture. The natural materials consisted of grass stems, Japanese honeysuckle, 3 *Rosa rubrifolia* and one *Mahonia japonica* leaf, and the silk flowers used were 9 rosebuds, 3 roses, 4 clematis sprays and 5 clematis flowers.

The garland is made by wiring silk flowers and leaves together into one continuous length, which is draped gracefully in loops along the front of the tablecloth and pinned in place. It was made with 20 clematis flowers, 16 groups of clematis leaves, and 2 wired bows.

Clematis flowers have been mingled with roses in the centrepiece, linking this with the garland.

DECORATING A MARQUEE BUFFET TABLE

1 *It is important to create this design in situ, because in addition to giving a better result, you may find it nigh on impossible to move the arrangement once it has been completed – it may be very heavy. Protect the table cloth as you work, preferably with some plastic sheeting placed under a large old cloth.*

2 *Assemble the mechanics. The base of the stone-coloured plastic urn is an upturned biscuit tin – it is wise not to use valuable china in a marquee, in case of accidents. Begin to build up the arrangement, keeping it simple, bold and elegant – three good principles for large designs.*

3 *The finished buffet table (right), with matching pedestals. Simple ribbon bows and ivy make an easy and economical garland for the table cloth.*

4 *An alternative pedestal design (left). Note the way in which these flowers and foliage create an entirely different atmosphere.*

Small Table Decorations

1 *A flower tree makes an attractive alternative to trees made from foliage and those with added flowers. The minimum of foliage is used to cover the mechanics, and then the flowers are added to create a very luxurious feeling.*

2 *This simple basket idea is very economical, in terms of both time and money. A ribbon bow covers the handle, a painted bird sits happily on the side, and a pretty daisy plant topped with moss has been placed in a plastic-lined basket.*

3 *When making this table design it is vital that you avoid giving it the appearance of a floral pudding! This pitfall is avoided by ensuring that there is sufficient depth and recession to the design. Interesting foliage is good here, as the guests will be looking at the flowers very closely. The design is created by taping a block of floral foam into a plastic tray and building up the flowers around it.*

DECORATING THE WEDDING CAKE

1   *The cake and its decoration are an important element of any wedding. Here a little silver chalice has been arranged with wired flowers to allow a greater freedom of design.*

2   *Arrange similar flowers between the cake tiers, then place the chalice on top of the cake. The garlands of ivy around the cake table continue the decorative theme.*

FLORAL ARCHWAYS

An ideal example of the effectiveness of letting the surroundings dictate the floral decoration is to create an archway. This one was built in a large garden, but it would look equally attractive if arranged in a church.

It is not important for an archway to be symmetrical when it is outdoors, but if you were to create it in a church you should follow the existing lines of the architecture. For this garden arch, Doris pinks, white campanulas, wild gypsophila and lavender sweet peas were combined with *Alchemilla mollis*.

An archway makes a most attractive frame for a bride and groom, especially when the wedding photographs are taken, and provides a very pretty focal point for any garden or walkway. If the garden in which the reception will be held already has a pergola or arch over which flowering plants have been trained, you might consider taking advantage of this and holding your wedding at a time when the flowers will be in full bloom.

MAKING AN ARCHWAY

1 *When choosing the branches for an archway you should first decide on the height and shape of the finished arch. You will find it much easier to use branches that are naturally bent rather than try to coax straight branches into curves. Once you have found suitable branches, place their bases in tubs of nylon-reinforced plaster and leave to set for at least 24 hours.*

2 *Cut a strip of wire netting about 15cm (6in) wide and 1.2m (4ft) long, then cut a block of wet foam into eight pieces and arrange these along the netting, separating them by gaps of 5cm (2in). Wrap the netting around them to form a roll and secure the ends together firmly. Then place the roll on a branch and wire securely in place. Make as many of these rolls as you need to run all around the archway.*

3 *Starting at the centre of the arch, begin to arrange the flowers and work down one side before beginning the other.*

4 *When you have finished decorating the sides of the arch, place a block of wet foam into the bottom of each container and arrange greenery in it. Here, blue thistles, grasses and ferns were used to soften the bottom of the arch and the top of the container. The flowers will keep fresh if frequently sprayed, but the arrangement will not last for much more than a day.*

The pretty colours and intriguing shape of this archway not only make it an attractive frame for the statue in the background but also create an ideal setting for photographs of the wedding party.

DECORATIVE STAIRS

A perfect way to trim a staircase for a celebration is to drape garlands and posies of flowers along the banisters.

However, you had better check first that the staircase is wide enough to allow guests to pass up and down without damaging the flowers. *Euphorbia marginata*, guelder roses, eucalyptus and roses were used here to make the posies, with garlands of smilax to link them along the banisters. To make the posies, cover quarter blocks of foam with wire netting and back them with plastic, then wire them on to the banisters and arrange the flowers in position. You can then loop the smilax between the posies. As alternatives, you could make garlands from ivy or ribbons, and the posies could be made from gypsophila or cow parsley for weddings.

Another charming decoration for a stairway is to cover one side of the stair treads with pillows of flowers, which are in fact made from black florists' trays. Once they are all decorated, they look like a continuous line of flowers.

To make them, tape one block of foam to each tray with florists' tape, then place one on each stair tread and arrange the flowers *in situ*. If this is not possible, then when arranging the flowers you should leave one end of the foam block flat and undecorated – in other words, cover the front, top and one side of the block. If the trays will be lined up against a wall you should leave the two sides undecorated as well as the back.

As with the posies and garlands, you should first check that the stairs are wide enough to accommodate this sort of decoration. We used cow parsley, sprays of coral roses, 'Bahama' roses, 'Cheer' narcissi, cream hyacinths, lily of the valley and laurustinus, which combined to create a wonderful perfume. If you put lily of the valley, narcissi, roses or cow parsley into foam, they will not last as long as they would do in water and wire netting, so you should leave it as late as possible before arranging them and then spray them continuously. The flowers should last for about 12 hours, unless the building is extremely hot.

When using flowers to decorate stairs, they should be as strongly scented as possible (lily of the valley, narcissi and hyacinths are all ideal), so that the scent will float up to the passers-by and circulate throughout the house.

WEDDING BOUQUETS AND HEAD DRESSES

As the wedding dress is usually considered to be one of the most important elements of the wedding decor, its design and colour will take precedence over the bridal bouquet and flowers. The style of your dress will also dictate your hairstyle, and therefore determine the flowers for the head dress. If you are unsure which flowers to choose, ask the florist for advice.

You may find it useful to make a list of your favourite flowers first, as well as any that you dislike, and if the florist has a shop you should visit it to have a good look at the stock. Discuss the list with them, as they will be able to tell you whether or not a particular flower will be available at the time of your wedding. It is sensible to return to the florist's shop two weeks before your wedding in case any flowers are being sold that you may prefer.

Unfortunately, some flowers, no matter how beautiful, are simply not suitable for bouquets or head dresses because they don't last long out of water, and certainly not throughout the day: peonies, sweet peas, lilac and anemones all come into this category. There is nothing worse than seeing a bride, coming out of the church or halfway through the speeches, who is carrying or wearing a sad collection of drooping, wilting flowers. If you've set your heart on using any of these flowers they will have to be incorporated into a table or pedestal arrangement instead. Amongst the many flowers and foliage that can be used in bouquets and head dresses with great success are roses, stephanotis, lily of the valley (if wired), rue, ivy, jasmine, ranunculus, tuberoses, chincherinchees, bridal gladioli, lilies and carnation petals.

If you will be having attendants, their colouring will play a large part in the choice of their outfits and of their flowers. For instance, you should avoid peaches and strong pinks for anyone who is redheaded, but most pastel colours will blend in well and look pretty. It is very attractive for all the flowers of the bridal party to coordinate, but that may not always be possible. Instead, you could ensure that one colour forms the theme that links you with your matron of honour, bridesmaids, pages, flower girl or ring bearer.

A mixed bouquet is a striking departure from wedding tradition.

The exotic forms of the flowers in the bouquet on the bed have been perfectly complemented by its trailing shape.

MAKING A WEDDING BOUQUET AND POSY

1 *Choose pretty and delicate foliage, then cut it down to pieces about 10cm (4in) long. For a trailing bouquet, use 17.5cm (7in) lengths of jasmine, ivy, honeysuckle or similar plants. Wire the flowers that will be used at the base of the trailing bouquet, as well as any heavy flowers, such as hyacinths, large roses or lilies, with 18-gauge stub wires. Use 22-gauge wires for the other items. Cover the foliage and flower wires with gutta percha.*

2 *Gather together about 10 stems of foliage so that the tops are roughly level. Bind together with silver reel wire very firmly, wrapping it around the stems about six times. This stage is very important as it forms the main construction for the bouquet or posy. Do not cut the reel wire as it will be easier to handle if kept on the roll.*

3 *Holding the wires firmly in your hand, gently pull outwards about five pieces of foliage to make a circle, and arrange the others to fill in the gaps from the top to the sides. Wrap the wire around twice more, for safety. The wire must be wound around the same part of the stems throughout, or the bouquet will lose its shape.*

4 *To make a trailing bouquet, follow steps 1, 2 and 3, then add the trailing foliage to one side of the circle to create a soft gentle flow. At this stage you may wish to enlarge the original circle by placing a wired piece of foliage flat against the circle, wiring it in and then shaping it.*

5 When adding flowers to the posy, insert them through the foliage one at a time. Once each flower is in position, wrap the reel wire round the stems to hold it in place before adding the next flower. Every time you add anything to the bouquet, you must bind it firmly in position with reel wire.

6 Once you have added all the flowers and foliage, secure the reel wire before cutting it off by threading it through the guttared wire stems and pulling it upwards. Next, trim off the stems to make a thinner handle for the bouquet. Make sure you cut them no closer than 5cm (2in) from the reel wire, and trim the wires so that they graduate to a point.

7 Now wrap the silver reel wire down over the handle to hold the wires in place, then cover the handle with gutta percha, working from the top of the handle down to the point. It is best to wrap it round with gutta twice to prevent any wires poking through.

8 Bend the handle into a curved shape. Using 12mm (½ in) satin ribbon, fold the top corner of the ribbon over, place this at the top of the handle and pin into place, pushing the pin upwards to avoid accidents – this will hold the ribbon in place. Wrap the ribbon tightly all the way down the handle and back up, securing it in the same way as before. Tie off with a bow.

173

MAKING A HEAD DRESS, COMB AND HALF CIRCLET

1 *You will gain maximum effect if you use a variety of shapes as well as colours when making a head dress, so try to choose at least five different types each of flowers and foliage and wire them all individually. Here, we used muscari, gypsophila, tea roses, moluccella, ranunculus, laurustinus, pussy willow, variegated ivy and peperomia leaves.*

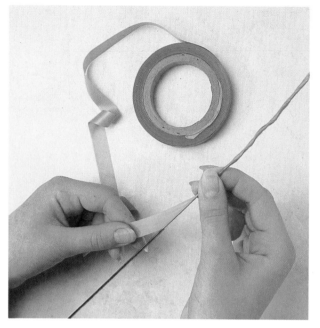

2 *To make the circlet, bind together two lengths of 18-gauge wire, then cover them with gutta percha.*

3 *Measure the circumference of the head, add an extra 10cm (4in) for the overlap, then cut the wires to the appropriate length. Curve into a hoop, overlapping the two wires until the circle is the desired size, and firmly bind the ends together with silver wire. Cover the join with gutta percha.*

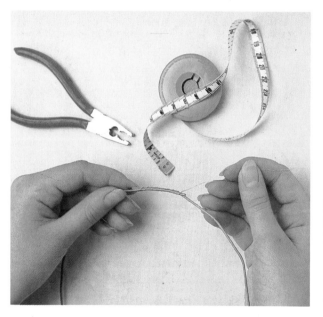

4 *Starting with an ivy leaf, place it flat on the hoop. Twist the wire around the hoop four or five times, then cut off any excess. Using gutta percha cut to half its normal width, bind the wire to the hoop. Continue working around the hoop in this way until you have wired all the flowers and foliage in place, leaving a gap of 2.5cm (1in) at the back.*

174

5 *Taking a length of ribbon in your hand, form it into a neat bow. Bind the centre tightly with silver wire and trim off any excess.*

6 *Tie a length of ribbon, about 50cm (20in), in the gap left at the back of the circlet, then place the bow on top of the knot and tie again to secure it in place.*

7 *Follow the instructions for steps 1, 2, and 4 when making a comb, but each time bring the wire and gutta percha through the teeth of the comb.*

8 *The same principles shown in step 4 apply when making a half circlet or band, except that you must bend the ends of the main wire together, bind them with silver wire and then cover with gutta percha. Work from the ends of the wire towards the middle, ensuring that this is the highest point.*

OTHER IDEAS FOR YOUNG BRIDESMAIDS

If you're looking for something different, a flower ball is a very pretty idea. It is easily made, using a mossed ball as a base, into which small and pretty wired flowers are inserted until every piece of moss is covered and the flower ball is a perfect sphere. Then a simple bow and loop should be securely pinned into the finished ball so that it can be carried in the hand. Don't make the flower ball too large or it will look somewhat clumsy and cumbersome.

A prayer book spray is another pleasing idea and is easy to carry. The spray should not be too large and is stitched on to a piece of pretty ribbon so that it can be used as a book marker. You can also wire and stitch some very small pips and foliage to the ends of the ribbons for added interest. Stitching the ribbon lightly where the piece is folded back will keep the design firm, but remember to fold the ribbon with the right side showing.

A pretty ball of silk flowers is made by pressing 14 scabious heads, 14–16 blossom florets and 14 ribbon loops into a foam ball 140mm (5½ in) in diameter. The carrying ribbon is secured by bending a wire into a hairpin shape, pushing it through the centre of the ball, then bending back the ends to form hooks. The end hooks are then pulled back into the foam, leaving a firm centre loop through which the ribbon is threaded.

MAKING A BRIDESMAID'S CIRCLET AND BASKET

1 *Make a circlet in the same way as you would a flower coronet (see pages 174–5), splitting the stem tape in half for a delicate finish. You can also make a long garland in the same way. This can then be carried by two small bridesmaids, or tied to their wrists for easy carrying.*

2 *Prepare the basket by lining it with plastic and wire a piece of wet floral foam into the bottom. You can also use a frog for extra stability.*

3 *Add the flowers and foliage, arranging them to hide the mechanics and sit neatly in the basket without obscuring the handle, by which it will be carried. This soft flowing design will not be easily damaged – young bridesmaids can be very active!*

4 *The finished circlet and basket, worn by a young bridesmaid.*

177

A Christening Party

Christening ceremonies are usually held at the morning service, though they are sometimes held in the afternoon, and are then followed either by a luncheon or a tea party.

Usually the party will be held in the home of the parents of the baby, and it follows that the new mother will often be so busy with her baby and with organizing refreshments for the guests that perhaps the thought of having to arrange the flowers as well might be a little daunting. It might well occur to her to leave the flower decorations out altogether, but just as with other forms of entertaining, flowers, however simple, turn the occasion into a party. With a certain amount of forward planning, there should be no problem.

The flowers should be unsophisticated and pretty – this is not the time for modern leaf designs or similar arrangements – and they should be suitable in both colour and form. Simple containers are preferable, and white china is very suitable, setting off the small, pastel flowers to perfection. Use low, pretty arrangements for the table, rather than large designs, which will be easily toppled. The flowers should be soft in colour and delicate in shape, and if possible slightly scented. Sweet peas or hyacinths are charming, though they may be a little heady in a crowd of adoring relatives. Lightly scented pinks and canterbury bells will be a delight.

If you arrange the flowers in small baskets these will make lovely gifts for the godparents and grandparents. There are some very pretty dried and silk materials that would look attractive in such designs, but dainty fresh flowers always seem so appropriate to the young.

The christening cake will be the centre of attention – after the baby – and similar flowers will look enchanting arranged in a garland around the cake. This is easily created with foam sausages wrapped in cling film, the materials being pushed through the plastic into the damp foam. The garland can be arranged at least a day before the event and placed ready to allow the cake to be put in the middle. White tablecloths or special crocheted or lace cloths are particularly lovely for this occasion. Sticky fingers are inevitable with very young guests, but the cloth can be washed and the day is very much for the young.

A garlanded crib is another lovely idea. To make the flower garland for the top of the crib, cut a block of wet foam into eight pieces, then wrap each one in wire netting and secure to the top edge of the crib with wire, ensuring that any sharp ends are facing outwards rather than inwards, and do not present a danger to the baby. If you are intending actually to place the baby in the cot, it might be a good idea to tie the blocks in place with string or ribbon, for safety's sake. Even though the flowers here are not poisonous, the baby should only be placed in the cot for photographs or short periods of supervised time, in case the baby tries to eat any of the petals or leaves. Garlands of smilax are arranged around the bottom edge of the crib, and finished off here with double bows of yellow satin ribbon.

Again, arrangements in the cloakroom or bedroom are lovely, and the atmosphere in a house with a new baby and flowers is a wonderful one. If the new mother really feels a little too busy then a kind granny or godmother will surely come to the rescue. A christening without flowers would be a little bleak.

A garland around the cake is always a simple but lovely idea. Foam sausages, wrapped in plastic, will keep the flowers fresh for some time. Here, small pink roses and cream tuberoses combine with ivies to create an enchanting design.

When planning the decorations for a party following a christening, as well as the more usual arrangements, one charming idea is to decorate a crib. It makes a very pretty feature for the corner of a room, or when placed beside the christening cake. A mixture of jasmine, anemones, lily of the valley, white azaleas, de-thorned tea roses, wax flower and smilax was used to garland this crib.

FLOWERS FOR A SILVER WEDDING

Silver weddings are a special celebration, when you wish to create a happy relaxed atmosphere, so that guests can enjoy reminiscing about the past twenty-five years.

Decorations for such gatherings are a joy, but they must be kept to a sensible size and number: remember flower arrangements and bouquets will be sent as presents, and if the house is already filled to overflowing it would be a pity to have nowhere to place them. However, even if the only flowers are the twenty-five red roses from husband to wife, it is far more effective to have one or two special designs than masses of flowers, none of which coordinate in any way, dotted all over the house.

Soft pinks and cream flowers look particularly attractive with silver, and it is a lovely idea to use silver containers at this time. If a buffet table is planned, then tall silver candlesticks look wonderful, with or without candles, depending on the time of day. A seated dinner party arrangement will be perfect in a silver salver or simple vases. It is a charming idea to arrange the flowers in the little silver vases that are so often used on the top of the wedding cake, and indeed the one originally used may still be available. These little vases can be arranged as simply or as formally as is required.

As with most celebrations, the cake will be an important feature, and if it is set on a table apart it will look most elegant with a simple garland of smilax looped up with small posies of flowers similar to those used on the main table. Flowers arranged on a cake are always a delight, and if the colouring echoes the rest of the decor the effect will be stunning.

The choice of flowers will be a very personal one and it is always lovely to choose your favourites if they are available. If not, then perhaps you might select according to your colour preferences, although soft pink and creams are the colours most generally chosen, because of their affinity with silver. Silver candles and ribbons are available and can be used to continue the silver theme, but with reserve – use too much silver, and it will seem as though Christmas has arrived a little early. If pink flowers or blush pink have been used, then candles that are shaded the palest of pink will be a delight. The soft warmth of the very pale pink will be very effective at night and will create a wonderful atmosphere.

Not everyone has a store of family silver from which to choose, but there are some wonderful silvered plastic candlesticks and vases. These are easily purchased and are very inexpensive, and if the party is a large one, perhaps at a hotel, you will be saved the worry that a valuable piece of silver might disappear.

White china is another very good foil for a silver wedding, and nothing could look lovelier than soft pink garden roses arranged informally in a white china vegetable tureen. If the party is to be held in the evening, pale pink candles in white china candlesticks are show-stoppers.

Remember to place a few flowers in the cloakroom and bedroom for the guests, and here it would be a lovely idea to continue the silver wedding colour scheme. They only need to be simple designs but they will make all the difference.

For those who would prefer an arrangement without silver bows and similar accessories the grey foliages are wonderful. *Senecio greyii* and artimesia are perfect, but there are many other wonderful grey foliages, including the blue grey-green eucalyptus, which will give a delightful silvery effect without the metallic glint or glitter. Just a little will be sufficient to give a highlight and create the silver effect required.

A silver wedding party is a time to meet with old friends and loved ones and the atmosphere has to be such that all those present enjoy a marvellous reunion. The flowers, although a very small part of the arrangements, will add greatly to the success of the party.

Soft colourings should not mean pallid insignificance, and it is important to add a touch of deeper colour to give the desired sparkle to the arrangement. The grey-green foliages are the perfect accompaniment. The arrangement at the side echoes the table design, and if other arrangements are desired they should be kept relatively small so that they do not compete with the main designs.

GIFTS

Flowers make wonderful gifts, but all too often they are presented unimaginatively, still wrapped in the paper of the shop where they were bought. Not only this, but they may be given without foliage, when it would have been better to have spent less on the flowers but provided some attractive foliage to set them off.

With a little forethought, however, flowers make heart-warming presents in themselves, or can be used to enhance the main gift. If you are giving a bunch of flowers, try to select shapes and colours that will complement the decor of the recipient's home. If you are arranging the flowers beforehand, choose a container that will transport easily and make sure that the mechanics are firm and secure.

If the chief present is a container – a china bowl, a mug, or even a pan or a casserole dish – it will look much more attractive filled with fresh flowers or plants than wrapped in paper. You might choose your flowers to pick out the colours of a painted pattern on china, for example, or fill a cooking utensil with culinary herbs.

The container – a copper pot – has been chosen and has floral foam firmly taped into it, ready to take the flowers and foliages to be used for a copper wedding anniversary gift.

183

BOUQUETS AND POSIES

Presentation bouquets and posies (shown overleaf) vary tremendously, depending on the flowers used and the particular occasion for which they are intended, but they are always much appreciated.

It must be said that presentation bouquets or boxes of cut flowers can be very expensive – unless you are fortunate enough to be able to pick all the material from your garden – so if you have to work to a tight budget you would be wise to choose a few really beautiful flowers rather than masses of cheaper ones. Don't forget to add some foliage, preferably choosing something unusual or particularly decorative.

Should you be unable to buy the right type of cellophane for a bouquet, then a low cardboard box covered in plain or patterned paper, and lined with crumpled tissue paper, is an excellent alternative. The flowers will stay fresher if placed in a box, as you can wrap damp tissue paper around the ends of their stems, and spray the flowers themselves with a light mist of water to give added moisture. If you will be transporting the flowers to their recipient yourself, the box will provide added protection as it will support the flowers and prevent them bruising. To protect open lilies or similar flowers, you should gently wrap each flower head in tissue paper to stop the petals breaking or being crushed.

When giving someone a present of cut flowers for them to arrange themselves, you can either wrap the flowers in cellophane or pack them into a box (below).

A tied posy needs no further arranging but can be placed in water as it is. This makes it an ideal gift for people who don't have the time or the facility to arrange the flowers themselves.

184

MAKING A TIED POSY

1 *Starting with two stems of foliage (rosemary was used here), cross the stems and bind them together with white or green gutta percha, making sure it is secure.*

2 *Keep adding the foliage. As you add more, continue to cross the stems and bind them with gutta. This is the only time in flower arranging that your stems should cross, as this will make the posy fan out.*

3 *Feed the flowers through from the top of the posy, also crossing the stems and binding them. For this posy, 'Porcelain' roses, white freesias, coral spray roses, laurustinus and rosemary were used.*

4 *Tie off the gutta percha by feeding it through the stems and pulling tightly. Cut off the stems evenly. The posy should be able to stand up on its own if you have crossed enough stems. Also, if you do not cross the stems you will find that the flowers will be crushed together in the centre of the posy and not evenly spaced. For a finishing touch, tie with satin ribbon.*

WRAPPING A BOUQUET IN CELLOPHANE

1 *Place a long length of cellophane on a flat surface. Arrange the bouquet in the centre of the cellophane, then carefully draw the rest of the cellophane over the bouquet.*

2 *Separate the cellophane from the remainder of the roll, then turn the two cut sides and staple them together. Gather the cellophane around the stems of the bouquet, ensuring that the flower heads are not being squashed or crushed, then fasten with a large ribbon in a colour that matches the flowers.*

LASTING FLOWER GIFTS

Flower arrangements make beautiful and thoughtful gifts, but the drawback to fresh flowers is that they are essentially ephemeral. If you want your present to be a little more permanent, dried or silk flowers offer the best of both worlds.

Whether a present to yourself or someone else, the selection shown encompasses easy and pleasing possibilities. Easiest of all is potpourri – it is too fiddly to arrange, except possibly in broad bands of colour, and so the only choice is one of presentation. Somehow the crumpled brown paper bags that potpourri is often sold in don't rise to the spirit of gift giving. A transparent container allows the colour to be enjoyed; shown here are three options.

A glass, such as the brandy snifter shown, can be an inexpensive receptacle for the potpourri or the real gift, with the potpourri in a supporting role. The pyramid-shaped clear plastic box, available from specialist stores, contains a tiny amount of potpourri, topped with slightly more extravagant dried rose heads sitting on a bed of white delphinium florets. And lastly, a circle of tulle is gathered to form a potpourri bag, tied at the neck with thin ribbon and embellished with a cluster of tiny flowers. Tulle or fine net potpourri bags are excellent if you have a large number of small presents to give, or perhaps to make for a Christmas bazaar; they will scent a drawer or cupboard for many months.

There is nothing unusual about the concept of dried-flower lollipop trees, but they can be customized in various ways. Spraying the flower pot with high-gloss emulsion to match the arrangement is one; adding toning ribbons is another. Even the surface finish beneath the tree leaves room for improvisation. A sphagnum moss or wood chippings finish is an easy solution; you could also use reindeer moss, as in the base of the red tree. The latter has its own miniature flower garden, repeating the choice of flowers in the tree. If you have enough material, try covering the entire base with flowers, so that no moss is visible. The base of the blue tree has a gravel finish; the bamboo cane stem is set in plaster and, when nearly dry, gravel is gently pressed into the surface. Tightly packed ash or hornbeam keys with some fir cones, their stems inserted into florists' foam, make an even more unusual finish.

The flower-filled tea pot and cup and saucer are self explanatory and, like the potpourri-filled brandy snifter, can range from the cheap and cheerful to the extraordinarily expensive. The fierce yellow and orange of tansy, Chinese lanterns, dyer's saffron and mimosa would be perfect for the similarly coloured 'Thirties and 'Forties china.

MINI BELL JARS

Floral displays in miniature bell jars make ideal small gifts for children, and require very little outlay. They are an excellent way of using up all the bits and bobs of dried flower heads that have parted from their stems, and even a single bunch of dried (preferably mixed) flowers goes a long, long way.

Choose the jars with care. Although there is a certain amount of ship-in-a-bottle manipulation, the wider the mouth of the jar, the easier the exercise. Avoid jars that are tall and slender, and obviously those that have numbers or writing embossed on the bottom, because the jars are displayed bottoms up. Faceted jars are particularly attractive, as are those with slightly tinted glass.

Paint the lid before starting, then attach a small frog to the inside, using mastic. Impale a small piece of floral foam to the frog. Alternatively, use a spot of quick-drying glue. Place the upturned jar over the lid, to check that the foam fits comfortably inside with room to spare all the way round. Begin to insert

These miniature bell jars – in reality inverted jam jars – are quick and easy presents for children to make.

Dried flowers make delightful gifts. The trees are created
by inserting the base of the dowel either into foam held
in position by a frog attached to mastic or into quick-
drying plaster. The top is inserted into a foam ball
which is then covered with wired flower and seed heads.

189

flowers into the foam, checking frequently for fit. Feed the flowers through the mouth, if it is narrower than the rest of the jar, by gently pressing them inwards; they will expand to fill the jar once inside. Hide any visible foam with moss, then secure the lid.

Use short, squat jars right-way up. Fill with potpourri and a small bunch of dried flowers, concealing the threads of a screw top with glued-on moss or thin ribbons.

The flowers – lily of the valley, roses and sweet peas (left) – are held in the decorative shells by a small piece of modelling compound into which the stems are inserted. The asparagus fern that accompanies the lily of the valley can be obtained from florists.

SILK FLOWER GIFTS

Like dried arrangements, silk flowers make highly acceptable small gifts or can be used to decorate the main item. The attractive houseplants shown here, for example, might be presented in a plain plant pot or in a collectable piece of china.

A shell decoration makes an equally attractive gift, ideal for a small birthday present for a friend, or for Mother's Day, or as something slightly out of the ordinary for the hostess of a dinner party.

Pelargoniums, African violets and cyclamen (below) – any of these would make a colourful gift. Select the container before you make the plant so that you can judge the number of flowers required and the length of the stems. These can be secured with brown foam.

FLOWERS FOR MOTHER'S DAY

What better way of spoiling your mother –
or someone who is your mother in all but
name – than to give her a pretty flower
arrangement to celebrate Mother's Day?

Very often the simplest designs are the most effective,
as they can display the flowers in their true beauty,
so don't worry if you can't reach a florist in time
– a few flowers picked from the garden can be just
as impressive and attractive as those bought from
a shop, especially if the recipient prefers them.

A large tied posy of feminine, scented flowers, held
together with a length of white satin ribbon, is
another idea for a Mother's Day present, although
it needs to be more carefully planned than a simple
vase of flowers. Nevertheless, once again the flowers
do not have to be bought from a florist, and a good

*Because a tied posy is arranged in the hand before being
bound with ribbon, it can be placed in water without
any further arrangement being necessary.*

hunt through the garden may produce a sizeable
bunch of suitable flowers. If possible, when collecting
the flowers, choose the ones that you know your
mother likes, rather than your own personal
favourites, unless, of course, the two coincide.

To make the tied posy illustrated here, strip off
their lower leaves, then gather the double pink tulips,
paper-white narcissi, pink ranunculus and eucalyptus
leaves together in your hand, tie them together with
a ribbon and finish them with a big bow. Then, all
the stems are trimmed to the same length, so that
the flowers can be placed in a container without
further arrangement. This always creates a very
natural-looking posy that is suitable for most types
of vase.

A PLANTED BOWL

Many people love the beauty of cut flowers, but feel that their joy is all too fleeting, in which case a bowl or basket filled with living plants is the perfect gift, especially if it contains flowering plants as well as those loved for their foliage alone. If you are intending to give a planted bowl to a busy mother on Mother's Day, you will help her immeasurably by choosing plants that are easy to care for. Another important consideration is to select plants that require roughly the same amounts of light and moisture, and which look good together. This bowl was filled with dracaena, jasmine, a white hydrangea and a white azalea, to provide a good contrast of white and green. This combination of colours always creates a strong impact and gives a very fresh feel.

When planting the bowl, always remember to leave a small trench around the rim where the soil meets the bowl, so that you can water the plants easily without having any spills. You should also choose a container that is watertight and deep enough to house the plants and soil, as well as sturdy enough to bear their weight. The hydrangea, azalea and jasmine can be left in the garden during the summer months and brought indoors again during the winter, but the dracaena would have to be replanted in a separate container as it would not be happy outside. As well as being an unusual gift for Mother's Day, a planted bowl also makes an ideal present for someone who is bedridden or in hospital, as they will be able to watch the plants grow and enjoy them coming into flower.

A small planted bowl makes a delightful Mother's Day present, but make sure that it is sufficiently deep for rooted plants.

193

MAKING A PLANTED BASKET OR BOWL

1 *If the basket does not have its own waterproof lining, it should be lined with thick plastic sheeting. Fill it about half-full with good quality potting compost.*

2 *Remove the plants from their plastic pots and arrange in the basket. Here, 'Cheer' narcissi, jonquils, polyanthuses, helxene, jasmine and trailing ivy were used.*

3 Once your plants are in position, fill in the gaps between their root balls with soil, making sure that they are all covered and firm. Do not fill the basket to the brim with soil as you will have trouble watering it – leave at least 2.5cm (1in) from the top of the basket. Trim off any excess plastic, leaving about 2.5cm (1in) above the top of the basket.

4 For the finishing touches, use bun moss and pebbles or bark. When placing the moss on the edge of the basket, ensure that the excess plastic is folded outwards. This catches any water that might otherwise drip on to a table top. Between waterings, keep the plants moist by spraying them with water.

FLOWERS FOR MEN

When talking of giving flowers one so often only thinks that they are for women, and yet there are many occasions on which flowers are given to men.

Father's Day and Valentine's Day both offer the opportunities to give flowers or plants to men. Certainly, some of the best flower arrangers, like so many of the best cooks, are men, and every gardener would be delighted with such a thought – you might perhaps give a posy of flowers with some special packets of seeds.

Masculine flowers do not readily spring to mind, perhaps because flowers appeal to all in many ways. The real masculine preference seems to centre on colour, and when asked for an opinion on arrangements, men will usually prefer brightly coloured flowers and foliages to those of the softer shades; there must be exceptions, but if the recipient is not well known or his colour preference uncertain, it will be a good idea to go for red.

Little pretty flowers do not seem appropriate, and a simple but elegant design will probably be the most suitable choice and will look attractive in the office or flat without seeming out of place. Scarlet lilies, hemerocallis and gerberas will easily create a bold and well defined line. The foliage used in such designs also needs to be elegant and clean shaven in appearance. Variegated iris leaves, with their long straight lines, look striking and can be folded or bent to create a geometric design in which to place the chosen flowers.

A container that has to be transported needs to be solid but light, and there are some excellent ashtray-type dishes that would be admirable. These are plastic and are therefore not practical for later use as an ashtray, but they can hold drawing pins

A Valentine basket is a delightful way to show your feelings. This has been arranged in the Victorian style, with the most fragrant flower at the centre. The basket was lined with plastic and then filled with floral foam, cut below the level of the rim so that the flowers, when arranged, would come up to the level of the container.

Very simple but strong in design and colours, the arrangement on the facing page has been made in a glass ashtray. Even if the recipient is a non-smoker, he will find this useful later for items such as pins or golf tees. A small block of floral foam was securely taped to the dish (glass does not take tape very readily, so it is best to take the tape right around the dish). Some wavy sticks and dried leaves cut into shapes provide a backdrop to clear-cut red flowers and large aspidistra leaves. If the leaves had been left upright, the arrangement would have looked too stiff, so they have been folded over and the stem pushed through to create a feeling of movement.

A posy may seem to be an unusual gift for a man, but there are many who enjoy having flowers in their home, and a tied posy is a lovely idea because it can be placed directly in a vase without further arranging. Here, the flowers are simple, elegant and long lasting.

or golf tees, when the flowers have faded and the foam and frog have been removed. Choose a black or dark brown colour for the tray, as this will continue the drama of the arrangement: pink or pale blue will certainly not promote the manly image.

Most men are very romantic, although not always prepared to admit it, and many would be as delighted with a Valentine posy basket filled with flowers as they would with a box of chocolates. (A golf ball or cuff-links hidden in the bottom would make a very acceptable surprise.) The basket would not go unnoticed in the office, and the fortunate fellow might be ribbed a little, but the rest will be hoping that they, too, might be as lucky.

Plants, of course, are always a safe option, and a pot plant will bring much pleasure to a man of any age. Grandfathers are always difficult subjects for presents, although they are always the most grateful. A plant for the flat will bring much pleasure, or if he has a garden or an allotment then here again plants are the ideal gift. The gift will only be perfect, however, if a little skilful research has been made. A plant that will only grow in cool damp surroundings will not suit a gentleman who likes to be warm and hates drafts. Neither is a shrub which will not mature for twenty or more years the most tactful of thoughts. Many elderly men love cacti and find them fascinating; similarly, bonsai trees are an unusual idea. Bulbs, both for the house or garden, are always acceptable, and if the bowl for the house is to be ready planted, then the addition of a fern and moss will give him something to enjoy while the bulbs gradually unfold.

The elderly man in hospital will love every gift, especially if it is a plant that he can watch growing and flowering. Gifts for hospital patients really must be in practical containers and easily maintainable. The nursing staff will not be very overjoyed if they have constantly to attend to a highly pernickety plant, so choose a reliable one that will be happy in hot, air-conditioned surroundings. Choose a plant, also, that the patient will be able to take home with him when better.

Arrangements of plants, still in their pots, are a very good suggestion for a single man who is a flat dweller, and here elegant and sculptured plants will be sure to please. Try to combine a variety of shapes and designs within the bowl and the gift will bring much pleasure for many years. A good nursery will be able to suggest suitable plants and those which will like similar conditions and perhaps withstand a certain amount of neglect.

Perhaps the most obvious gift for men is a button-hole. This can be simply a carnation or rose from the garden, but if given with love it will be worn with pride.

CHRISTMAS GIFTS

There can be no happier time to give presents than at Christmas, but so often the age-old worry of what to give or buy threatens the most even-tempered of us and the season of goodwill takes on a decidedly unloving air. A Christmas flower arrangement could well be the solution.

Many people would love to have attractive decorations but are too busy to make them. If any of your friends fit into that category an attractive arrangement that could decorate either the dining table or a low table in the sitting room would make an ideal gift, and one that will give much pleasure. This is a small present that would be equally well received at an old folks' home and would greatly add to the appearance of their festive table.

Transporting a gift of flowers is not always easy, and sometimes a basket is a good idea, but there are other ways of ensuring that an arrangement arrives safely at its destination. A table decoration in the form of a wreath with a large candle to place in the centre makes a delightful gift. A garland that can be draped down the centre of a table is always charming and sufficiently versatile to be used as a decoration elsewhere. Unless the Christmas arrangement is to be given close to the actual day, it is preferable to make it from artificial Christmas materials or to combine long lasting foliages with silk flowers, such as artificial Christmas roses and poinsettias (see pages 232–3 and 243–4). The ring or garland can then be made well ahead of the pre-Christmas panic, which will solve another common problem.

Christmas tree decorations are also lovely, and spice posies – small bunches of scented herbs and flowers, tied with ribbons – are easy to make. Also known as tuzzie muzzies, these small nosegays are a delight to receive.

Pomanders are another charming gift and look very decorative when tied with green or red velvet ribbons and hung up, perhaps on the Christmas tree or else on the mantelpiece, where the warm air will help to release their aroma. Like spice posies, they are easily made. Use a thin-skinned orange; tie tape around it where you will later put the ribbon, then cover the remaining area with cloves; put the pomander in a paper bag with a teaspoon of orris root powder and a teaspoon of powdered cinnamon; tie the bag tightly, and leave it in a box for at least two weeks. When the pomander has matured, remove the bag and tape; tie the pomander with ribbon, and you have a delightful Christmas gift which, like the artificial garland, can be prepared well in advance.

Another attractive Christmas gift would be a floral foam tree (see page 116). If you were giving this to a household with children you might incorporate some lollipops in the foliage. If the person receiving the gift is a keen cook, perhaps you might think in terms of a kitchen decoration incorporating spices, such as nutmegs and cinnamon sticks, tied with red ribbon bows.

Candle garlands or wreaths make simple but pretty Christmas gifts. You can use a wide range of materials – silk or dried, plastic or fresh – the method is the same in each case. Each piece of material must be wired, as for a larger garland, and they are then taped together to form a ring. It is always a good idea to make a matching pair of garlands, as there are so often two candlesticks on the table.

200

WEDDING ANNIVERSARIES

Wedding anniversaries are a time for nostalgia and a time for the future, for plans fulfilled and plans to be made. To give flowers for a wedding anniversary is certainly an old practice, and as, by tradition, each anniversary has its own special symbol, a few ideas are suggested here for floral themes that might be appropriate for the year.

The first anniversary is special, and roses are the usual choice, but as this is traditionally a paper anniversary, paper roses would be fun. The Mexicans and Portuguese make beautiful paper flowers, which will last a long time, longer than those of the second anniversary, which is cotton. For this, it might be amusing to make an arrangement with cotton bolls, which can be purchased from florists. These bolls make a wonderful decoration when incorporated with other dried materials. The third anniversary is leather, and here, perhaps, an arrangement in a lovely leather cigarette case (well-lined, of course) might suffice, or perhaps you could find a leather covered water bottle or flask.

With the fourth anniversary, which is fruit and flowers, there will be no problem at all. The fifth, which is wooden, conjures up the thought of wonderful designs with driftwood. From the sixth to the eleventh anniversaries, the container will set the scene, but with the twelfth, silk flowers must be the answer. Then follow lace and ivory, with crystal as the fifteenth anniversary. The next notable one is the silver wedding, which is, of course, the twenty-fifth. The thirtieth is pearl; the thirty-fifth is coral, and the fortieth is ruby, all of which can be beautifully translated in terms of flowers with appropriate colourings. Thereafter, the sapphire, golden, emerald and diamond anniversaries can be represented by simple and elegant designs, with just a hint of the special occasion. With age comes restraint and dignity and the time to enjoy every precious minute.

You will find many lovely ideas to emphasize each anniversary: glycerined leaves, for example, give a very leathery effect, and cow parsley is often referred to as Queen Anne's lace.

A wedding anniversary gift should be a thoughtful one, not necessarily expensive or extravagant, and to give an arrangement that has been carefully thought out will bring much pleasure and perhaps a little fun and amusement. In the case of the special anniversaries, the container may be a part of the gift, remaining after the flowers are finished. This will be particularly appropriate if the container has been bought to match the anniversary: for example, a copper cooking pot for the seventh. All this could make the fun of giving even greater fun than the receiving, which is perhaps the way it should be.

If special containers are to be used for the arrangements, then care must be taken to line them before they are used. A plastic liner is easily fitted into a silver mug or a china dish, and it would probably be wise to allow the foam to drain a little before it is used in an arrangement of this type. Everything will then be appropriate and beautiful, which is as it should be when celebrating an anniversary of any kind.

The language of flowers is also amusing, and it would be a lovely idea to incorporate it into a wedding anniversary arrangement. The Victorians were well aware of the meaning of flowers, and a lady would be able to read much into the posy that was sent to her. Nowadays, we are not so aware of the special significance of the flowers that we are given, though there must be few who do not recognize the meaning of red roses.

There are several symbols, however, which are rather unkind or sad, so if you wish to send a message to your loved one through flowers, be sure to send the correct variety. One plant that is always lovely to include is, of course, the rose, but did you know that the rose leaf means 'you may hope'? Take care when sending tulips – red ones will mean a declaration of love, but yellow symbolizes hopeless love! One plant that must obviously be included is ivy, which stands for friendship and marriage. The uninitiated may not find the idea of a young husband sending ox-eye daisies and love-lies-bleeding very romantic, but those who know will realize that he is sending with his gift of flowers a beautiful token of undying love.

A book about the lovely art of saying it with flowers makes fascinating reading, and it is interesting to discover the origins and customs from which the ideas stem. It is also interesting to know the reaction of the recipient, as this, too, has a meaning. For example, to let the flowers that you are given touch your lips means 'yes', but let a petal fall to the floor and the answer is 'no' – another reason for going to a good florist!

Here, an arrangement has been made in a copper pot as a gift for a seventh wedding anniversary. The foliages have been chosen to emphasize the copper container. The rose suits every occasion, but is especially appropriate to a wedding anniversary, as is the variety used here, which is 'Darling'.

In a design for a silver anniversary, stocks add their beautiful scent to a combination of cow parsley, 'Little Silver' roses, moluccella, eucalyptus and pittosporum. An arrangement of this type may present transport problems, but you may well be able to bring the flowers and vase and arrange them in situ, perhaps using foliages taken from your own garden to complement purchased flowers.

FLOWERS FOR A NEW BABY

The arrival of a new baby is a very special time for family and friends, and flowers can add greatly to the delight of the event. A bouquet of flowers for the new mother is a lovely thought, but in hospital these are usually placed unexcitingly in a glass vase and then dumped unceremoniously on the bedside locker. The new mother will have little time to re-arrange them with all the hospital routines and the new arrival to get to know.

An arrangement that can be brought to the hospital is a far more acceptable present, and one that will look very much better than an expensive bouquet, slowly turning the water green. The flower arrangement can, of course, be sent from a florist, but there is something much more personal in making your own, especially if you are able to incorporate very special treasures from the garden or select flowers for their fragrance or colour.

The container is important, and a basket is a good idea: it can be easily moved and will not be excessively heavy, and if it is pretty, then it will be lovely to take home when the family are allowed out. There are many very attractive baskets that can be purchased inexpensively and can be used as part of the design. For example, the very pretty baskets that are made with moss or straw look highly attractive when filled with dainty, spring-time flowers. The choice of basket will be yours, but aim to select one with a reasonably tall handle. If the handle is too short, then the arrangement will be very squat (unless the handle has been completely hidden). As with all arrangements, there must be some recession, so try not to overfill the basket or the flowers will look very stiff and pudding-like. A pretty, relaxed basket of soft colourings will be a pleasure to make and then to receive.

The mechanics for a basket are fairly straightforward. If the basket has not got a plastic liner then one will have to be made. This is easily managed with a plastic bag of the type used by supermarkets (check that it does not have holes in the bottom or the exercise will be pretty useless). Fix a plastic frog in the base, and place a block of floral foam cut to size, on the frog. Florists' tape will hold all these firmly in place to the basket. After this, all you need do is to arrange the flowers, checking that the foam and plastic bag are not visible when the arrangement is completed. If some of the mechanics are still visible then tuck in a little moss to cover them. Do not be tempted to tuck in masses of foliage to hide the mechanics – this will only create a very heavy design when you are aiming for simplicity.

It is a good idea to allow the foam a good soaking and then a short draining time. The draining time is important because you will otherwise find that when you arrange the flowers, water will fill the bag and will make it more difficult to transport the basket. Once delivered to the new mum, then it will be quite easy for her to keep the foam damp with water from the jug on the locker.

Very often, the family will be back at home when you visit them and then I think that almost any type of arrangement will be welcome, even one for the dining table, as a new mother does not often find the time for these luxuries. Many people will be visiting her to see the new baby, and a thoughtful idea like this will be very welcome. As with a hospital visit, I think that this is a better time to give an arranged design – there will be plenty of time to send the bouquet when junior is a little older.

Although you will not use a great deal of foliage in delicate arrangements like these, it is still important to have some variety, to provide interest and contrast.

Appendix I

Dried Flowers

Growing for Drying

Although statice and immortelles or everlastings – ammobium, helichrysum, acroclinium, helipterum and xeranthemum – are fairly easily grown, sun-loving annuals, harvesting them at the peak of their beauty does rob the garden, especially if the garden is an ordinary size. If there is enough space, treat these flowers for drying like the crop that they are, and grow them in rows in the vegetable garden, where their absence won't be an eyesore. In any case, everlastings are easy to buy, and it would be more sensible to grow some of the rarer annuals for drying.

Celosia, or cockscomb, with its velvety, old-fashioned appeal, is a good choice; there are mixed seeds available with red, pink, salmon and gold flower heads. Bells of Ireland, annual scabious or moon flower, love-in-a-mist, love-lies-bleeding and zinnias – if you are prepared to preserve them in a desiccant – are other good choices.

Seed mixtures of annual flowers that are suitable for drying are available. They include gomphrena and rhodanthe as well as the usual immortelles. Mixtures of ornamental grasses are also available. Perennial seed mixtures of plants for drying usually contain Chinese lantern, poppy, sea holly, *Iris foetidissima*, achillea, echinops, anaphalis, thrift, allium and sea lavender. It seems a less satisfactory idea than the annual mixture, though, as the plants' heights, spreads, cultivation needs and growth rates vary. A moderately strong echinops could swamp a clump of slow-growing thrift or iris in no time at all.

Whatever the choice of flowers, a good seed bed needs to be prepared, as some seeds do not germinate easily. Use very little fertilizer, or too much foliar growth will be made at the expense of flowers.

If space is limited, concentrate primarily on making a nice garden, with one proviso: use attractive plants suitable for drying or preserving, which are not so easily bought, and which continue to look attractive after harvesting. There are many shrubs with foliage that can be preserved in glycerine, and gentle pruning provides the raw material without denuding the garden. Among the most reliable are spotted laurel, beech, box, camellia, choisya, cotoneaster, elaeagnus, eucalyptus, fatsia, griselinia, ivy, evergreen shrubby honeysuckle, magnolia, mahonia, laurel, rhododendron and laurustinus. Broom can be air dried, as can eucalyptus and various artemisias.

Good, all-round ground cover plants with foliage which can be treated include ferns; Corsican hellebore and stinking hellebore; pachysandra and Solomon's seal. You can, by discreet and self-controlled harvesting – one or two leaves, for example – have a pleasant garden and good dried material. Hosta leaves – always lovely in a garden unless the slugs gain control – can be air dried, and assume attractively twisted shapes. Preserved foliage is especially difficult to buy, and the raw material is quite easy to grow, even in the shadiest garden.

Seed pods of poppy, hypericum, peony, some iris, mullein and allium are also good value, as the pleasure of the flowering period is not cut short. The flowers of popular dried pods such as Chinese lantern and honesty are insignificant, and their only garden value is in the pod stage.

Harvesting

There are a few general rules about harvesting. Always harvest on a dry day, as morning dew or rain clinging on the flowers and foliage can cause rot. To ensure best results, always harvest during a spell of warm, dry, sunny weather – a long wet spell results in turgid, soft plant growth, which is difficult to dry, and which will show excessive shrinkage.

Harvesting of some seed pods and the annual flowers that dry naturally in autumn can be tricky. In cool temperate climates, summers are often disappointing, and every last bit of sunlight is needed, but the first hard frost can turn the hoped-for crop into a useless, sodden, blackened pulp, and gale-force winds will produce only weather-beaten skeletons. Be aware of impending local frosts and avoid growing plants for drying in known frost pockets, areas exposed to high winds or to early morning mists.

Preserving inferior material is a waste of time. Any discoloration, tears or holes in the petals or foliage, become very obvious when dried or preserved. Obviously, one or two damaged leaves can be discreetly removed from an otherwise perfect branch before preserving.

Some plants can be picked at various stages in their development. Wild grasses, for example, can be picked while in flower and yellow with pollen or when fully ripe and going gold. Dyer's greenwood can be picked when its fat buds are all green, or when they have opened to reveal bright orange centres. Teasel and burdock can be picked when green or when fully ripe and brown.

Many flowers, such as hollyhock and yellow loosestrife, have equally attractive flowers and seed pods. For flowers with one optimum moment for

harvesting, it is usually just before the flowers are fully open and before the colour fades. Visible pollen or seeds, or wilting or missing lower florets on flowers spikes, indicate an overmature flower. If it is the seed pod that is being collected, it should not show signs of splitting open. To prevent dropping, harvest fluffy material, such as clematis and pampas grass when the seed pods are hairy but not yet fluffy. They continue to ripen and become fluffy as they dry; if harvested when fully ripe and fluffy, they fall apart. An aerosol fixative, such as hair spray, can help prevent very fragile and delicate seed heads shattering.

Foliage preserved with glycerine or antifreeze needs to be mature – mid to late summer is usually the best time to collect it. Young green foliage will not absorb the solution adequately, and either wilts or shrivels. Autumn is usually too late, because the sap is no longer rising and natural senescence has started so the solution will not be drawn up through the stems. Leaves with autumn colouring have already stopped taking in sap, and so are unsuitable for glycerining, although they can be pressed between layers of newspaper. Evergreens take up antifreeze solution at a slower rate in winter, and tend to have new, soft growth in spring, so late summer is best for them too.

WILD PLANTS
Collecting wild plants for drying, like the collecting of edible wild plants, has a small but devoted following. The irony is that, once preserved and presented in a domestic setting, wild flowers, foliage and seed pods take on a rarity value, rather like the wild mushrooms lavishly described on a restaurant menu.

Some plants are protected by law and no part – roots, flowers, seeds, stems or foliage – may be taken. Protected plants vary from place to place; local authorities can supply a list, and larger local libraries may also have this information. Permission must also be gained from the land owner of fields or woodlands before entering to search for suitable plants for preservation. This is not always easy to do, and taking common roadside or hedgerow materials is unlikely to cause any offence. Use a pair of secateurs when collecting, for a quick, clean cut. Pulling up plants is unnecessary and very destructive, and against all environmental preservation principles. The plants suggested below grow wild in most temperate climates, but equivalent plants can be found in other climates.

Among common wild plants particularly useful for their seed heads are cow parsley; teasel; rosebay willowherb, or fireweed; various grasses; hops; polygonum; dock and sorrel; plantain; mullein; foxglove; rushes; sedges; thistles; burdock; clover; bulrushes, or cattails; meadowsweet and nipplewort. Buttercups; various mints; sneezewort; yarrow; wild chamomile; heather; knapweed; yellow loosestrife; purple loosestrife; feverfew and tansy are common and attractive wild flowers.

Because some time can elapse between collecting wild flowers and starting the drying process, place delicate specimens, which might wilt, in a plastic bag, then seal. Don't leave them in the bag indefinitely, or they may rot instead.

Ferns can be pressed between sheets of newspaper placed under the carpet, a pile of books or a mattress, as can bracken, a lovely autumnal filler for dried arrangements. Wild rose hips, thorn haws and guelder rose berries can be preserved with glycerine, varnished or left as they are, to wither very slowly.

Tree and shrub branches are indispensable for large-scale arrangements and, on a smaller scale, for adding personal touches to the florist's mixture of dried flowers. Obviously native trees vary from one locality to the next, but those with coloured bark, such as red-tinged dogwood or green-tinged spindle; an elegant habit of growth, such as hazel or birch; or attractive cones, such as alder, are good choices.

PRESERVING FLOWERS AND FOLIAGE

There are basically two ways to preserve plant material, although there are several different techniques for each method.

Most plant preservation involves drying, either by exposing the material to a combination of air and heat, or by surrounding it with a desiccant, such as sand, alum or silica gel, which absorbs moisture from the plant cells. Some types of foliage are preserved by standing them in diluted glycerine or antifreeze, which is drawn up into the plant by osmosis and replaces the plant's own water content, thus preserving it.

Although there are tried and true techniques for preserving certain flowers – drying garden roses in a desiccant, for example – experiment with different methods can produce interesting results.

Different techniques may be used on the same material for varied effects. Eucalyptus leaves, for example, remain blue grey, but brittle, when air dried; and remain pliable, taking on rich mahogany tones, when treated in glycerine. Some plants are best dried using one technique at one stage of growth, and a different technique at another. Hydrangeas in their full bloom should be dried with desiccant, while those already starting to dry naturally on the bush, towards the end of summer, need to be dried with their stems resting in a small amount of water.

PRESERVING BY AIR DRYING

Air drying is as simple as it sounds, and involves no special techniques or equipment. The drying period can range from a week to several months, depending on the type of material, when and where it was harvested, and the humidity of the place where it is drying. Dried flowers, however, tend to become rather brittle and those dried by being hung upside down can have unnaturally straight stems.

The most obvious choice is the everlasting flowers – members of the *Compositae* family, such as straw flowers, helipterums and xeranthemums, which originate in hot sunny climates and have paper-thin petals or petal-like bracts. These contain very little moisture and will often dry of their own accord in the garden.

Other suitable candidates include seed heads, such as honesty; the globe-shaped head of communal garden chives, onions and leeks; and the large, flat seed heads of members of the *Umbelliferae* family, such as cow parsley, or Queen Anne's lace, angelica and fennel. Large spiky seed heads include those of mullein and hollyhock. Grasses – both wild and ornamental – generally have much smaller seed heads but are also ideal for air drying.

Flowers with heads composed of many tiny blossoms, such as gypsophila, lady's mantle and achillea, are suitable, as are those whose beauty comes from petal-like bracts, such as acanthus; or leaf-like calyces, such as Chinese lantern or the woolly-grey *Helichrysum petiolatum*.

TECHNIQUE

The goal is to dry the plant material as quickly as possible, because the longer it takes a flower to dry, the more colour is lost. Warmth, protection from direct sunlight (which fades the colour of some flowers), a dry atmosphere and plenty of ventilation are necessary. Bunches of flowers might look nice hanging up to dry in a kitchen, but the steamy atmosphere can be counterproductive.

Attics or dark corners of unused rooms are possibilities, provided there is an adequate circulation of air. Outbuildings, such as garages or sheds, are usually damp and without adequate ventilation. The space used should also be dust free.

If you are drying flowers, strip the leaves as soon as possible after picking, as they retain moisture and slow down the drying process. They are also easier to remove when fresh than when brittle and dry. Large flowers should be dried individually, and bunches of flowers should ideally contain one type only, as drying times vary. The bunches should be small enough to allow the air to circulate freely and loose enough not to entangle or crush the inner flowers.

Drying time depends on the type and moisture content of the material and the conditions in which it is drying. Drying time for a particular plant can vary from one year to the next, depending on the weather. Material that is fully dry should feel crisp and the stems should snap. Check the 'neck' of the stem, just under the flower, as this is usually the last place to dry out. Stand a sample upright for a day or two; if it is still moist, the flower head will droop.

Because stems tend to shrink as they dry, it is often necessary to re-tie bunches or individual flowers part-way through the drying process. Stout twine is traditional, tied round the stems twice, so it is self adjusting, then in a bow. Rubber bands are also self adjusting, but they need to be attached to wire for hanging. Plastic-coated wire, such as garden ties and freezer bag ties, can also be used.

Suitable foliage for drying includes *Magnolia grandiflora*, silver artemisias, aspidistra and bamboos, which are actually giant grasses.

For drying flowers and foliage upside down, an old-fashioned wooden drying rail, which can be raised and lowered by a pulley, is useful in a high-ceilinged room. Alternatives include cup hooks fixed to the underside of beams; coat hooks or nails fixed to walls; telescopic wall hung towel rails; ordinary clothes lines; and the open trusses of an attic. If the truss is high, you can suspend wooden dowels, broom handles or even stout garden canes from it, to get a second level for drying. Chromium-plated dress rails, free-standing coat racks and hat racks are other possibilities. Bunches and single flowers can be hung on coat hangers first, to make maximum use of space.

Some flowers, such as astilbe, leeks, lady's mantle and goldenrod, and grasses can also be dried right-way-up, after being hung 'feet first' for a few days, to counteract the natural wilting that occurs. (Leeks, for example, entirely dried right-way-up develop a 'parting' at the top of the flower head.)

Chinese lanterns are best dried right-way-up from the start, so the lanterns don't finish pointing upwards. Hang the stem on a clothes line, using the uppermost lantern as a hook. Wire mesh on a wooden frame placed across two trestles can support single flower heads while the stems hang beneath. Bracken stems can be placed in a cardboard box or large jar, with the fronds free standing in their natural shapes.

Many of the straw flowers – xeranthemum and helipterum, for example – have flower heads heavier than the dried stems can support. These stems are usually cut short and the heads wired before being hung to dry. Because the stem shrinks around the wire the latter is fixed firmly in position. However, staining and rust sometimes result – this is particularly noticeable in pale-coloured flowers – and a sensible compromise is to wire up partially dried flowers, while the stems are drier but still flexible.

PRESERVING IN A MICROWAVE
This relatively new method has proved successful with miniature roses or those with clusters of small flowers, such as 'Dorothy Perkins', in tight bud, small-flowered gypsophila and grasses. Other flowers may respond well to this method, and it worth experimenting. Though the material must be air dried afterwards, microwaving speeds up the process and also helps retain colour.

TECHNIQUE
Strip away the foliage, then place the flowers or grasses in a single layer on several sheets of kitchen towel in the microwave. Use the medium setting (400–500W); three minutes is about right for gypsophila, and two and a half minutes for roses. Check after three minutes and replace the kitchen towel if it is soaked. Wipe the microwave after each use, as a lot of moisture is released. Remove the material, then hang it upside down, as for air drying, for about three days.

PRESERVING IN WATER
This is really a variation of preserving by drying in air. Suitable candidates include fully mature, almost papery, heads of hydrangea; bells of Ireland; proteas and heathers. Achillea is sometimes dried in this way, as are hosta leaves.

TECHNIQUE
Strip the leaves, then place the flower stem in 2.5–5cm (1–2in) of water and, ideally, in warmth, to dry as quickly as possible. Do not top up the water as it evaporates and is absorbed.

DRYING IN DESICCANTS
Drying flowers in a desiccant is the least predictable method of preservation, which is why such flowers are extremely expensive to buy. It is also a connoisseur's method which, when successful, produces exquisitely lifelike flowers, in both form and colour. Desiccated flowers are more fragile and more vulnerable to atmospheric moisture than those preserved by other methods, and are best displayed in airtight glass domes.

During desiccation, the water content of the flower is completely absorbed by the surrounding desiccant material. This can be silica gel, borax, alum, sand, or yellow cornmeal. Combinations of desiccants, such as equal parts by volume of cornmeal and borax, are sometimes used, as is clothes washing powder. Desiccants vary in weight and size of grain, and some are better for certain flowers than others. The desiccant should be heavy enough to keep the petals in position, as arranged, but light enough not to crush them. All desiccants can be re-used, provided that they are sieved regularly to remove any particles of dried flowers, and are thoroughly dried.

Silica gel is the most expensive desiccant, but gives the most reliable results. It is available from chemists and drug stores in both granular and powdered form; the granular form can be pulverized with a rolling pin or in a food processor to provide the alternative powder. Silica gel is the quickest acting desiccant; thin-petalled and delicate flowers, such as pansies, may only need one day. Dry such flowers in powdered silica gel. Other, more rigid and substantial flowers can be dried in the granular form, and can take up to three weeks.

Borax and alum are powdery, lightweight and relatively inexpensive, but tend to form lumps when damp. If a petal is slightly wet on the surface, borax and alum sometimes harden and crack, exposing the petals to air; for this reason it is sometimes mixed with a rough substance, such as cornmeal. Flowers take nearer a week than a day to dry.

Sand is an old-fashioned desiccant, which needs careful preparation before use. It must be fine grain, clean and free of silt or salt; commercially packaged river sand is best. Sand is relatively heavy, which

makes it unsuitable for many flowers, and takes a long time – up to three weeks – to thoroughly dry the flowers.

Suitable flowers include garden roses, zinnias, delphiniums, daffodils, dahlias, carnations, marigolds, camellias and pansies. All should be picked in perfect condition, just before fully mature and on a dry day. The time lapse between cutting and inserting in a desiccant should be as short as possible. Cut the stem to within 2.5cm (1in) of the head. You can insert a short length of wire into the remaining stem, or wire it after drying. If the stem is woody, insert the wire directly into the base of the flower. Remove any remaining leaves.

The desiccant must be dry to start with; some silica gel is sold with a humidity indicator, or turns a colour if damp. If necessary, spread the desiccant in a thin, even layer in a shallow roasting tin and warm it for half an hour in a low oven, 120°C/250°F/gas ½. Dry desiccant after each use in the same way.

Put a 2.5cm (1in) layer of desiccant in the bottom of a plastic storage box or biscuit tin. Gently turn each flower in the desiccant to coat it, then place the flowers in the desiccant, in a single layer and not touching one another. Most flowers dry best when placed head up; bend any wires as necessary. Lay delphiniums and other spiky flowers lengthways on the desiccant. Dry one type of flower at a time, as some flowers take longer than others.

Slowly pour a thin stream of desiccant over each flower, so that the space between every petal is filled and the flowers are covered. With open roses, carnations and dahlias, use a cocktail stick to separate the petals as you pour. Gently shake or tap the container from time to time, to get rid of any air pockets.

Continue sifting until there is a 2.5cm (1in) layer of desiccant over the flowers. Replace the lid tightly, then store in a warm, dry place. The warmer the desiccant, within reason, the quicker the drying, and the less colour loss. Desiccants, especially sand, are sometimes heated in a very low oven immediately before using; and sometimes a flower-filled box or pan is heated immediately after being prepared, to hasten the drying process. There is obviously potential for microwaving, although any experimenting should be done with care and in a plastic, glass or ceramic container; never experiment with material you are not prepared to lose.

Thin-petalled, small and single flowers take less time to dry than thick-petalled, large and double-flowered forms. When the approximate drying time is reached, slowly pour out the desiccant through your hands. Catch and inspect the first flower. If it feels papery, remove it and the others; if not return them for a few days to continue drying. A trick is to place one test flower slightly shallower than the others, but still covered, in the tin or plastic box, with a little marker. That way, it can be inspected without disturbing the others.

Flowers left too long in silica gel become very brittle and dark; those dried in other desiccants can be stored there without harm, although it is likely that the desiccant is needed for regular re-use.

Any desiccant clinging to the petals can be shaken away or brushed off with a fine paint brush.

PRESERVING WITH GLYCERINE AND ANTIFREEZE

Glycerine, diluted with water, is the traditional method for preserving mature foliage, especially beech, elaeagnus and eucalyptus. Glycerined material, whether whole branches or single leaves, retains its natural shape and flexibility, but glycerine is very expensive. Antifreeze diluted with water works in much the same way, and is less expensive. They are not, however, always interchangeable. Laurel leaves, for example, work well with antifreeze and not at all with glycerine.

Material treated with glycerine or antifreeze lasts indefinitely, and because of the leathery texture of the leaves, they can be dusted or even wiped with a damp cloth without risk.

Unlike air-dried material, which often retains much of its original colour, material treated with glycerine and antifreeze changes colour completely. Some material becomes pale and straw coloured, other materials turn a rich mahogany brown or almost black, and there are various hues in between. Material treated in the dark tends to be a darker, richer shade than the same material preserved in a bright, sunny spot. The yellow or blue dye in antifreeze has no effect on the resultant colour of the foliage.

TECHNIQUE

Choose only perfect leaves, and if preserving branches, remove any blemished or crowded leaves. To help stems take up the liquid, strip the bark off and split or crush the bottom 5cm (2in). Try to insert the stems into the preservative as soon as possible after cutting; if there is a delay, it is better to make a fresh cut. Foliage that is wilted before you start is high risk. To test whether a stem will take up glycerine or antifreeze, take a sample and stand it in water for a couple of hours; if the foliage wilts, discard it.

Dilute the glycerine or antifreeze with hot, or even boiling, water; the harder the stem, the hotter the water should be. Some people advocate two-thirds water to one-third glycerine or equal parts antifreeze and water, a proportion which is less expensive. As the glycerine is very thick, mix it thoroughly with water, or it will settle at the bottom of the container.

Choose a narrow, rather than a wide container, as only 7.5–10cm (3–4in) of preservative is needed. Narrow containers holding large branches may tip over, so support them if necessary. Top up the liquid as it is absorbed, making sure that it never dries out while the material is being preserved. Thick leaves can also be wiped with glycerine occasionally during the preserving process.

Large leaves, such as fatsia, mahonia, ivy and aspidistra, which are preserved individually, can also be floated in the solution of equal parts glycerine and cold water. Make sure they are fully submerged.

Glycerining or antifreezing can take from one to six weeks; generally, the thinner and smaller the leaf, the quicker it is preserved. Sometimes material – eucalyptus, for example – is very attractive before it is fully preserved, when only the veining is picked out in a contrasting colour. Semi-preserved foliage will not last indefinitely, though.

When the foliage feels smooth and has fully changed colour, and before drops of preservative appear on the leaf tips or surfaces, the material is finished. Because the preservative is absorbed up the stem, leaves at the top are the last to be preserved; it is best not to attempt very large branches, as the uppermost leaves may wilt before the preservative reaches them. Wiping the leaves with glycerine from time to time helps to prevent curling and wilting.

Foliage that droops or oozes glycerine or is 'overdone', is liable to go mouldy in storage, or continue oozing liquid if there is any moisture in the atmosphere. Clean the leaves by washing them in warm soapy water and dry thoroughly.

Cotoneaster berries and rose hips can also be preserved by placing the stems in diluted glycerine.

GUIDE TO PRESERVING INDIVIDUAL PLANTS

PLANT LATIN NAME	COMMON NAME	MATERIAL TYPE S = Seed head F = Flower L = Leaf B = Branch Material Type	RECOMMENDED TREATMENT PROCESS A = Air dry G = Glycerine T = Antifreeze P = Pressing Treatment Process	Special notes on harvesting
Acanthus spp	Acanthus	S	A	After flowering of top buds, when stem tip starts to harden
Acer saccharinum	Silver maple	L	A, G	Just before full autumn colouring, as leaves start to fall naturally, dry flat
Achillea spp	Achillea	F	A	Best bloom, before fully open and colour fades
Achillea millefolium	Yarrow or milfoil	F	A	Prime bloom, before whiteness fades
Acroclinium	Australian everlasting	F	A	Mid to full bloom, before all yellow centre stamens visible
Aegopodium podagravia	Ground elder	S	A	At full green seed head
Agrostis spp	Bent grass	F, S	A	Mature stem
Agrostemma githago	Corn cockle	S	A	After purple flower, seed head stage
Alchemilla mollis	Lady's mantle	F	A	Mid to full bloom before yellow fades
Allium schoenoprasum	Chive	F	A	Just at full purple bloom
Allium spp	Ornamental onion	F, S	A	Prime bloom petals all round the 'ball', or after petal fall at green seed stage
Allium spp	Leek	F, S	A	Prime bloom petals all round the 'ball', or after petal fall at green seed stage
Alopecurus pratensis	Meadow foxtail	F, S	A	In flower or after, at brightest green colour of stems
Althaea rosea	Hollyhock	F, S	A	Top stem flowers in bloom, fully formed green seed pods at bottom of stem
Alstroemeria spp	Alstroemeria	S	A	After petal fall, when green seed pods just coming to maturity (do not leave too late)
Ammobium alatum	Winged everlasting daisy	F	A	Two-thirds bloom open
Anemone hupehensis	Japanese anemone	S	A	After petal fall
Anthemus cupaniana	Chamomile shrub	F, L	A, G	Full leaf, and at fading flower, pluck out petals
Antirrhinum spp	Snapdragon	S	A	Seed pod stage, green stems turning to brown
Aquilegia × hybrida	Columbine	S	A	After flowering, mature green seed pods
Arctium lappa	Burdock	S	A	After flowering, and plant is fully mature at growing tips
Artemisia vulgaris	Mugwort	F, S	A	Mature plant at growing tips, still silver grey/green
Aruncus diolcus	Goat's beard	F, S	A	Immediately after flowering
Astilbe arendsii	False goat's beard	F, S	A	After flowering
Avena sativa	Oats (field)	S	A	Green fully formed ears, as green/yellow, and golden before corns drop
Barbarea spp	Sweet rocket	S, A	A	After petal fall, before seed pods split
Betula pendula	Silver birch	S, B	G	Catkin stage with leaves, or mature leaves only
Borago officinalis	Borage	S, F	A	At flowering, and past flowering
Brassica napus	Rape (field)	S	A	Green seed pod stage, or later green going brown, as seeds shatter
Briza media	Pearl/quaking grass	F, S	A	After flowering, as pearls fully develop, well before natural die back
Buddleia spp	Buddleia	S	A	At flowering, and as ripe brown, before seed pods split
Buxus sempervirens	Box	L, B	T	Mature leaves
Calendula officinalis	Pot marigold	S, F	A	Green mature seed formation, flower prime bloom
Campanula carpatica, persicifolia	Bellflower	S	A	After flowering, as pods turn green/buff, before seed pods open, or after opening

Carpinus betulus	Hornbeam keys	S	A	Mature, before natural shedding from tree
Catananche caerulea	Cupid's dart	F	A	Mid bloom
Centaurea cyanus	Cornflower	S, F	A	Flower half open to prime, or after petal fall for seed head only
Centaurea spp	Knapweed/hardhead	F, S	A	In mid flower, or pods dark nut brown
Chrysanthemum parthenium	Feverfew	F, S	A	Mid bloom, or late bloom and pluck out petals
Clarkia elegans	Clarkia	F, S	A	After flowering, when seed pods full but still green or later when dried brown and seeds shatter
Clematis spp	Clematis	S	A	Pick at whirl stage, before fluffs form
Clematis vitalba	Old man's beard	S	A	Pick when whirls formed, but not in fluff
Coriandrum sativum	Coriander	S	A	Seed pod stage
Cortaderia selloana	Pampas	F, S	A	As plumes protrude from stem tops, and before becoming fluffy
Crocosmia, masonorum	Montbretia	S, L	A	Seed pods going orange/brown; leaf mature
Cupressus spp	Cypress		A, T	Mature green fronds, or mature variegated fronds
Dactylis glomerata	Cocksfoot grass	F, S	A	After flowering, brightest green colour of heads
Daucus carota	Carrot (wild)	S	A	Naturally dried off, deep brown seed heads and stems
Delphinium hybrids spp	Delphinium	S	A	After petal fall, before seed turn dark brown and split
Delphinium spp	Larkspur	S	A	After petal fall, before seed turn dark brown and split
Dianthus barbatus	Sweet William	F	A	Head two-thirds open bloom
Digitalis purpurea	Foxglove	S	A	After flowering, green maturing brown stems, before seed shatter
Dispacus spp	Teasel	S	A	Green turning brown, late after frost dark brown as seeds disperse
Dronicum cordatum	Leopard's bane	S	A	Pluck out petals for green seed back; hang dry upside down
Echinops ritro	Echinops	S	A	Just after blue flowering, as thistle ball spikes become mature
Eleagnus spp	Elaeagnus	L	A, T	Mature leaf at growing tips
Erigeron spp	Garden fleabane	F, S	A	In flower
Endymion non-scriptus	Bluebell	S	A	Crisp brown seeds and stems, at seed dispersement
Epilobium angustifolium	Rosebay willowherb	F, S	A	Quick dry in purple full bloom, or cut at green seed stage, before fluffing occurs
Erica, spp calluna vulgaris	Heather (wild garden)	F	A, G, T	Just before full bloom
Eryngium spp	Sea holly	F, S	A	Mature stems, mid to full bloom, and when dried off naturally
Eschscholzia californica	Eschscholzia	S	A	Green fully formed seed stage
Eucaluptus spp	Eucalyptus/gum tree	L	G	Mature leaf up majority of stem
Euonymus europaaeus	Spindle berry	S	A	Mature pink seed pods, do not leave too late
Fagus sylvatica	Beech (copper/green)	L, B	G	Mature leaves
Fagus sylvatica	Beech nuts	S	A	Mature, before natural splitting and seed shatter
Foeniculum vulgare	Fennel	F, S	A	Green seed stage
Fraximus excelsior	Ash keys	S	A	Mature, as natural shedding from tree starts
Galeopsis tetrahit	Common hempnettle	S	A	After flowering, fully mature and natural leaf drop stage
Geranium ibericum	Crane's bill	S, F	A	After petal fall, stems turning green/brown
Godetia grandiflora	Godetia	F, S	A	After flowering, when seed pods full but still green or later when dried brown and seeds shatter
Hedera spp	Ivy	L	A, T	Mature leaf
Helichrysum bracteatum	Straw flower	F	A	Full bloom, before yellow centre stamens too visible
Helipterum, manglesii	Helipterum daisy	F	A	In mid to full bloom, before all yellow centre too visible
Helleborus spp	Hellebore	F, L	T	Full green flower, or mature leaf
Heracleum sphondylium	Hogweed, cow parsnip	S	A	Mature, green/brown, before seeds disperse; later at brown dead stage
Holcus lanatus	Yorkshire fog	F, S	A	Pink flowering stage for colour, or buff colour naturally dried off
Hordeum vulgare	Barley (field)	S	A	Green fully formed ears, as green/yellow, but before heads turn over
Humulus lupulis	Hop	F	A	Flowers pale green in mid to full bloom, only small buds remain on stem tops
Hydrangea spp	Hydrangea	F	A	Cut as petals start to feel papery
Hypericum calycinum	St Johns wort	S	A	Black seed stage, brown mature leaf
Iberis saxatilis	Candytuft	S	A	When naturally dried off, at seed stage
Ipomea hybrids	Morning glory	S	A	Seed pod stage, green going brown
Iridaceae	Iris	S	A	Ripe seed pod, before seed shatter
Lagurus ovatus	Hare's tail	F, S	A	After flowering, as green tails, or silver/green tails when more mature
Lapsana communis	Nipplewort	S	A	Mature, going brown, at seed shatter stage
Lavandula angustifolia	Lavender	F	A	Mid to prime bloom
Leucanthemum vulgare	Oxeye daisy	F, S	A	Mid to full bloom before white petals discolour, or pluck out for seed back only
Ligustrum ovalifolium	Privet	L, B	T	Mature leaves
Limonium sinuatum	Statice	F	A	Mid to best bloom, before head fully open
Linum usitatissimum	Common flax	F, S	A	Past flowering, when yellow seed case becomes fully visible

Lunaria	Honesty	S	A	Green seed pods stage, or fully mature, when seed case opens, silver centre exposed
Lychnis dioica	Campion	S	A	Pods mature, green, going brown, before seed shatter
Lychnis spp	Rose campion	S	A	After flowering, and starting to dry naturally. For silver colouring do not leave too long
Lysimachia punctata	Yellow loosestrife	F, S	A	After flowering
Lythrum salicaria	Purple loosestrife	S	A	After petal fall, with good autumn brown colour of stem
Mahonia spp	Mahonia	L	A, T	Mature leaf, or in autumn colours
Matricaria recutita	Mayweed	S, F	A	Prime bloom
Mentha spp	Garden mint	F	A	Two-thirds stem in prime bloom
Moluccella laevis	Bells of Ireland	F	G	Just maturing, green
Muscari spp	Grape hyacinth	S	A	Crisp buff colour and seeds shed
Nigella damascena	Love-in-a-mist	F, S	A	At full bloom, mature green seed pod stage, before splitting, or brown ripe as seeds shatter
Oenothera spp	Evening primrose	S	A	Mature green tip of stems, or going brown and seed pods opening
Origanum vulgare	Marjoram (wild)	S	A	Mid pink bloom for three-quarters of stem, do not leave too late, as flowers become fluff
Papaver spp	Poppy	S	A	Fully formed green seed pod, before splitting
Pastinaca sativa	Parsnip (wild)	S	A	After flowering, before browning and seeds shed from stems
Petroselinum crispum	Parsley	L, F	A	Prime bloom, and mature green leaf
Phalaris arundinacea	Canary grass	F, S	A	After flowering, as tops are good green, before turning to beige
Phleum pratense	Cat's tail/timothy	F, S	A	In flower or after, at brightest green colour of stems
Physalis alkekenji	Chinese lantern	F	A	Orange pod stage, do not leave too late for good colours
Phragmites communis	Great reed	F, S	A	In flower
Plantago lanceolata	Ribwort	S	A	After flowering, at green seed stage
Plantago media	Hoary plantain	S	A	After flowering, at green seed stage
Polygonatum multiflorum	Solomon's seal	F, S	G	Mature stem
Polygonum bistorta	Bistort	F	A	Full pink bloom
Polygonum persicaria	Redshank, willow weed	F, S	A	Prime flower, and well before seed shatter
Prunus laurocerasus	Laurel	L, B	T	Mature leaves
Pyrethrum spp	Pyrethrum	S	A	After flowering, or pluck out faded petals
Rheum rhaponticum	Rhubarb	F,S	A	At full flower, or immediately after
Rosmarinus officinalis	Rosemary	L, F	A, T	Mature leaf, or early flowering
Rudbeckia spp	Rudbeckia (annual)	S	A	At full/past bloom, pluck out petals, retain brown centre knob only
Rudbeckia laciniata	Rudbeckia (perennial)	S	A	After petal fall, seed head hard dark green/brown
Rumex spp	Sorrel	F, S	A, G, T	At flowering, and good colour red/brown seed stage, well before natural seed shatter
Rumex crispus	Curled dock	F, S	G, T	Mature stem, good colour seeds, before fully ripe
Rumex obtusifolius	Dock (field)	F, S	G, T	Flowers mature good colour red/brown seeds, well before dispersement
Salvia officinalis	Sage	F, S	A	Full purple flower, or after flower for seed pod stage
Santolina chamaecyparissus	Lavender cotton	F	A	At yellow flower ball stage
Scabiosa hybrid	Paper moon scabious	S	A	Seed head 'parachute' ball fully formed, before natural die back
Secale cereale	Rye (field)	S	A	Mature green heads, or later as green going yellow before seeds shed naturally
Sedum spp	Stonecrop	S	A	After flowering, when leaves start to drop from stem, and mauve/red colour of head still evident
Silene spp	Campion (red/white)	S	A	Pod mature green, going brown, before seed shatter
Sinapis alba	White mustard	S	A	Green seed stage
Sisyrinchium striatum	Satin flower	S	A	Flowering stems turn from green to brown, at seed disbursement
Solidago canadensis	Golden rod	F	A	Mid to prime bloom
Sparganium erectum	Blanched bur reed	F, S	A	At full flowering
Spiraea × *billiardii* 'Trimphans'	Spiraea	F, S	A	Mid bloom or just mature; quick dry to hold pink colour
Stachys tanata	Lamb's tongue	S	A	Brown seed stage
Tagetes erecta	French marigold	F, S	A	In mid to full bloom, or green seed head stage
Tanacetum vulgare	Tansy	F, S	A	Mid to full bloom before yellow fades to ochre, or later when brown head
Tripleurospermum maritimum	Mayweed	S, F	A	Past bloom, pluck out faded petals, keep yellow centres
Triticum aestirum	Wheat (field)	S	A	Green milk ear stage, as green/yellow, and golden before corns drop
Typha latifolia	Great reed mace	F, S	A	Best when small portion of stem top still protrudes above brown swelling
Various ferns spp	Ferns (woodland)	L	A, P	Mature green at growing tip, before spores set on underside
Veronica longifolia/spicata	Speedwell	F, S	A	In mid flower, and after flowering as spikes turn good brown
Xeranthemum abbum	Everlasting flower	F	A	Mid to perfect bloom
Zea mays	Corn on the cob (maize)	S	A	After tassel, at harvest of mature cobs, with pale green going gold husks

Appendix II

Making Silk Flowers

Equipment and Materials

The basic equipment needed for silk and ribbon flowermaking is not specialized and consists of items which you probably have already for other purposes or can obtain quite easily. The marking and cutting equipment is as follows:

Transparent plastic ruler: marked with metric or metric/Imperial measurements.

Pencil: to mark measurements on the ribbons. Choose one which is neither too hard nor too soft, to avoid either scoring the ribbon surface or discolouring it with the pencil lead.

Craft scissors: with wire-cutting edges at the centre of the blades. Alternatively, you can equip yourself with medium-sized sharp scissors and a separate pair of wire cutters. Pliers are occasionally useful for bending heavy stem wires to shape and these often incorporate wire-cutting blades.

For texturing petals you can obtain a special set of heads that can be fixed to a soldering iron, but much of the texturing can be done by hand if necessary.

Making Flowers from Silk

Fabric flowers are commonly called silk flowers although often the fabric from which they are made is not real silk. The examples shown here are made from specially manufactured flowermaking ribbons. If you wish to create the flowers from silk, it is necessary to treat the material to prevent it from fraying, using the following recipe:

Boil 900ml (30fl oz/1.0 US pints) of water in a saucepan. Mix 15g (½oz) starch with 1 teaspoon of water. Add to the boiling water and stir until it thickens. Leave to cool slightly and add 20g (¾oz) glue. Brush the mixture over the silk.

Flowermaking Ribbons

The materials used to make the flowers illustrated are ribbons of various weights and textures: all consist of man-made fibres and are treated to resist fraying. Their qualities are specially designed for flowermaking and they should be obtained from a craft shop or by mail order. Hair and dressmaking ribbons are not always acceptable substitutes as some are likely to fray easily and may not give the required effect.

Flowermaking ribbons are available in a wide range of colours and finishes, so that almost any type of flower can be simulated.

Acetate ribbon: is satin-faced on one side and matt-textured on the other. It is a firmly woven ribbon with a resin finish. It is normally used to show the satin side but the matt side is sometimes displayed to create particular effects. Green acetate is frequently used for leaves and sepals, and the lovely yellows, pinks and reds are ideal for rose petals.

Shaded acetate ribbon is also available. This has two bands of colour running lengthwise, one band is white or cream and the other a stronger hue. The colours merge at the centre of the ribbon.

Lantern ribbon: is a firm acetate ribbon with pre-cut vertical slits which enable it to be used for making very fine petals and effects of loose fringing.

Silky ribbon: is the most versatile flowermaking material, used for a wide variety of petals, florets, buds and leaves. It is a fine, lightweight ribbon available in a wide range of beautiful colours.

There are various types of silky ribbon which are used to imitate the particular colours and textures of natural flowers. Shaded silky ribbon has two colour bands running lengthwise which merge at the centre of the ribbon. One band is white or cream and the other a distinct colour. There is also a version of this ribbon with very subtle colour gradation from light to dark and a decorative metallic shaded ribbon with woven-in gold or silver lurex threads.

Two-colour silky ribbon is similar to the shaded ribbon but the bands are both distinct colours, again merging at the centre, so the colour variation is not necessarily from light to mid-tone or dark. This is available in two degrees of colour gradation, one slightly more subtle than the other.

Another variation of silky ribbon is a beautiful marble-effect shading of the colours.

Velvet silky ribbon: has a smooth pile, or nap, on one side and should be used to show the velvet side. It is used to imitate the richness of texture in some natural petals, such as those of magnolia.

Organdy ribbon: is finer than silky, available in plain colours with one band of white or cream.

Poplin ribbon: is firmer than silky but less heavy than acetate. It is available in plain and shaded colours and has a silky sheen.

Cotton ribbon: is slightly heavier than poplin and has a matt finish. It is available in a range of lovely colours.

Seal ribbon: is a relatively heavy ribbon of ribbed velvet on one side.

PRE-FORMED MATERIALS

Tiny florets, such as those in forget-me-not flowerheads, are available in pre-cut form and they can be shaped by moulding with a heated tool (see page 220). These pre-cut florets are very useful for making up delicate sprays and posies to be inserted as fillers in arrangements or in decorative sprays made mainly with larger flowers.

Individual pre-formed leaves are available in different ribbon types for certain flowers. Rose leaves are made from green velvet, metallic or silky ribbon, chrysanthemum leaves from velvet ribbon, and poppy leaves from seal ribbon.

Ivy, caladium, geranium and spotted laurel leaves are obtainable in the form of printed rolls. The individual leaves are cut to shape and reinforced with wire before they are applied to a flower stem or inserted in an arrangement. The printed leaf patterns, as well as providing a realistic effect in individual flower stems or sprays, contribute a useful extra element to the design of a silk flower arrangement.

STAMENS

There are several different types of ready-made flower stamens – round- or pointed-tipped, dull, pearlized, frosted, sparkle or gloss finish – in various sizes and a range of colours. Stamens are usually supplied as double-headed strings which can be cut or doubled over to form short-stemmed stamens, with the exception of lily stamens, which have long stems and a single head.

CONSTRUCTION MATERIALS

The following materials are in constant use when you are making silk flowers and it is advisable to acquire a good stock of the items you will need.

STEM TAPE

This is the tape commonly used by florists and is directly adaptable to silk flowermaking. It is a strong, flexible paper tape impregnated with a substance that makes it self-adhesive. Stem tape is used to cover stem wires and to fasten components of the flowers together. There are several shades of green and brown for use on stems, and also a range of lovely colours. From time to time you will need stem tape matching the flower colour in order to neaten flower bases, bind stamen stems and make buds of flower centres.

WIRES

Several different thicknesses of wire are used in silk flowermaking. They are specified in the flowermaking instructions by the British Standard Gauge number.

Uncovered wires: are used in gauges 30, 22, 20 and 18. The 30-gauge wire is relatively fine and is used for wiring petals and fastening flowers and leaves to stems. The lower gauges are mainly used as stem wires. All these wires are sold in standard gauges but the wire is covered with paper of a particular colour. Green or white covered wires are available in gauges 33, 30, 28, 26 and 24. Light green, pink, red, wine red, beige, brown, blue and yellow are available in 26-gauge only.

Padded craft wire: in 16-gauge is useful for making thick stems and simulating branches, if covered with an appropriate colour of stem tape.

ADHESIVE MATERIALS

Because you are working with fine materials and often on a small scale, it is essential that adhesive materials are not only effective in their adhesive property but also give a clean finish.

Flowermaking adhesive: is a white polyvinyl compound which becomes transparent as it dries. Proprietary brands are available in small bottles or tubes, or in tins. However, you will need to use very little at one time and it is important that the container is properly sealed when not in use.

Double-sided adhesive tape: is obtained by the roll, like ordinary adhesive tape, but because it is a very fine film which is adhesive on both sides, it is backed by a paper strip. This must be removed after the tape is applied to one component and just before another component or material is attached. It is effective in securing together two pieces of ribbon, with or without a reinforcing wire in between. It is available in 5mm ($^3/_{16}$in), 24mm ($1^5/_{16}$in) and 36mm ($1^7/_{16}$in) widths.

BASIC TECHNIQUES

This chapter describes all the flowermaking techniques which recur in the instructions for individual flowers. These are the basic skills of silk flowermaking and if you are new to the craft, it may be helpful to try out these techniques before you start to make the flowers. Where a special technique is needed to create a particular effect, this is explained in the step-by-step instructions.

CUTTING

Shapes can be cut from ribbon either freehand or by using a template. Freehand cutting is quicker and produces a more natural result. The use of templates is perfectly acceptable and is probably advisable with some of the more complicated shapes until you feel confident of cutting accurately. Templates of the main components of each flower are provided on the relevant pages.

In order to reduce material wastage to a minimum, it is important to consider the most economical way of cutting the ribbon before you start making the flower. The width of many flowermaking ribbons is 72mm ($2^1{}_3/{}_1{}_6$ in) and, wherever possible, the size given for a petal or leaf is calculated on a proportion of this measurement which will allow you to cut shapes side by side across the width of the ribbon. If you are working with ribbons larger or smaller than 72mm ($2^1{}_3/{}_1{}_6$ in) width, it should be possible to make minor adjustments to achieve a petal or leaf of suitable size and proportions.

For some single or multiple elements, such as narrow leaves or multi-tipped petals, the simplest way to cut them is to fold a large piece of ribbon into the appropriate number of sections and cut a single shape out of the folded layers.

When cutting a petal or leaf, it is best to start at the tip. Follow the steps shown, turning the ribbon as indicated to arrive at the final outline. Keep the cutting action smooth; this is particularly important when cutting rounded shapes. Hold the scissors straight and, using the full length of the blades, feed the ribbon steadily into the scissors.

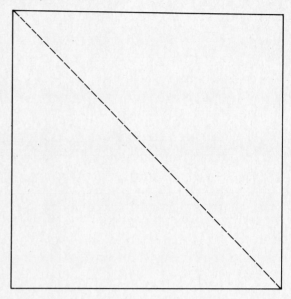

Five-point fold

Fold the square along the diagonal to form a triangle

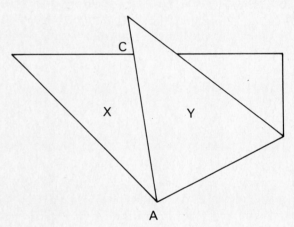

Fold along line AC to bring X behind Y

FIVE-POINT FOLD

Many petals and calyces have five segments to the overall shape. It can be difficult to cut these freehand but there is a simple technique of folding the ribbon which simplifies the cutting and creates a uniform shape. The instructions are based on a 72mm ($2^1{}_3/{}_1{}_6$ in) square but you can adjust the dimensions

Cutting petals and leaves

1st cut	2nd cut	3rd cut	4th cut	petal/leaf shape
petal tip	turn over	turn over		

218

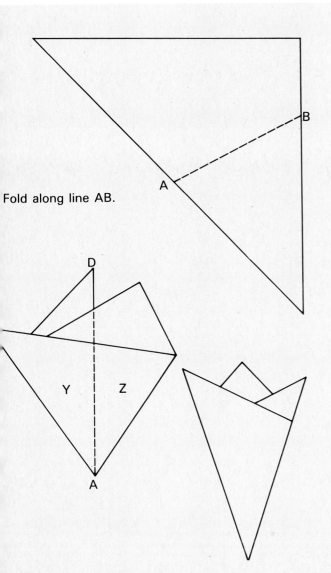

Fold along line AB.

Fold along line AD to bring Y over on to Z, making the more compact shape shown right

throughout to work on a larger or smaller scale. With practice, you will find it easy to make the folds; it is advisable to try out the technique with thin paper before using the ribbon.

Where the five-point fold is used in making a particular flower, a diagram is provided, marked with the cutting line for the individual component.

STRETCHING

Many flowers have frilled or fluted petals. To achieve this effect, stretch the ribbon just inside the edge of the petal between your finger and thumbs. The most pronounced flare is achieved if the petal is damp. However, care is needed, as it is possible to tear the ribbon, especially when stretching on a cut edge.

TEXTURING

Flower petals and leaves show different qualities of form and texture which are part of their natural growth patterns. In ribbon flowermaking, special techniques of texturing are used to simulate these qualities, to give a natural-looking result in the finished flower. Several of these techniques can be done either by hand or using a heated tool designed for the purpose.

CUPPING

Cupping of petals, for example in the rose or poppy, is best achieved if the petal is bias-cut across the grain of the ribbon. Hold the centre of the petal between thumbs and forefingers and pull against the bias. When wiring a cupped petal, emphasize the shape as you gather the ribbon at the base.

ROLLING

Roll the edge of a petal over a short length of heavy wire or a fine knitting needle. Withdraw the wire and alternately roll and pull the curled edge until it automatically springs back into place when released. Rose petals require this effect.

CURLING

Petals, leaves and fringing can be curled by drawing the ribbon firmly across the closed blades of a pair of scissors.

CRINKLING

In nature, many petals and leaves have a crinkled texture running across the whole surface. This can be created by either of two methods:
DAMP CLOTH METHOD (see overleaf, left) Use a handkerchief or piece of lightweight cotton fabric. Dampen the cloth and spread it on the work surface. Fold the petal (or leaf) in half lengthwise and place it on the cloth. Fold the cloth down over the petal.

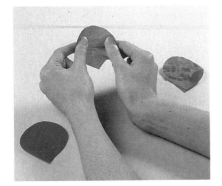
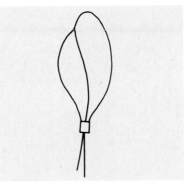
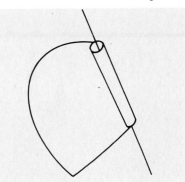

Place the heel of one hand firmly on the covered petal. Gather the corner of the cloth in the other hand and pull slowly but firmly through 180 degrees, maintaining firm pressure on the petal.

If you are working with a thick material, such as flocked ribbon, it is best to use a heavier cloth; a damp facecloth is particularly effective.

SPIRAL TWIST METHOD (below centre) Fold the petal or leaf in half along its length and twist it into a spiral. Hold it firmly to press in the crinkled texture, then open it right out.

Both of these methods should be applied before reinforcing a petal or leaf with wire, as the wire may be dislodged during the process. However, if the item is fully lined and the wire is secured between two layers of ribbon, the crinkling can be applied to the completed petal or leaf (below right).

TOOLING

A soldering iron fitted with special flowermaking heads can be used to texture petals and leaves. There are two mushroom heads for cupping medium-sized and large petals, and a ball head for cupping small petals (facing page, left). A blade head is used for marking veins on petals or leaves. Of the two heads with curved tips, one is smooth, for making a channel or curling a petal over on itself; the other is ridged, for making a furrowed channel or parallel veins. The rose-petal curling head is a curved, pointed tool used for curling petal edges (facing page, centre). The forget-me-not head is a small curved mould which can be impressed on the shape of very small pre-formed petals.

When using the heated tool, it is best to work on a heat-resistant tray or on a well-protected table or work surface. You will need a soldering iron stand or a heatproof dish and a soft fabric pad about 150mm (5⅞ in) wide, filled with down or foam.

Select the head required and fit it to the shaft of the soldering iron. Make sure the screw is secure. Switch on the iron and leave it to heat.

When tooling a petal or leaf, lay the ribbon on the pad before applying the heated tool.

Cupping   Press the selected tool head on the ribbon for a few seconds. If the area to be cupped is large, move the head around a little to cover the area required.

Veining   Draw the blade head firmly along the ribbon to draw the line of the vein; usually, you should work from the outer edge towards the centre of the leaf or petal.

Channelling   Depending upon the position of the channel, draw the smooth curved head down the petal or leaf from top to bottom, or around the outer edge. If you move the tool slowly through the centre of the shape, the whole petal will curl over.

To make a ridged channel, draw the ridged curved head across the ribbon in the required position. This technique can also be used to mark parallel veins or to curl the whole petal over.

Rolling and curling   Firmly stroke the edges of the petal with the rose-petal curling tool from the outer edge inwards.

Moulding   Simply hold the forget-me-not head on the petal to mould the shape. It normally takes just a few seconds to texture with the heated tool heads and care must be taken not to burn the ribbon by holding the head on it for too long. When working with some intricately cut petals, it may be helpful to put one or two plain pins through them to anchor them in position on the pad.

When you finish working with a tool head, switch off the electricity supply to the tool, unscrew the head and put it into the heatproof dish to cool. Always leave the heated tool on a stand or in the heatproof dish until it has cooled completely.

REINFORCING AND LINING

It is often necessary to reinforce a petal or leaf because of its size, or the way it 'sits' on the flowerhead or stem. A simple way to do this is by sticking a wire on the back of the ribbon; this wire can then be gently curved to achieve the desired effect. The ribbon may be lined to strengthen it or to provide a different texture on one side of a petal or leaf; for example, a silky lining on the underside of a velvet leaf.

REINFORCING

Cut a length of covered wire a little longer than the petal or leaf. Apply adhesive to the underside of the wire and lay this on the wrong side of the piece of ribbon, starting about 5mm (³⁄₁₆ in) from the top. Make sure the wire is on the side of the ribbon which

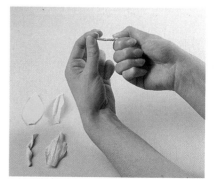

will not be visible in the finished flower. Instructions for individual flowers state which is the correct side.

If an individual stem is required for a flower or leaf, cut the reinforcing wire to about twice the length of the petal or leaf shape and adjust the length when taping it to a main stem.

STRIP-LINING

To strip-line a petal or leaf, cut a narrow strip of ribbon to match the shape and apply narrow double-sided adhesive tape to this. Peel the backing paper from the tape and lay a piece of covered wire on it, about 5mm ($\frac{3}{16}$ in) below the top of the strip. Lay the wired strip on the petal or leaf and press down firmly to attach the adhesive tape.

FULL-LINING

In full-lining, a wire is sandwiched between two layers of ribbon which are stuck together with flowermaking adhesive or double-sided tape. The leaf or petal shape is cut after lining.

Lay double-sided adhesive tape over the whole area of one piece of ribbon, making sure it is on the wrong side if using velvet silky or acetate ribbon. Press the reinforcing wire down on the tape, then cover it with the second piece of ribbon and smooth this down firmly.

With fine or lightweight ribbons, it is not always necessary to attach the full shape of the lining piece. The reinforcing wire can be attached to a strip of double-sided tape running down the centre of the leaf or petal and the lining can also be attached to this strip only.

When positioning reinforcing wires on petals or leaves, make sure the top of the wire is at least 5mm ($\frac{3}{16}$ in) from the edge of the ribbon, otherwise it is noticeable in the finished flower. If using a heavy gauge wire for reinforcing, allow twice that measurement to ensure that the tip of the wire does not show.

USING ADHESIVE

Flowermaking adhesive is specially formulated for use with ribbons. It cannot be softened once it has begun to dry, so it is essential to keep the lid on the container when you are not using the adhesive.

To apply the adhesive, put a small blob on a matchbox top, or on the back of your hand if you are right-handed, or vice versa. Make a hook at the top of a piece of wire and use this as an applicator to transfer the adhesive to the ribbon. Be careful not to apply too much or the excess will ooze out between glued sections. If the ribbon pieces to be stuck together are large, then it is easier to squeeze the adhesive out of the bottle directly onto the centre of one piece and use the wire hook to spread it.

To stick two pieces of ribbon together, press them firmly between your fingers. To stick wire to ribbon, gently dot the underside of the wire into the blob of adhesive on your hand, so that only the underside of the wire is wet, position it on the ribbon and hold it in place for about 30 seconds.

Do not continue work with the wired ribbon until the adhesive has dried; this usually takes about 30 minutes.

USING DOUBLE-SIDED ADHESIVE TAPE

Double-sided tape is ideal for sticking two pieces of ribbon together, for example, when making fully-lined petals or leaves. The tape must be kept in a plastic bag when not in use, otherwise it will dry out and lose its adhesive property.

When making a fully-lined leaf or petal (below, right), lay one piece of ribbon on the table or worktop and carefully place on it a strip of double-sided tape of the appropriate width and length. Press it down firmly, especially at the corners, and peel off the backing paper. Immediately place the second piece of ribbon on top, making sure that you apply it smoothly. Do not remove the backing paper from the tape until you have the second piece of ribbon ready to be applied. The adhesive tape attracts dust and fibres very quickly and if left exposed will become dirty and lose its adhesion.

If you are applying a reinforcing wire to the ribbon, put this in place as soon as you remove the backing paper from the tape and cover it with the piece of lining ribbon immediately. Smooth down the ribbon to cover the wire cleanly.

When you are working with fine ribbons, a narrow strip of double-sided tape holds quite large pieces of ribbon together effectively. Lay a strip of 5mm ($\frac{3}{16}$ in) tape down the centre of the ribbon shape. Press down firmly, then remove the backing paper

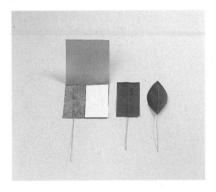

and place the second piece of ribbon on top. If this shape is to be reinforced with wire, lay the length of wire in position before the second piece of ribbon is applied.

TAPING

Stem tape is used to cover bare wires and provide a neat finish to stems, and for fastening together several parts of a flower during construction. The tape is used full-width, half-width, and sometimes quarter-width. To make half-width tape, peel a few layers of tape from the roll, press them evenly together and cut lengthwise through the centre. If you require quarter-width tape, divide one of the batches of half-width tape again in the same way.

If you have never used stem tape before, it is best to practise using full-width tape. Stretch a short length at one end of the tape and lay it across the top of a stem wire. Squeeze the tape onto the wire. Hold the wire in one hand and the tape in the other at an acute angle to the wire. Roll the wire into the tape, making sure that the tape is stretched as it is applied. This reduces the quantity of tape needed and makes a neat finish.

When assembling some flowers, or grouping flowers into a plant or spray, separate wires are taped together to form the main stem. To avoid the wires becoming twisted during taping, it is advisable to secure them firstly by rolling a little tape around all the wires at intervals up the stem. They will not then slip out of place or twist as you tape the whole stem.

Always keep stem tape in a plastic bag to prevent it from drying out.

WIRING

Four main methods of wiring are used to gather and secure the bases of petals or leaves, to assemble them in sequence, or to attach them to a stem. A fine and flexible wire is needed, usually 30-gauge wire.

Hairpin method (below left) This is suitable for wide-based petals and leaves or those made from a thick material such as flocked or velvet silky ribbon.

Make a hairpin shape with 30-gauge uncovered wire (above right) and place this around the base of the petal or leaf, about 10mm (⅜in) above the bottom edge of the ribbon. It is important to keep this allowance of ribbon even.

Starting from the left-hand side of the shape, make small, even gathers in the ribbon. It is important to maintain tension on the wires while doing this, which you can achieve by winding the wires around your fingers. Secure the petal by holding the two lengths of wire tightly and turning the petal over to twist the wire. Bring the ends of the wire down to form a stem and tape for a length of about 20mm (1³⁄₁₆in).

Wiring in sequence It is often necessary to link petals together before arranging them on a stem. There are two methods of wiring in sequence.

Single-row sequence (below centre) Take two lengths of 30-gauge wire and hold them horizontally a little apart. Twist the two wires together towards one end, leaving about 100mm (3¹⁵⁄₁₆in) free at the side, with the greater length of the wires extending on the other side. Hold the greater lengths of wire slightly apart and insert a petal. Gather the base of the petal neatly. Hold the two lengths of wire firmly and turn the petal to secure the wire.

Open the wire back to one twist after the first petal and insert the second petal next to the first, making sure the allowance of ribbon below the wire is even. Repeat the process of wiring until all the petals are secured by the wires. Each petal should slightly overlap the one before at the broadest part. When the sequence is complete, hold the wires firmly where the last petal is fastened and turn the linked petals to secure the wires. Do not cut the wires.

To maintain tension in the wires, wrap the long lengths around your fingers while gathering the petal bases. Alternatively, you can apply this method using a single length of wire bent to form a loop at one end. Twist the looped end and insert the petals as described above. It may help to maintain tension on the wires if you hook your little finger into the loop of wire. This method is suitable for wiring small numbers of petals, particularly if the petals are small and delicate.

Double-row sequence (below right) Use 30-gauge wire to link the petals as described in the single-row sequence but create the double row by positioning the petals very closely together, alternately in front of or behind the one before.

Twisting method This is a method of securing individual components together and is particularly suitable for narrow-based petals or leaves. It is very

useful when adding a leaf, calyx or bract directly to a stem or flowerhead.

To join a leaf to a stem by this method, hold the base of the leaf against the stem and place a short end of 30-gauge wire against the leaf. Hold the wire end and leaf in position with your thumb and firmly wind the long end of 30-gauge wire once or twice around the stem. To secure the leaf, hold the long and short ends of wire together and twist them by turning the stem. Trim the wires and cover the ends with a stem tape.

The same procedure may be used to attach petals to a flower centre or stem tip.

MAKING FLOWER CENTRES

Some flower centres are almost concealed by the petals, while others are an important aspect of the flower's visual attraction. Whichever is the case, it is important to form the flower centre correctly as it is the basis of the way the petals are grouped and attached to the stem. Pre-formed stamens are used in most flower centres. Fringing is also frequently needed to create the right effect. The button centre is appropriate for flowers with flat, open faces. Special variations are given with the step-by-step instructions.

Stamen centre (below centre) Stamens are supplied as double-headed strings. Normally, to make a flower centre the stamen strings are folded in half and a piece of 30-gauge wire is passed through the loop to fasten them together. The two ends of the wire are secured by holding them firmly and twisting the stamens, and are then neatened with stem tape, full- or half- width depending on the thickness of the bunch of stamens.

If a long stem is required for the stamen centre, one head is cut off the stamen string to utilize the full length. The cut ends of the stamens are secured by the twisting method, using 30-gauge wire. The wire base is neatened with half-width stem tape.

Large stamens can be made from uncovered wire by taping the top of the wire with coloured stem tape to make a little ball, then taping down the wire to form the stamen stem. To make a cluster of wire stamens, tape or wire them together at the bottom of the stems.

Fringed centre (below right) A piece of ribbon is fringed by cutting vertically from one long edge at narrow intervals, leaving an uncut base strip along the opposite edge of the ribbon. Place a piece of double-sided adhesive tape along the uncut strip (or this can be applied before you cut the fringing).

To attach a fringed centre to a stem, take a length of stem wire taped down about 30mm ($1\,^3/_{16}$ in) of its length, or use covered wire, and form the top of the wire into a hook. Remove the backing paper from the double-sided tape attached to the fringe, hook the wire into the fringe and squeeze tightly. Roll the fringed strip firmly and evenly around the wire hook, keeping the top and bottom edges level. Fasten the base with 30-gauge wire and tape over and down the wire with coloured stem tape.

Button centre The size of the button depends upon the size of the flower but normally one slightly larger than a shirt button will do. Bend a length of 30-gauge wire into a hairpin shape and thread it through two holes in the button. Hold the two ends of wire under the button and twist the button to secure the wires. Cover the button completely with full-width stem tape in the appropriate colour. Join in a stem wire and secure the join with stem tape.

THICKENING STEMS

It is sometimes necessary to thicken the full length of a stem, or the end near the flower centre, or at the leaf nodes, as for the carnation (see page 229). This can be done by applying several layers of stem tape, by adding more wires and taping them, or by winding 10mm ($3/8$ in) strips of tissue tightly around the taped stem. Tissue thickening should be finished by covering the stem with full-width stem tape.

ASSEMBLING

There are various methods of assembly which depend on the size and construction of the flower, and the number of components to be assembled.

Petals and leaves which have been wired and taped individually can be held in position around a flower centre or on a stem and taped in place directly with stem tape. It is not necessary to use wire to secure them.

Leaves or bracts which have not been individually wired are usually attached to a stem or flowerhead by the twisting method.

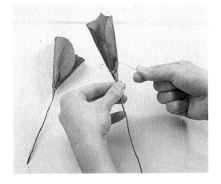

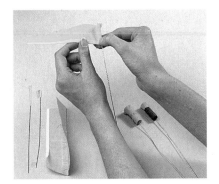

Petals wired in sequence are attached to the flower centre using the ends of the wires that link the petals, the flower centre being already attached to a stem wire. Hold the ring of petals around the flower centre, bring the short ends of wire down the flower stem and wrap the long ends right around petals and centre at the base of the flower, just above the wire linking the petals. Pull tightly and bring the short ends of wire up to meet the long ends. Twist the flowerhead to secure. Care should be taken to ensure that the allowances of ribbon at the petal bases are all smoothed downwards and that the ring of petals has been kept level. Trim the wires to different lengths so that they do not create a lumpy effect on the stem, and cover them with stem tape.

When making very small flowers, use only one long length of 30-gauge wire to secure the petals to the flower centre or stem. Pull as tightly as possible and hold the wire below the flowerhead while you turn the head to secure the wire. When taped, this makes a neat finish to the small flower.

MAKING INDIVIDUAL FLOWERS

The instructions for making each flower specify the best type of ribbon for achieving the required effect. In many cases silky ribbon can be substituted for the green material, but when making African violets and Easter lilies you will only achieve the right result by using the same type of ribbon as shown in the instructions.

The quantities of ribbon needed to make each flower as shown are listed on page 253.

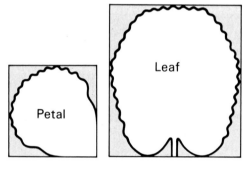

AFRICAN VIOLET
(Saintpaulia)

MATERIALS

Velvet silky or flocked ribbon in deep purple
Flocked ribbon in green
Lemon yellow stamens
Green stem tape
30-gauge wire
24-gauge green covered wire
Flowermaking adhesive

1   Cut 24mm ($1\frac{5}{16}$ in) squares of purple velvet ribbon, five for each flower and two for each bud. Cut one petal shape from each square and crinkle, using the spiral twist method.

To make one flower, wire five petals together in single-row sequence, using 30-gauge wire, with velvet sides facing you. To make one bud, wire two petals together in sequence, velvet sides facing.

For each flower or bud, cut a stamen string in half and tape below the head with half-width stem tape to thicken.

Wrap stem tape around the end of a length of green covered wire to thicken it into a small closed bud. Continue taping down the stem.

2   With velvet pile on the inside, wrap the wired flower petals around the stamen. Secure by winding one long end of wire round the flower base, hold the wires together, twist the flowerhead and tape. Tape the flower to a length of green covered wire using half-width stem tape and open out the petals.

Repeat to make a second flower.

Assemble the bud in the same way but do not open

the petals.

3 Cut a 36 x 40mm ($1\frac{7}{16}$ x $1\frac{9}{16}$ in) rectangle of green flocked ribbon and shape the leaf. Crinkle, using the spiral twist method. Using flowermaking adhesive, stick a length of green covered wire to the centre of the leaf on the shiny side. Tape the base of leaf and stem with half-width stem tape.

Cut smaller leaves from 24 x 30mm ($1\frac{5}{16}$ x $1\frac{3}{16}$ in) and 20 x 26mm ($1\frac{3}{16}$ x $1\frac{1}{16}$ in) rectangles. Arrange flowers, buds and leaves into a cluster and tape the stems together to finish.

If you wish to assemble a full plant, make at least nine flowers and four buds, and surround them with leaves in varying sizes, the smaller leaves at the centre.

BRIAR ROSE
(Rosa rubiginosa)

MATERIALS

Shaded silky ribbon in white/pale pink
Silky ribbon in green
Brown-tipped yellow stamens
Ready-made rose leaves
Stem tape in yellow and green
30-gauge wire
28-gauge white covered wire
20-gauge stem wire
Flowermaking adhesive
Cotton wool

1 Cut five 60mm ($2\frac{3}{8}$ in) squares from shaded silky ribbon and shape petals. Tool with the large mushroom head where indicated. Turn the petals over and tool the centres.

Turn each petal back and use adhesive to stick the length of white covered wire halfway up the petal, leaving an equal length as stem. Allow the adhesive to dry.

Thicken the top 20mm ($1\frac{3}{16}$ in) of a length of 20-gauge stem wire with yellow stem tape.

Put twenty stamen strings together and fold them in half. Arrange them around the thickened wire tip to make the flower centre. Secure with 30-gauge wire by the twisting method and bind with half-width yellow stem tape.

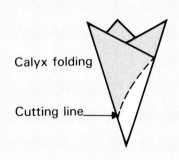

Calyx folding

Cutting line

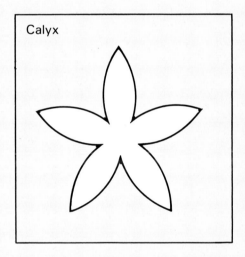

Calyx

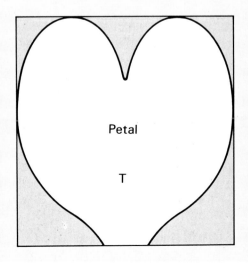

Petal

T

225

Arrange the petals around the flower centre to overlap sequentially. Secure with 30-gauge wire by the twisting method and neaten with yellow stem tape.

2   To make the bud, cut five 50mm (2in) squares of shaded silky ribbon and cut one petal shape from each square. Tool in the same way as for the large petal but using the small mushroom head.

Loop a length of 30-gauge wire around a piece of cotton wool, hold the wire and twist the cotton wool to secure it. Shape the cotton wool into a bud.

Using adhesive, stick one petal to the bud and fold the petal tips over the cotton wool to conceal it. Allow the adhesive to dry.

Stick on the remaining petals individually to build up the bud, curling back the tips of the petals. Secure the base of the bud with 30-gauge wire by the twisting method and neaten with half-width green stem tape.

3   Cut one 48mm (1⅞in) square of green silky ribbon and one 36mm (1⁷⁄₁₆in) square. Fold each square by the five-point fold as shown and cut to make the calyces. Pierce a hole in the centre of each calyx using 20-gauge wire. Push the large calyx up the flower stem and secure underneath the flower with green stem tape. Repeat with the bud calyx.

Arrange the leaves in groups of three and tape to flower bud and stems. Tape flower and bud together and finish taping the stem.

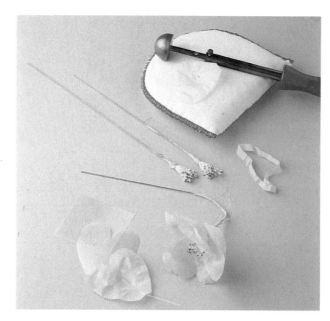

CARNATION (Dianthus)

MATERIALS

Silky ribbon in pale yellow and grey/green
Stem tape in yellow and green
30-gauge wire
20-gauge wire

1   Cut nine 72mm ($2^{13}/_{16}$ in) squares of yellow silky ribbon. Fold and cut each square as shown to make the petals. Fringe the edges finely. Cut along one fold in each petal section to a little more than halfway down and refold concertina fashion.

Hold the base of a petal and dampen the thumb and forefinger of your free hand. Twist the petal sections alternately in different directions to stretch the outer edges. Treat all the petals in this way.

Secure the base of each petal by the twisting method using 30-gauge wire. Cut the ends of wire to different lengths but no less than 50mm (2in) long. Cover about 20mm ($^{13}/_{16}$ in) of the wire with half-width yellow stem tape.

2   Cluster the wired petals together evenly to form the flowerhead. Secure them with half-width stem tape, making sure that each petal stands free. Join in a 20-gauge stem wire and secure it with green stem tape. Wrap green stem tape around the top of the stem wire close to the base of the flower.

Cut one 48 x 72mm ($1\frac{7}{8}$ x $2^{13}/_{16}$ in) rectangle of grey/green silky ribbon and fold concertina fashion at 6mm ($\frac{1}{4}$ in) intervals. Cut the leaf shape as shown to make twelve leaves. Attach pairs of leaves to the flower stem by the twisting method using 30-gauge wire. Tape with half-width green stem tape to thicken the point where the leaves attach to the stem. Curl the leaves over closed scissor blades.

Thicken the end of a 20-gauge stem wire with green stem tape to form a bud. Join the bud to the flower stem and continue taping, adding further pairs of leaves at intervals down the stem. Tape to the end of the stem.

To make the spray carnation, make up smaller flowers by the same method, using only five petals cut from 48mm ($1\frac{7}{8}$ in) squares in each flowerhead. Join three small flowers and two buds to form the spray.

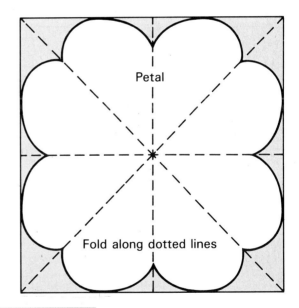

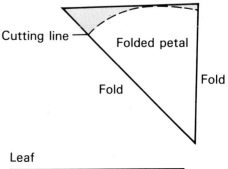

CHRISTMAS ROSE (Helleborous niger)

MATERIALS

Silky ribbon in white
Shaded silky ribbon in white/pale green
Acetate ribbon in green
Yellow pointed stamens
Stem tape in yellow and red brown
30-gauge wire
28-gauge white covered wire
24-gauge green covered wire
20-gauge stem wire
Double-sided adhesive tape in 5mm ($^3/_{16}$ in) and 36mm
  ($1^7/_{16}$ in) widths

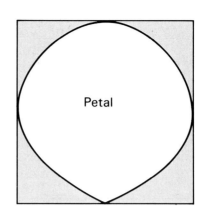

Petal

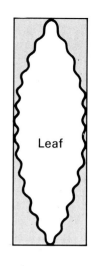

Leaf

1 Cut five 48mm (1⅞ in) squares of white silky ribbon. Apply 5mm ($^3/_{16}$ in) double-sided tape diagonally across the centre of each square.

Cut a 24mm ($1^5/_{16}$ in) strip from the white side of the shaded ribbon, leaving a predominantly pale green section. Cut five 48mm (1⅞ in) squares of shaded ribbon.

Cut short lengths of white covered wire. Attach a wire to the adhesive tape across the centre of each white square of shaded ribbon. Cut one petal on the diagonal of each square.

Stretch the petals just inside the edges and gently curve the wires to cup the petals slightly. The pale green colouring should be on the outside of each petal.

Wire the five petals in single-row sequence, using 30-gauge wire. Leave an even allowance of 15mm ($^9/_{16}$ in) below the securing wire at the base of each petal.

2 Thicken the end of a 20-gauge stem wire with yellow stem tape.

Cut thirty-two stamen strings in half and divide the stamens into four bundles. Secure the base of each bundle with 30-gauge wire, using the hairpin method. Position them evenly around the thickened

stem end, with the base of the stamens just below the taped section and the stamen tips just above the stem end. Tape to hold them in place and secure with 30-gauge wire by the twisting method. Cover the wiring with tape.

Wrap the petals around the flower centre, keeping the concave curves in shape. The fifth petal should just overlap the first. Wind a long end of 30-gauge wire around the base of the petals and bring together all the ends of wire at the flower base. Twist the flowerhead to secure wires and trim excess lengths.

3 Tape the base of the flowers with red-brown stem tape and continue taping down the flower stem to the required length.

To make a smaller flower, cut five petal shapes from 36mm ($1\frac{7}{16}$ in) squares of silky ribbon. Line the petals and make up the flower as above.

To make a small bud, cut five petal shapes from 24mm ($\frac{15}{16}$ in) squares of white silky ribbon. Do not line them but stretch them gently as for the larger petals. Wire the petals in single-row sequence. Make the bud centre by taping the end of a stem wire to form a small node but do not attach stamens. Wrap the petals around the node and secure as for the full-size flower.

Cut two 60 x 100mm ($2\frac{3}{8}$ x $3\frac{15}{16}$ in) rectangles of green acetate ribbon. Apply 36mm ($1\frac{7}{16}$ in) double-sided tape to one of these rectangles on the matt side of the ribbon.

Cut five 100mm ($3\frac{15}{16}$ in) lengths of green covered wire. Attach them to the adhesive tape, evenly spaced across the width of the rectangle and starting about 10mm ($\frac{3}{8}$ in) from the top edge.

Place the second triangle of green acetate ribbon over the first, shiny side up, and press down firmly. Divide the strip into five equal sections and cut a leaf from each one. Tape the leaf stems together to make a fan of leaves.

Using red-brown stem tape, attach the smaller flower and bud to the main flower stem and join in the leaves below the flowers.

CLEMATIS MONTANA

MATERIALS

Silky ribbon in pale pink and green
Yellow heavy cotton thread
Green embroidery silk
Stem tape in green and red brown
30-gauge wire
30-gauge green covered wire
30-gauge white covered wire
18-gauge stem wire
5mm ($\frac{3}{16}$ in) double-sided adhesive tape
Red felt-tip pen

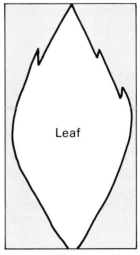

Leaf

Petal

1 Cut off four 36mm ($1\frac{7}{16}$ in) squares of pink silky ribbon. Fold each square in half, crease the fold and open out the square.

Apply double-sided tape down the centre of one half of each square. Attach one 70mm ($2\frac{3}{4}$ in) length of 30-gauge white covered wire to each piece of tape. Fold over the other half of the square and press down firmly. Cut one petal from each rectangle.

Tool the petals down either side of the wire with the ridged head. If the tip of the petal looks square, trim to round it.

2 Cut a 70mm ($2\frac{3}{4}$ in) length of green embroidery silk and loop it around one finger. Wrap a length of yellow cotton thread three times around your finger to cover the green loop. Slip the combined threads off your finger and hook a short length of 30-gauge wire through the loops. Twist the wire to secure. Twist a small piece of 30-gauge wire around the threads just above the first wire. Cut the top of the looped thread to make a silky tassel. Spread the tassel and trim the green threads to short lengths. Neaten the base of the tassel with green stem tape.

Arrange the petals around the tassel centre, tooled side inwards, and secure with a half-width red-brown stem tape.

Repeat to make a second flower.

3 Cut three 65 x 72mm ($2\frac{9}{16}$ x $2\frac{13}{16}$ in) rectangles of green silky ribbon. Fold in half widthways and place a strip of double-sided tape down the centre of one half of each rectangle. Attach a length of 30-gauge green covered wire to each piece of adhesive tape. Fold over the other half of the rectangle to line the first.

Cut the leaves and mark the leaf veins with scissor blades or the tool blade head. Colour the edges with the red felt-tip pen. Tape the three leaves together in a trefoil grouping.

Repeat to make two more leaf groupings.

To assemble, tape flowers and leaves to an 18-gauge stem wire and cover the wire with red-brown stem tape. This clematis flowers profusely, so if you are making a large stem or full plant, it may be necessary to tape together several wires to provide support. A natural effect is achieved by varying the leaf sizes if several groupings are made.

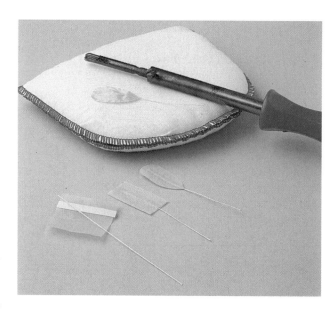

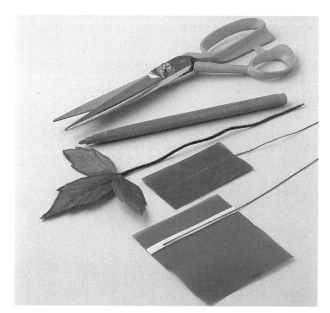

Cyclamen

Materials

Silky ribbon in cyclamen pink and green
Velvet silky ribbon in green
Pink stamens
Red-brown stem tape
30-gauge wire
28-gauge white covered wire
24-gauge green covered wire
20-gauge stem wire
Double-sided adhesive tape in 5mm ($^3/_{16}$in) and 24mm ($^{15}/_{16}$in) widths
Yellow crayon

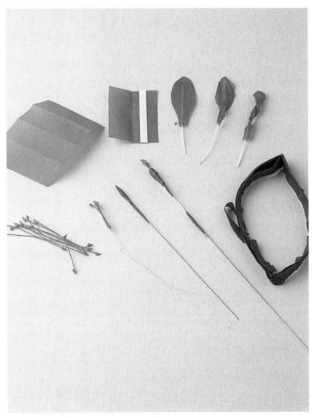

1 Cut a 36 x 50mm ($1^7/_{16}$ x 2in) rectangle of pink silky ribbon and fold it in half lengthwise. Apply a strip of double-sided tape down the centre of one half. Cut an 80mm (3⅛ in) length of white covered wire. Attach the wire to the adhesive tape. Fold over the other half of the ribbon and press down firmly.

Make five petals for the flower and three for the bud. Crinkle by the spiral twist method.

Fold two stamens in half and secure the base with 30-gauge wire. Tape the base with half-width stem tape. Cut a stem-length of 20-gauge wire and position the stamen centre at the top, with the stamen heads just above the end of the wire. Secure the stamens with stem tape and continue taping to thicken the stem end.

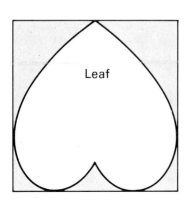

Leaf

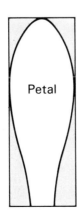

Petal

231

2 Assemble the five petals around the flower centre, overlapping each other slightly, and tape them in place. Thicken the length of the stem below the flowerhead with stem tape.

Turn back the flower petals to show the flower full face. Bend the stem about 25mm (1in) below the base of the flower.

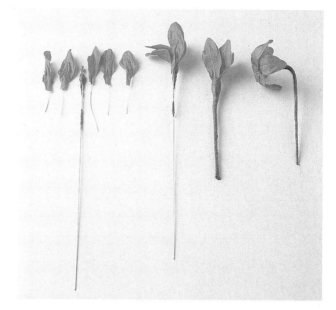

3 To make the bud, thicken the end of a length of 20-gauge stem wire. Position three petals around the thickened stem end and secure with stem tape. Thicken the full stem and bend it below the bud as for the flower.

To make the closed bud, thicken the end of a length of stem wire to form a pointed bud shape. Thicken and bend the stem as before.

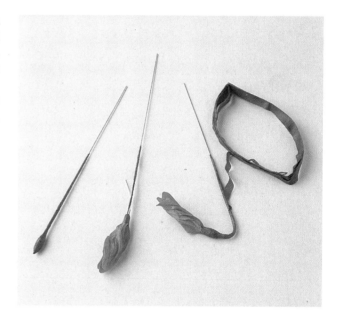

4 Cut one 45mm (1 $^{13}/_{16}$ in) square of green velvet ribbon and one of green silky ribbon. Apply double-sided tape to the wrong side of the velvet ribbon square. Position a length of 24-gauge green covered wire down the centre of the square and cover with the silky ribbon square.

Cut the leaf shape and apply the leaf markings using the yellow crayon. Tape the leaf stem with red-brown stem tape.

Make second and third size leaves from 36mm (1 $^{7}/_{16}$ in) and 30mm (1 $^{3}/_{16}$ in) squares respectively.

Arrange the flower buds and leaves in a neat grouping and secure the stems with tape.

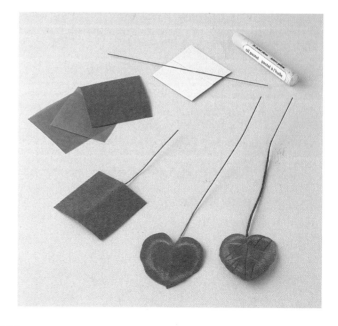

232

EASTER LILY (Lilium longiflorum)

MATERIALS

Acetate ribbon in white and green
Large lily stamens
Stem tape in white, pale green and mid green
26-gauge white covered wire
24-gauge green covered wire
18-gauge stem wire
Double-sided adhesive tape in 5mm ($^3/_{16}$ in) and 36mm
  ($1^7/_{16}$ in) widths
Yellow felt-tip pen

1 Cut nine 36 x 120mm ($1^7/_{16}$ x 4¾ in) rectangles of white acetate ribbon. Cut nine narrow strips of white acetate ribbon and attach 5mm ($^3/_{16}$ in) double-sided tape to each strip on the shiny side. Strip-line the centre of each rectangle, inserting a length of white covered wire under each lining strip. Cut the petal shapes and stretch them between thumb and forefinger on either side of the petal tip.

To make the flower, place strips of 5mm ($^3/_{16}$ in) double-sided tape on both long edges of three of the petals. Peel the backing paper from the tape and join six petals together, alternating one taped petal and one untaped. Join the petals into a trumpet, keeping the wires on the outside.

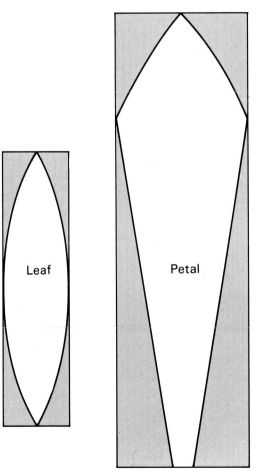

Leaf

Petal

2 Colour the tips of six stamens with the yellow felt-tip pen. Tape down each stamen stem with half-width white stem tape to strengthen.

To make the pistil for the flower centre, cut three 120mm (4¾ in) lengths of white covered wire. Bend them over to make loops and cover with white stem tape. Join in a 120mm (4¾ in) length of white wire and tape all the wires together with half-width white stem tape.

Assemble the six stamens with the pistil in the centre, standing 10mm (⅜ in) above the stamens. Attach this stamen centre to a length of 18-gauge wire and thicken with pale green stem tape. Insert the flower centre into the throat of the flower.

Cover the base of the flower with green stem tape and continue taping down the flower stem.

3 To make the bud, join the remaining three petals as for the flower, keeping the reinforcing wires on the inside.

Thicken the end of an 18-gauge stem wire with yellow stem tape and tape down 100mm (3¹⁵⁄₁₆ in) of the wire. Insert the wire into the bud, with the thickened end forming the bud centre. Secure the bud base with green stem tape and tape down the stem.

Cut a 36 x 72mm (1⁷⁄₁₆ x 2¹³⁄₁₆ in) rectangle of green acetate ribbon. Fold it in half lengthwise and apply double-sided tape to one half of the ribbon. Attach a length of green covered wire down the centre of the taped half. Fold over the other half of the rectangle on the matt side of the ribbon. Attach a length of green covered wire down the centre of the taped half. Fold over the other half of the rectangle and smooth it down. Cut out the leaf.

Make four more leaves and tape them singly to the bud and flower stems at intervals.

LARGE ROSE

MATERIALS

Shaded poplin ribbon in pink/cream
Acetate ribbon in green
Green stem tape
30-gauge wire
24-gauge green covered wire
18-gauge stem wire
36mm (1⁷⁄₁₆ in) double-sided adhesive tape

1 Cut thirteen 72mm ($2\frac{13}{16}$ in) squares of shaded poplin ribbon and cut a petal shape from each one.

Stretch the petals at the centres between thumbs and forefingers to cup them slightly. Tool the top edges of the petals with the rose petal curling head or roll the edges over a stem wire.

Roll two petals together to form a centre and secure by the twisting method using 30-gauge wire. Neaten with half-width green stem tape and join in an 18-gauge stem wire.

Wire three petals in single-row sequence, with the concave surface of the cupping facing you. Wrap these around the petal centre and fasten the ends with 30-gauge wire, taking the long lengths right around the flower base to join with the short ends. Twist the flower to secure. Trim the wires and neaten with half-width stem tape.

Wire eight petals in a double-row sequence and wrap these around the inner petals. Secure as above and tape the flower base.

2 Cut five 5 x 40mm ($\frac{3}{16}$ x $1\frac{9}{16}$ in) rectangles from green acetate ribbon and cut sepals. Apply a very small piece of double-sided tape to the base of each sepal on the right side of the ribbon. Peel the backing paper from the double-sided tape and stick the sepals evenly around the top of the flower stem, just below the petal base. Tape to secure. Hold very firmly and curl the sepals downwards over closed scissor blades.

Cut ten 36 x 60mm ($1\frac{7}{16}$ x $2\frac{3}{8}$ in) rectangles of green acetate ribbon. On five pieces, apply double-sided tape to the matt side.

Cut five 100mm ($3\frac{15}{16}$ in) lengths of green covered wire. Attach a wire down the centre of each acetate rectangle. Cover with the other five rectangles.

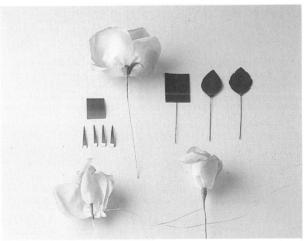

Cut the leaf shapes and serrate the edges. Mark the leaf veins with scissor blades or the tool blade head.

Make a group of five leaves by taping them together with half-width green stem tape. Join the leaves to the flower stem with full-width tape and continue taping down the flower stem. (If the stem is long, it is advisable to add at least one of the group of leaves.)

3 Make a bud rose by rolling two petals to form a centre and surrounding them with three petals wired in single-row sequence, as for the flower. Secure the bud to a stem wire and add sepals and leaves. Tape to the end of the stem.

The size and number of petals can be increased or decreased to make larger or smaller flowers. A stamen centre can be used in place of the petal centre.

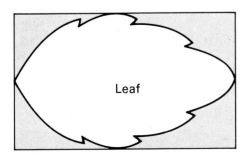

Leaf

Sepal

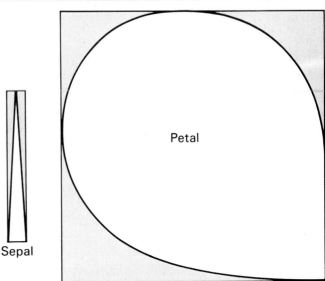

Petal

LILY OF THE VALLEY (Convallaria majalis)

MATERIALS

Lily of the valley petals (pre-formed)
Acetate or silky ribbon in white
White round stamens
Green stem tape
30-gauge wire
22-gauge stem wire
Flowermaking adhesive

1 Tool the centre and each section of all the petals on the dull side with the small ball head. Make a small hole at the centre of each petal with a darning needle or piece of fine wire.

2 Cut the white stamen strings in half and push one stamen through the centre of each petal. Dab adhesive on to the petal around the hole and hold the stamen head in place for 30 seconds. Allow the adhesive to dry.

Make eight small florets in this way. Stick together the edges of the petals to close up the florets. Tape the stamen stems with a half-width stem tape.

3 To make a bud, cover a very small piece of cotton wool with a 24mm ($^{1}5/_{16}$in) square of white acetate ribbon. Secure by the twisting method, using 30-gauge wire and tape with half-width green stem tape.

Use a stamen as a tiny bud and attach the buds to one end of the 22-gauge stem wire. Secure with half-width green stem tape. Trim the stem wire to half-length. Continue taping down the stem, adding in the flowers at intervals of about 15mm ($^{9}/_{16}$in).

NERINE

MATERIALS

Silky ribbon in pink and green
Pink round stamens
Green stem tape
30-gauge wire
30-gauge white covered wire
18-gauge stem wire
Flowermaking adhesive

1 To make one floret cut six 12 x 65mm ($^{7}/_{16}$ x $2^{9}/_{16}$in) rectangles of pink silky ribbon and shape petals. Use adhesive to stick a 120mm (4¾in) length of white covered wire down the centre of each petal. Allow the adhesive to dry.

2 Tool down each wire from top to bottom of the petals with the smooth curved head to curl the petals naturally.

3 Assemble seven stamens and cut off the heads at one end. Secure the cut ends with half-width stem tape.

Position the petals around the stamen centre and secure by the twisting method using 30-gauge wire. Cover the wire with half-width stem tape. Continue taping to thicken the stem just below the floret and tape to the end of the floret stem.

4 For one flowerhead, make up six florets in all. Position them at the top of an 18-gauge stem wire and secure them in place with stem tape. Make sure that each floret stands 30mm ($1^{3}/_{16}$in) from the main stem on its own. Tape down 20mm ($1^{3}/_{16}$in) of the main stem to hold the floret stems firmly and bend them gently outwards to make an evenly radiating pattern from the stem tip.

5 Cut two 12 x 50mm ($^{7}/_{16}$ x 2in) rectangles of green silky ribbon and shape leaves. Attach the leaves to the main stem at the point where the florets are attached, on opposite sides of the stem. Secure by the twisting method, using 30-gauge wire. Neaten with stem tape and continue taping down the main stem.

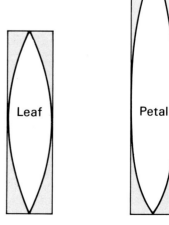

Leaf   Petal

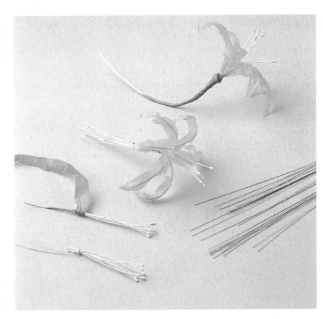

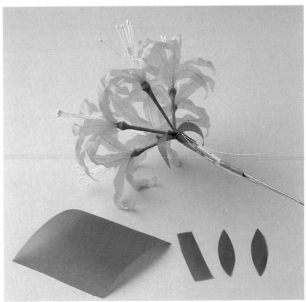

PELARGONIUM

MATERIALS

Silky ribbon in pale pink and green
Green stem tape
33-gauge white covered wire
28-gauge green covered wire
20-gauge stem wire
Double-sided adhesive tape in 5mm ($^3/_{16}$in) and 36mm ($1^7/_{16}$in) widths
Purple crayon
Brown felt-tip pen

1 Cut five 30 x 36mm ($1^3/_{16}$ x $1^7/_{16}$in) rectangles of pink silky ribbon. Fold in half and place a strip of 55mm ($^3/_{16}$in) double-sided tape down the centre of one half of each rectangle. Attach a length of white covered wire to each strip and fold over the other half of the rectangle to line the first. Cut five petals.

Mark two petals near the base with two purple lines. Stretch the tips of all five petals.

Use purple crayon to colour a length of white covered wire and cut three 20mm ($^{13}/_{16}$in) lengths to use as stamens. Tape the stamens together with half-width green stem tape.

Assemble the petals around the stamen centre, with the two purple-striped petals side by side and secure with half-width stem tape.

Repeat to make a second flower

2 Cut a 72 x 110mm ($2^{13}/_{16}$ x $4^5/_{16}$in) rectangle of green silky ribbon. Fold it in half lengthwise and cover one half with 36mm ($^7/_{16}$in) double-sided tape.

Cut five lengths of green covered wire and attach them to the double-sided tape in a radial pattern, coming together about 10mm ($^3/_8$in) from the edge of the rectangle. Fold over the second half of the rectangle, slitting the edge of the ribbon to ease it round the wires. Cut the leaf veins with scissor blades or the tool blade head and colour the edge of the leaf with brown felt-tip pen.

Make leaves in pairs and join the pairs together with green stem tape to form a single stem about 50mm (2in) below the leaf bases.

Cut a 10 x 24mm ($^3/_8$ x $1^5/_{16}$in) rectangle of green silky ribbon, fold it in three and shape the calyx. Cut three calyces for each flower and two for each pair of leaves. Attach them to the edge of the strip of 5mm ($^3/_{16}$in) double sided tape in groups, leaving space for cutting. Lay second strip of double-sided tape on top.

Attach the calyces to the stems where leaves or flowers join. Arrange the flowers and leaves into a spray and secure with green stem tape. Join in a 20-gauge stem wire if necessary to strengthen the main stem. Finish off the taping.

Make smaller leaves from 45 x 60mm ($1^{13}/_{16}$ x $2^3/_8$in) and 30 x 45mm ($1^3/_{16}$ x $1^{13}/_{16}$in) rectangles.

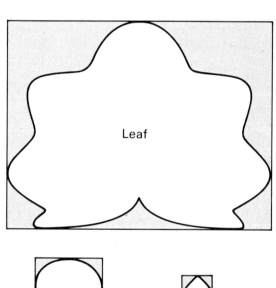

Leaf

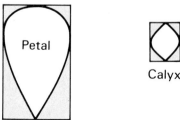

Petal

Calyx

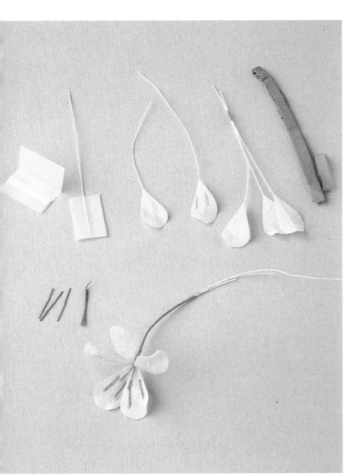

POINSETTIA (Euphorbia pulcherrima)

MATERIALS

Velvet silky ribbon in bright red and green
Silky ribbon in bright red and green
Red berry stamens
Stem tape in yellow, light green and green
24-gauge green covered wire
Double-sided adhesive tape in 24mm ($1\frac{5}{16}$ in) and 36mm
  ($1\frac{7}{16}$ in) widths

Bract

1 Cut five 24 x 72mm ($1\frac{5}{16}$ x $2\frac{13}{16}$in) and five 36 x 90mm ($1\frac{7}{16}$ x $3\frac{9}{16}$in) rectangles of red velvet ribbon. Cut five 36 x 90mm ($1\frac{7}{16}$ x $3\frac{9}{16}$in) rectangles of green velvet ribbon.

Cut the same number of rectangles of the same sizes in red and green silky ribbon.

Cover the wrong side of each velvet ribbon rectangle with double-sided tape. Attach a length of green covered wire to the centre of each rectangle and fully line with the appropriate piece of silky ribbon.

Cut a bract shape from each rectangle and crinkle all bracts using the spiral twist method.

2 Cut five red berry stamens in half. Tape with half-width yellow stem tape covering just over half of each stamen head. Tape again with half-width light green stem tape, allowing a narrow strip of yellow to show at the top edge.

Cut twelve 60mm ($2\frac{3}{8}$ in) lengths of green covered wire and tape each at one end with half- width light green stem tape to form a node.

Assemble the berry stamens and green nodes into five groups and tape one group to each small red bract using half-width light green stem tape. Allow 10mm ($\frac{3}{8}$ in) of the stamen stems to stand free. Tape the small bracts together using full-width stem tape.

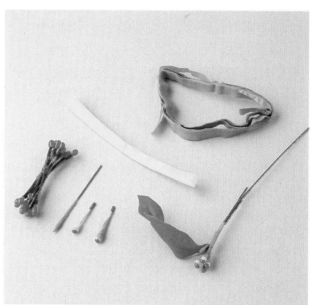

3 Attach the large red bracts below the small ones, filling the spaces between. Tape the green bracts below the large red bracts as above. Tape the wires together to form a single stem.

To make the small poinsettia, cut bracts from 24 x 36mm ($1\frac{5}{16}$ x $1\frac{7}{16}$in) and 24 x 48mm ($1\frac{5}{16}$ x $1\frac{7}{8}$in) rectangles. For the metallic ribbon version, cut all bracts from 24 x 72mm ($1\frac{5}{16}$ x $2\frac{13}{16}$in) rectangles; this should be lined with silky ribbon.

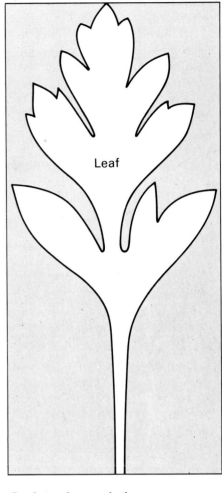

Leaf

Petal template overleaf

MATERIALS

Silky ribbon in bright red and green
Black stamens
Stem tape in black and green
30-gauge wire
30- and 40-gauge green covered wire
18-gauge stem wire
36mm ($^7/_{16}$in) double-sided adhesive tape

1   Cut eight 72mm ($2^1{}^3/_{16}$in) squares of bright red silky ribbon and shape petals. Crinkle by the damp cloth method. Stretch the edges gently between your fingers and cup the petal centres.

   Hairpin wire the base of each petal and neaten with half-width green stem tape.

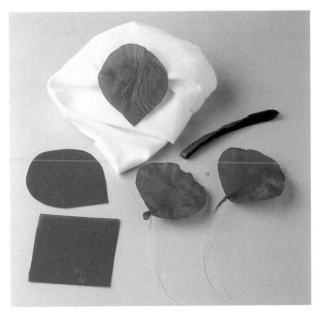

2 Assemble twelve lengths of 30-gauge green covered wire and tape them together at the centre with black stem tape. Thicken with tape to form a pod. Turn the wires evenly back over the pod from one end and secure below the pod with green stem tape.

Make up four groups of sixteen stamen strings, fold them in half and secure with 30-gauge wire. Cluster the stamens around the pod and secure by the twisting method using 30-gauge wire. Neaten with green stem tape.

Join in two lengths of 18-gauge stem wire to form a stem below the flower centre. Secure with green stem tape.

Place two petals on opposite sides of the flower centre and secure with stem tape. Position the next two petals to cover the spaces between the first two and tape. Repeat with the remaining four petals to form the full flower.

Tape down the flower stem to the point where leaves will be joined.

3 Cut two 72 x 125mm (2^{13}/$_{16}$ x 4^{15}/$_{16}$in) rectangles of green silky ribbon. Cover with double-sided tape and attach the leaf shape as shown.

Mark the leaf veins with the tool blade head or scissor blades. Tape the base of the leaf with half-width green stem tape.

Make at least three leaves per flower stem and tape them to the stem at intervals on alternate sides.

Ready-made leaves can be used for the poppy, reinforced and taped at the base before joining to the stem.

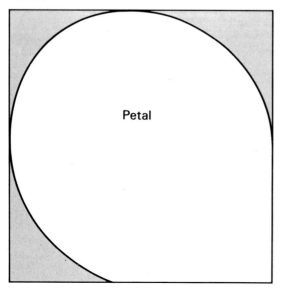

Petal

SCABIOUS

MATERIALS

Silky ribbon in pale mauve and green
Bright green stem tape
33-gauge green covered wire
30-gauge wire
20-gauge stem wire
Flowermaking adhesive

1 Cut fifteen 18 x 24mm ($1^{1}\!/_{16}$ x $^{15}\!/_{16}$ in) rectangles of mauve silky ribbon and shape petals A. Cut eighteen 18 x 36mm ($1^{1}\!/_{16}$ x $1^{7}\!/_{16}$ in) rectangles of mauve silky ribbon and shape petals B. Crinkle by the spiral twist method.

Wire petals A together in a single-row sequence, using 30-gauge wire. Repeat with petals B.

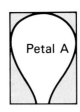

Petal A

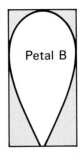

Petal B

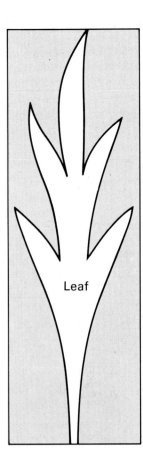

Leaf

2 Cut one hundred and eighty 36mm (1$\frac{7}{16}$in) lengths of green covered wire. Thicken 5mm ($\frac{3}{16}$in) at one end of each wire with quarter-width green stem tape to form stamen heads. Tape all the stamens together at the base and join in a 20-gauge wire on either side of the stamen centre.

Wrap the wired petals A around the stamen centre. Pull the 30-gauge wires tightly and twist the flower to secure. Neaten with stem tape.

Add the wired petals B in the same way. Neaten with stem tape and continue taping down the stem.

3 Cut two 36 x 110mm (1$\frac{7}{16}$ x 4$\frac{5}{16}$in) rectangles of green silky ribbon and shape leaves. Use adhesive to stick a length of green covered wire down the centre of each leaf. Mark the leaf veins with scissor blades or the tool blade head.

Tape the base of each leaf with half-width green stem tape and tape them to opposite sides of the flower stem.

SMALL ROSE

MATERIALS

Silky ribbon in yellow
Acetate ribbon in green
Green stem tape
30-gauge wire
24-gauge green covered wire
18-gauge stem wire
24mm ($1\frac{5}{16}$in) double-sided adhesive tape
Flowermaking adhesive
Cotton wool

244

1 Cut twelve 48mm (1⅞ in) squares of yellow silky ribbon and shape petals. Curl back the top edges by tooling with the rose petal curling head or roll the edges over a wire. Turn over the petals and cup the centres between thumbs and forefingers or tool with the small mushroom head.

Form a piece of cotton wool into a bud shape. Use flowermaking adhesive to stick one petal around the cotton wool bud to enclose it. Allow the adhesive to dry.

Stick one petal on either side of the cotton wool centre, applying adhesive over half of each petal, followed by three petals evenly spaced.

Stick another three petals to the flower base, using less adhesive so the petals open out a little from the previous layer. Repeat with the remaining three petals and allow the adhesive to dry.

Secure the base of the flower with 30-gauge wire by the twisting method. Neaten with half-width green stem tape and join in a length of 18-gauge stem wire.

2 Cut five 5 x 40mm (³⁄₁₆ x 1⁹⁄₁₆ in) rectangles of green acetate and cut sepals. Attach small pieces of double-sided tape to the bases and press the sepals around the flower base, shiny side inwards. Secure with green stem tape and curve the sepals gently downwards with closed scissor blades.

Cut ten 24 x 45mm (1⁵⁄₁₆ x 1¹³⁄₁₆ in) rectangles of green acetate ribbon. On five rectangles, apply double-sided tape to the matt side. Attach an 80mm (3⅛ in) length of green covered wire to the centre of each taped rectangle and cover with a second rectangle of acetate. Cut the leaf shapes.

Serrate the leaf edges and mark the leaf veins with scissor blades or the tool blade head.

Group the leaves as shown, with one at the tip of the leaf stem and two pairs below. Secure the stems with green stem tape and join the leaves to the flower stem.

To make a bud, proceed as for making the rose, but using only six petals. The size of the rose can be varied by increasing or decreasing the size and number of petals.

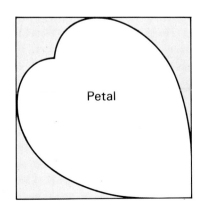

Petal

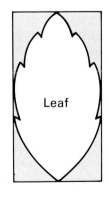

Leaf

Sepal

245

Spring Blossom

MATERIALS

Silky ribbon in pink, white and green
Yellow round stamens
Stem tape in green and dark brown
30-gauge wire
18-gauge wire
5mm (³/₁₆in) double-sided adhesive tape
Cotton wool

1 Cut one 36mm ($1\frac{7}{16}$ in) square from each of the pink and white silky ribbons. Fold by the five-point fold method and cut the floret. Fold each floret in four and crinkle by the spiral twist method.

Open out the florets and place a small piece of double-sided tape near the centre of the pink floret. Attach the white floret to the tape, slightly off-centre. Make a hole at the centre through both layers, using a darning needle or fine wire.

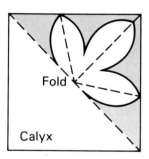

Fold

Calyx

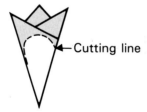

Folded floret

←—Cutting line

Floret

2 Fold twelve stamen strings in half and secure the base with 30-gauge wire. Neaten the wire with green stem tape to form a short stem.

Push the stamen centre through the hole in the double floret, with the white floret uppermost, so that the stamen heads project about 10mm (⅜in) from the floret centre. Secure the base of the floret by the twisting method using 30-gauge wire. Leave a wire stem about 30mm (1³⁄₁₆in) long and neaten with half-width green stem tape.

Make at least ten florets for one blossom twig. Two or three can be made all-white or all-pink.

To make a bud, cover a small ball of cotton wool with pink silky ribbon. Fasten the base with 30-gauge wire by the twisting method and neaten with half-width green stem tape.

Alternatively, cut one floret from a 24mm (1⁵⁄₁₆in) square of silky and crinkle as above. Fold it into a triangle and secure as for the cotton wool bud.

3 Cut a 36mm (1⁷⁄₁₆in) square of green silky ribbon, fold it diagonally and cut the calyx as shown. Join two florets with stem tape and wrap the calyx around the stem join. Secure by the twisting method, using 30-gauge wire. Trim the wire ends and neaten with green stem tape.

To make a short spray of blossom, join and tape 18-gauge stem wires to the required thickness with brown stem tape and attach the blossom stems. Alternatively secure the blossoms to a natural dry twig using stem tape.

SWEET PEA (Lathyrus)

MATERIALS

Silky ribbon in pink and green
Green stem tape
30-gauge wire
28-gauge green covered wire
20-gauge stem wire
5mm (³⁄₁₆in) double-sided adhesive tape
Cotton wool

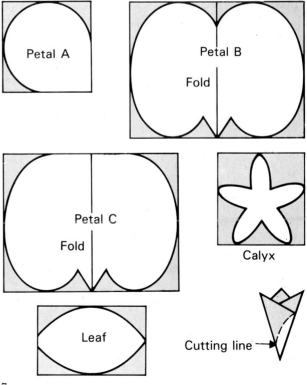

1 Cut a 24mm ($1\frac{5}{16}$ in) square of pink silky ribbon and shape petal A. Fold it in half, fill the centre with cotton wool and secure the edges with adhesive.

Cut two 36 x 48mm ($1\frac{7}{16}$ x $1\frac{7}{8}$ in) rectangles of pink silky ribbon. Cut petal B from one rectangle.

2 Stretch the edges of petal B. Apply the adhesive to the folded edge of petal A and attach it to the centre of petal B, with the point at the top.

Cut one petal C from the second rectangle of silky ribbon and stretch the edges. Make a pleat down the centre and secure with adhesive.

Attach petal C to petals A and B by wrapping 30-gauge wire around the base. It is not necessary to twist the wires. Neaten with quarter-width stem tape.

3 Cut a 24mm ($1\frac{5}{16}$ in) square of green silky ribbon. Fold by the five-point fold and cut as shown to make a calyx. Tool with the smooth curved foot, working from tips to centre.

Make a small hole at the centre of the calyx with a darning needle or fine wire. Push the calyx up the flower stem to the base of the flower and secure with quarter-width stem tape.

Make a bud by cutting and filling one petal A, as above. Wire the base with 30-gauge wire and neaten with stem tape. Attach a calyx to the bud.

To make a small flower, use only petals A and B.

Cut a 30 x 36mm ($1\frac{3}{16}$ x $1\frac{7}{16}$ in) rectangle of green silky ribbon. Fold in half and apply double-sided tape down the centre of one half. Attach a length of green covered wire to the double-sided tape and fold over the other half of the silky to line the first. Cut the leaf shape. Make two leaves.

To make the tendril, cover a length of 30-gauge wire with quarter-width green stem tape and wrap this around a 20-gauge stem wire. Slide off the 30-gauge wire to form a loose, coiled spring effect. Cut to length required. Tape together the tendril and the pair of leaves.

To form a spray, tape one bud, one small flower and two large flowers to a 20-gauge stem wire. Cover the stem with green stem tape and tape in two leaves and a tendril below the flower.

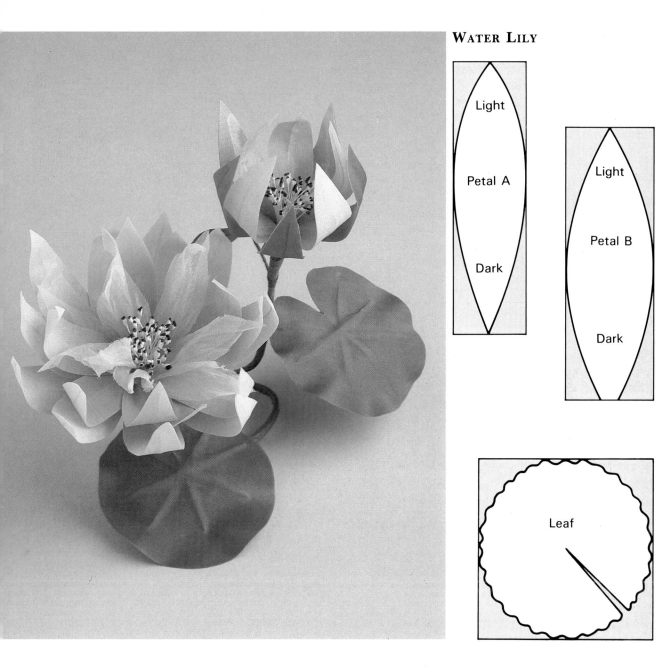

Light

Petal A

Dark

Light

Petal B

Dark

Leaf

Light

Petal C

Dark

MATERIALS

Shaded organdy ribbon in cream/pink
Shaded poplin ribbon in cream/pink
Poplin ribbon in green
Pointed dark-tipped stamens
Green stem tape
30-gauge wire
24-gauge green covered wire
24-gauge white covered wire
18-gauge stem wire
36mm (1⁷⁄₁₆ in) double-sided adhesive tape

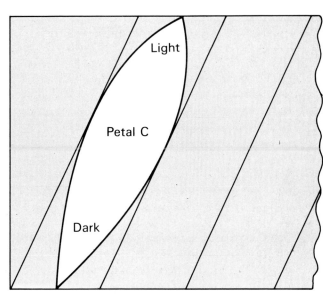

1   Cut ten 24 x 72mm ($1^5/_{16}$ x $2^{13}/_{16}$ in) rectangles of shaded organdy ribbon and shape petals A. Crinkle by the spiral twist method.

Cut two 72 x 200mm ($2^{13}/_{16}$ x $7^7/_8$ in) rectangles of shaded poplin ribbon. Cover one piece with double-sided tape. Attach ten 80mm ($3^1/_8$ in) lengths of white covered wire, evenly spaced, across the taped ribbon. Cover with the second rectangle. Cut the strip into ten pieces, each with a wire down the centre, and cut ten petals B.

Cut two 72 x 275mm ($2^{13}/_{16}$ x $10^7/_8$ in) rectangles of shaded poplin ribbon. Cover one rectangle with double-sided tape. Attach ten 90mm ($3^9/_{16}$ in) lengths of white covered wire, evenly spaced across the rectangle and slanted at an angle of about 70 degrees to the ribbon edge. Cover with the second rectangle of poplin. Cut ten petals C.

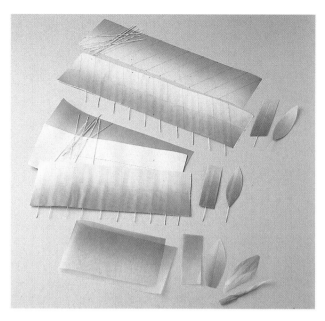

2   Wire each group of petals in double-row sequence, using 30-gauge wire. Make sure the allowance of ribbon below the wires is even.

3   Assemble thirty stamens and fold them in half. Secure the base with 30-gauge wire. Neaten with full-width green stem tape and join in an 18-gauge stem wire.

Wrap the wired petals A around the stamen centre and secure by holding the ends of 30-gauge wire and twisting the flower. Trim the wires short and neaten with stem tape. The stamens should stand about 15mm ($9/_{16}$ in) above the petal centres.

Wrap the wired petals B around the flower and secure and tape them as above. Add the petals C, secure them and tape the base of the flower. Pull the petals back from the flower centre and gently curve inwards the reinforcing wires of the B and C petals.

4   To make the bud, cut a 72 x 100mm ($2^{13}/_{16}$ x $3^{15}/_{16}$ in) rectangle of green poplin ribbon and one of shaded poplin. Cover the green rectangle with double-sided tape and attach five 80mm ($3\frac{1}{8}$ in) lengths of white covered wire evenly spaced across the rectangle. Cover with the shaded rectangle.

Repeat using two rectangles of shaded poplin ribbon. Cut five petals B from each lined rectangle, each with a wire at the centre.

Wire the bud petals in double-row sequence using 30-gauge wire, alternately one shaded and one green petal, with the green sides facing away from you.

Make a stamen centre as for the full flower and join in an 18-gauge stem wire. Wrap the bud petals around the flower centre, green sides outside, and secure by holding the ends of 30-gauge wire and twisting the bud. Trim the wires and neaten with stem tape. Curve the bud petals inwards.

5   Cut two 48mm ($1\frac{7}{8}$ in) squares of green poplin ribbon. Cover one with double-sided tape.

Cut one 75mm (3in) and six 20mm ($^{13}/_{16}$ in) lengths of green covered wire. Attach the long wire to the taped square across the diagonal and position three short lengths on either side to form a radiating pattern from the centre of the square. Cover with the second square of green poplin.

Cut the leaf shape and stretch the edges between the wire ends. Tape the leaf stem with half-width green stem tape. Bend the stem at right angles to the leaf.

Leaves vary in size to 72mm ($2^{13}/_{16}$ in) square and 96mm ($3^{13}/_{16}$ in) square. To make the largest leaf, it may be necessary to join ribbon sections. To do this, cut two 48 x 96mm ($1\frac{7}{8}$ x $3^{13}/_{16}$ in) rectangles and join them into one using double-sided tape to hold the edges together. Make the large leaves in the same way as the small leaf, adjusting measurements of the wires to fit the dimensions.

To make a curled leaf, roll the edges over a stem wire.

To assemble, tape the bud, flower and leaf stems together and curve the individual stems to form a base on which the water lily sits.

BEECH LEAVES

MATERIALS

*Shaded silky ribbon in yellow/brown, or plain silky ribbon
   in green*
Stem tape in brown or green
30-and 26-gauge covered wire in brown or green
5mm ($\frac{3}{16}$in) double-sided adhesive tape

1 To make one leaf, cut a 60mm (2⅜ in) square
of silky ribbon in the chosen colour. Fold in half and
apply double-sided tape down the centre of one half
inside the fold. Attach a 120mm (4¾ in) length of
26-gauge covered wire to the tape and fold over the
other half of the rectangle to line the first. Cut the
leaf shape.

For a full branch of beech leaves, make leaves of
varying sizes.

Mark the leaf veins with the tool blade head or
scissor blades.

2 Cut a 40mm ($\frac{9}{16}$ in) length of 30-gauge covered
wire and tape the end with half-width stem tape to
form a node. Tape the node to the base of the leaf.

For a full branch of beech leaves, make leaves of
varying sizes.

Assemble leaves singly or paired and tape them
together to form a single stem. It may be necessary
to join in an 18-gauge stem wire to provide enough
support.

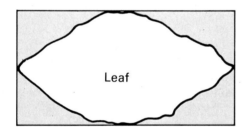

Leaf

RIBBON MEASUREMENTS

All measurements refer to 72mm ($2^{13}/_{16}$in) wide flowermaking ribbons unless otherwise stated. These quantities make the flowers as shown in the main picture of each step-by-step sequence.

AFRICAN VIOLET
Velvet silky ribbon: 100mm ($3^5/_{16}$in) deep purple
Flocked ribbon: 70mm ($2\frac{3}{4}$in) green

BRIAR ROSE
Silky ribbons: 550mm ($21\frac{3}{4}$in) white/pale pink; 100mm ($3^{15}/_{16}$in) green

CARNATION
For the full flower
Silky ribbons: 650mm ($25\frac{3}{8}$in) pale yellow, 50mm (2in) grey/green
For the spray
720mm ($28\frac{3}{8}$in) pale yellow; 50mm (2in) grey/green

CHRISTMAS ROSE
Silky ribbons: 425mm ($16\frac{3}{4}$in) white; 350mm ($13\frac{3}{4}$in) white/pale green
Acetate ribbon: 250mm ($9\frac{7}{8}$in) green

CLEMATIS MONTANA
Silky ribbons: 145mm ($5\frac{3}{4}$in) pale pink; 585mm (23in) green

CYCLAMEN
Silky ribbons: 200mm ($7\frac{7}{8}$in) cyclamen pink; 85mm ($3\frac{3}{8}$in) green
Velvet silky ribbon: 85mm ($3\frac{3}{8}$in) green

EASTER LILY
Acetate ribbons: 720mm ($28\frac{3}{8}$in) white; 220mm ($8\frac{3}{4}$in) green

LARGE ROSE
Poplin ribbon: 1300mm (51in) pink/cream
Acetate ribbon: 640mm ($25\frac{1}{4}$in) green

NERINE
Silky ribbons: 390mm ($15\frac{3}{8}$in) pink; 25mm (1in) green

PELARGONIUM
Silky ribbons: 150mm ($5\frac{7}{8}$in) pale pink; 500mm ($19\frac{3}{4}$in) green

POINSETTIA
For the large flower
Velvet silky ribbon: 390mm ($15\frac{3}{8}$in) bright red; 270mm ($10\frac{5}{8}$in) green
Silky ribbon: 390mm ($15\frac{3}{8}$in) bright red; 270mm ($10\frac{5}{8}$in) green
For the small flower
Velvet silky ribbon: 135mm ($5^5/_{16}$in) bright red; 100mm ($3^{15}/_{16}$in) green
Silky ribbon: 135mm ($5^5/_{16}$in) bright red; 100mm ($3^{15}/_{16}$in) green
For the metallic effect flower
Metallic shaded ribbon: 240mm ($9\frac{1}{2}$in) pink
Silky ribbon: 240mm ($9\frac{1}{2}$in) white (for lining)

SCABIOUS
Silky ribbons: 325mm ($12\frac{7}{8}$in) pale mauve; 110mm ($4^5/_{16}$in) green

SMALL ROSE
Silky ribbon: 580mm ($22\frac{7}{8}$in) yellow
Acetate ribbon: 180mm ($7\frac{1}{8}$in) green

SWEET PEA
Silky ribbons: 205mm (8in) pink; 80mm ($3\frac{1}{8}$in) green

WATER LILY
Organdy ribbon: 290mm ($11\frac{1}{2}$in) cream/pink
Poplin ribbon: 1250mm ($49\frac{1}{4}$in) cream/pink; 390mm ($15\frac{3}{8}$in) green

BEECH LEAVES
For autumn stem
Silky ribbon: 780mm ($30\frac{3}{4}$in) yellow/brown
For green stem
360mm ($14\frac{1}{4}$in) green

GLOSSARY OF TERMS USED IN FLORISTRY

Abstract A modern style of arrangement, in which plant material is used to create a bold, stark design.

Arrangement The completed flower design, including the container, base and drape, if used.

Balance The visual weight of the flower design when correctly arranged.

Base An article, such as a wooden board, placed underneath the container to improve the design or height.

Bloom A single flower.

Blossom Massed flowers on a branch, such as apple blossom.

Bouquet Flowers placed together to form a bunch. There is a considerable variety of styles of bouquet.

Candlecup A plastic or metal container that fits into the top of a candlestick to hold flowers and a candle.

Conditioning The process by which the life of cut flowers and foliage is prolonged prior to arranging.

Cones Metal or plastic tubes that are used to give greater height in a design.

Container The name given to any article used for flower arranging that will hold water, mechanics and the flowers.

Design The style of a flower arrangement and the way in which it is thought through.

Drapes The fabric used to enhance an arrangement.

Driftwood Wood that has been weathered by nature.

Focal point The centre of the design to which one's eye is inevitably drawn.

Fruits The term usually applied to apples, pears and so on, but it can include berries, grasses, seed pods, cones, fungi and nuts.

Garland Plant material assembled to form a rope of flowers and/or foliage.

Harmony The pleasing and good arrangement.

Informal The description for simply-styled arrangements that are usually bunched together.

Line A traditional arrangement created in a particular shape, such as horizontal, vertical, and so on.

Mass A traditional arrangement created with many varied and interesting plant materials.

Material The flowers and foliage used in an arrangement.

Mechanics The means by which flowers and foliage are held in position in the arrangement.

Modern The use of very little plant material to create a pleasing design.

Outline Plant material chosen to create the shape of the design. It is usually lighter-coloured or finer plant material.

Pinholder A lead-based shape with protruding pins that are long and sharp. It is used as a mechanic for keeping plant material in place.

Plastic-covered wire A mechanic used to keep plant material in place.

Posy frill A pretty edging for posies.

Pot-et-fleur A combination of growing plants and cut flowers in the same container.

Proportion The correct distribution of plant material in terms of weight, colour and texture.

Reel-wire The wire used for securing netting and containers.

Ribbon The mechanic used for decoration or for tying bouquets.

Stem tape The tape used to cover wired materials.

String This is used to secure mechanics and garlands.

Stub wire The wire used for mounting plant material for bouquets etc. It is available in many gauges.

Swag A collection of plant materials, without a visible background, that is used as a hanging decoration.

Transition The term used when plant material is so arranged that it links the heavier and lighter elements, or the outline and centre, of a design.

Wire netting Chicken wire which is used to hold plant material in place. It is crumbled or rolled and then pressed into the container to give several layers and plenty of spaces into which the stems can be pushed.

INDEX